A History of the

TURBO CHARGED

Racing Car

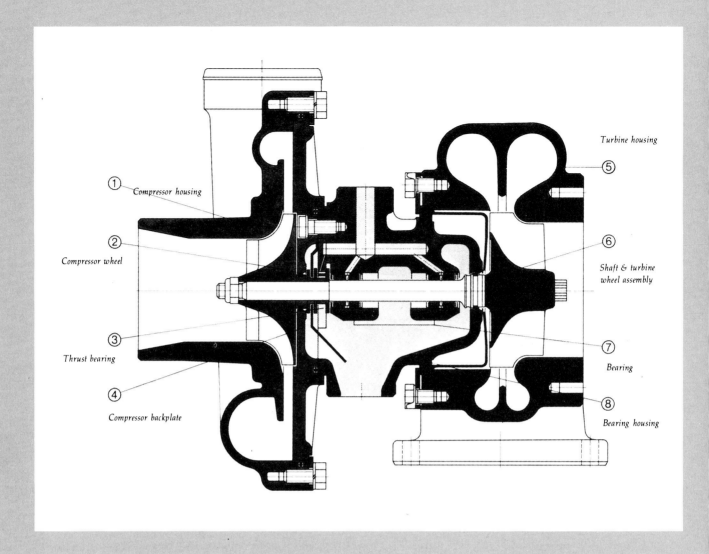

① Compressor housing

② Compressor wheel

③ Thrust bearing

④ Compressor backplate

⑤ Turbine housing

⑥ Shaft & turbine wheel assembly

⑦ Bearing

⑧ Bearing housing

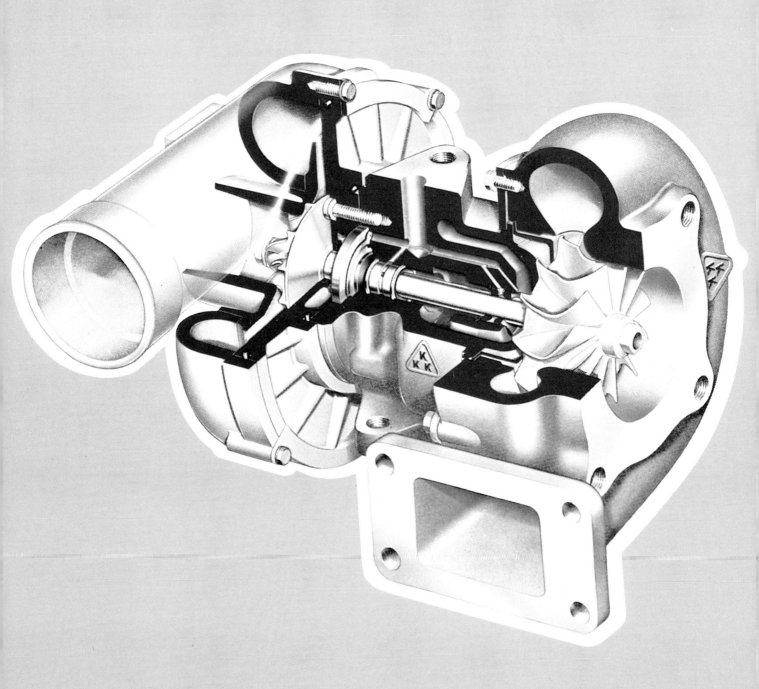

A History of the

TURBO CHARGED

Racing Car

Ian Bamsey

A KIMBERLEY Motor Racing Book

First published 1989

© MIURA PUBLICATIONS LTD

Published by:
Haynes Publishing Group, Sparkford, Near Yeovil,
Somerset BA22 7JJ, England

Haynes Publications Inc., 861 Lawrence Drive,
Newbury Park, California 91320, USA

Produced for William Kimberley Ltd. by
MIURA PUBLICATIONS LTD
6 Foundry House, Stars Lane, Yeovil, Somerset,
BA20 1NL, England

The colour photographs in this book have
primarily been supplied by LAT, London.
Formula One research assisted by Mike
Lawrence, Enrico Benzing and Allan Staniforth.

British Library Cataloguing in Publication Data

Bamsey, Ian
    The history of turbo-charged racing cars.
    1.   Racing cars, history
    I.   Title
    629.2'28'09

ISBN 0-946132-64-X

Library of Congress Catalog
Card number 89-85910

Printed in England by:
Wincanton Litho, Wincanton, Somerset
Typesetting & Artwork by:
Photosetting, Yeovil, Somerset

Contents

The Development of Turbocharging

Turbocharging is a form of supercharging, which is the process of forcing more air into the cylinders of an internal combustion engine. Early in the development of the motor vehicle engineers realised that engine power was increased if compressed air was fed to the carburettor. Air compressors had been used in industrial applications in the 19th century and in 1902 Louis Renault patented a system whereby a centrifugal air pump blew air into the mouth of a carburettor. In 1907 American Lee Chadwick developed the first proper supercharged engine, the carburettor receiving compressed air directly from a single stage centrifugal air compressor – soon dubbed 'the blower' – driven at nine times engine speed via a belt from the flywheel. Chadwick quickly progressed to a three stage blower and in 1908 he used the technology to win a major hillclimb. This feat brought the power potential of supercharging to the attention of a wide audience.

Already, turbocharging was under development. Towards the end of the 19th century Swiss engineer Alfred Buchi had patented an engine with an air compressor and an exhaust driven turbine coupled to it via a shaft. Ten years on, in 1905, Buchi had patented what became the common form of 20th century turbocharger – a device having no mechanical drive connection with the engine that coupled an exhaust driven turbine to a centrifugal air compressor by a short shaft. The idea was that the turbine harnessed the waste energy of the exhaust to drive the compressor which in turn crammed more air into the engine. Correctly, this process is known as turbo-supercharging.

Compared with supercharging, turbo-supercharging has the advantage of using waste energy in the exhaust pipe rather than engine power to drive the compressor. The compressor boosts power since in effect it improves an engine's capacity to accept air. While at any given engine speed more fuel can be fed in almost at will, there must be a corresponding increase of air to burn with it if power is to be improved. Both the engine driven supercharger and the exhaust driven turbo-supercharger employ a compressor to pressurise the charge air prior to intake so as to increase its density and thus the quantity that can be crammed in each cylinder per cycle.

The turbocharger that found widespread acceptance in the 20th century employs a single stage centrifugal compressor to provide the air pressurisation. The turbine driving it creates a flow restriction in the exhaust system so exhaust manifold back pressure increases. However, provided sufficient exhaust energy is converted into compressor work for charge air delivery pressure to equal or exceed pressure at the turbine inlet the engine's breathing should not be adversely affected. The inlet manifold is under pressure and this will help push the pistons down on the intake stroke as surely as back pressure hinders the exhaust stroke. Back pressure is only a problem in so far as it can hinder the entry of a fresh charge into a cylinder. However, if an engine breathes well and charge air pressure at least equals pressure at the turbine inlet there should be no problem getting the exhaust gas out and a fresh high density charge in.

Running with a positive pressure relationship the turbocharged engine is able to exploit the potential of very dense charge air assuming, of course, the density increase is matched by additional fuel. However, it should be noted that the density increase will not necessarily match the degree of pressurisation imparted by the compressor since raising the pressure of a gas increases its temperature as well as its density. Any temperature rise is at the expense of density.

The heating effect is unwelcome and the actual pressure felt in the inlet manifold is what counts and this is often measured as gauge boost pressure – the amount added to the normal intake manifold pressure. Normally aspirated engine manifold pressure is typically just a whisker below the 1.0 bar measure of atmospheric pressure at sea level, pressure falling with altitude. An alternative measure of intake manifold pressure is absolute pressure – the total pressure felt in the manifold. Unless otherwise indicated figures quoted hereafter are for absolute pressure.

Since atmospheric pressure falls with altitude – at the rate of around 0.1 bar for each 1000 metres – an air compressor is potentially of great benefit to an aero engine. Buchi had done his pioneering work on turbocharging in the diesel field and the first commercial application of his technology was for ships in the late Twenties. Meantime the young aviation industry had rapidly been developing conventional supercharging for aero engines. Not only was power loss with altitude avoided but more power for takeoff meant greater payloads could be carried while the possibility of cruising at higher altitude in thinner air meant reduced drag and consequently better fuel consumption, extending range.

The aviation world looked at turbocharging in the Twenties but the inherently higher exhaust gas temperature of a spark ignition engine compared to a compression-ignition engine shortened turbine life. Suitable turbine materials capable of withstanding in excess of 800 degrees centigrade were not yet available. Not until the Second World War was the aviation industry able to start to exploit turbo-supercharging, which offered higher thermal and mechanical efficiency thanks to its harnessing of waste energy.

To help counteract the temperature problem early turbo aero engines had the turbine wheel in the open air with only the inlet nozzle set into a cowling! However, in 1940 a new alloy known as Haynes Stellite 21 made it possible to form blades capable of withstanding up to 950 degrees centigrade. Nevertheless, the gas turbine engine was set to take over the world of aviation...

Not until the Fifties were compact turbochargers suitable for road vehicles commercialised. Nevertheless, in the late Fifties and Sixties turbocharging was widely employed as a means of extracting additional power from diesel engines for road haulage work. In 1962 the first turbocharged mass production petrol engined car was announced – the Oldsmobile Jetfire. This was followed in 1964 by the Corvair Spyder. General Motors used turbochargers supplied by Garrett AiResearch in California. Garrett had established itself as the largest turbocharger manufacturer feeding the growing diesel engine market. Other major manufacturers were the Schwitzer Corporation of Indianapolis, Holset in the UK and IHI Ishikawajima-Harima Heavy Industries Co. Ltd. – in Japan. Holset had joined the field in 1954 and from 1957 produced a Schwitzer design while from 1962 the Eberspacher company in Germany also started manufacturing Schwitzer designed units.

The type of turbocharger developed for commercial

vehicles clearly had to be relatively cheap to manufacture and dependable. Consequently the standard configuration was that of conventional single stage radial flow gas turbine linked by a short rotor shaft (running an inboard bearing system) to a single stage radial flow centrifugal compressor.

The typical turbine impeller was of high temperature steel welded to a shaft to form the rotor assembly. The turbine had to withstand exhaust temperatures of up to 900 degrees centigrade and ran within a cast iron housing. Spinning at up to 90,000r.p.m., the shaft revolved in plain bearings fed with engine lubrication oil. The compressor impeller was of aluminium alloy clamped to the shaft by an end nut. It spun in an aluminium housing which incorporated the volute (a carefully shaped outer housing). The impeller blades accelerated the incoming air so as to impart a high velocity to it by centrifugal force, then the air was diffused into the volute, reducing its velocity and thus building up pressure.

It should be noted that compressor action is essentially aerodynamic: the turbocharger is not a positive displacement device trapping air in sealed chambers before it is compressed. Consequently, as engine speed and load increase its aerodynamic qualities are severely tested. Critically important is the relationship between airflow and pressure. If flow is too low for the pressure build up in a system the air can stall and change direction – the phenomenon of 'surge' which can occur violently, causing serious damage. At the other end of the spectrum is flow that is disproportionately high for the pressure build up. Air flow can go supersonic at the inlet, which is inefficient and causes dangerous charge heating. If flow is too high there will be excessive impeller speed

for a given pressure delivery, and it is possible to overspeed the impeller, causing it to burst.

Clearly it is desirable to run a compressor as closely as possible to its peak efficiency at all times. Running a compressor below its peak efficiency implies a greater power requirement for a given pressure rise. Low efficiency causes a disproportionate temperature rise. A compressor's overall efficiency – its adiabatic (effectively its 'pumping') efficiency – is reflected in the temperature rise it creates. 100% efficiency is a pure adiabatic condition with no heat entering or leaving the system but in practice some temperature rise is inevitable and around 75% efficiency is the best that can be achieved. Further, the turbocharger typically has to serve an engine operating over a wide range of speed (r.p.m.) and load (throttle opening).

Different turbochargers have different characteristics (usually illustrated by plotting the relationship between pressure and flow on a compressor 'map') and it is difficult to produce a turbocharger which combines high efficiency with the map width needed to accommodate an engine with a wide r.p.m. and throttle range. Essential is careful matching of compressor to engine, of engine to turbine and of turbine to compressor. Whereas gas flow through the compressor diffuses, flow through the turbine does the accelerating, and turbine speed is a function of exhaust gas temperature and speed, and of pressure in the exhaust manifold. A turbine can use all the heat it can get provided it can withstand the temperature.

Exhaust gas speed as felt by the rotor is influenced by the turbine entry nozzle: reducing the size of a nozzle will accelerate the gas at low throttle levels. On the other hand, as engine speed increases the gas can choke at the

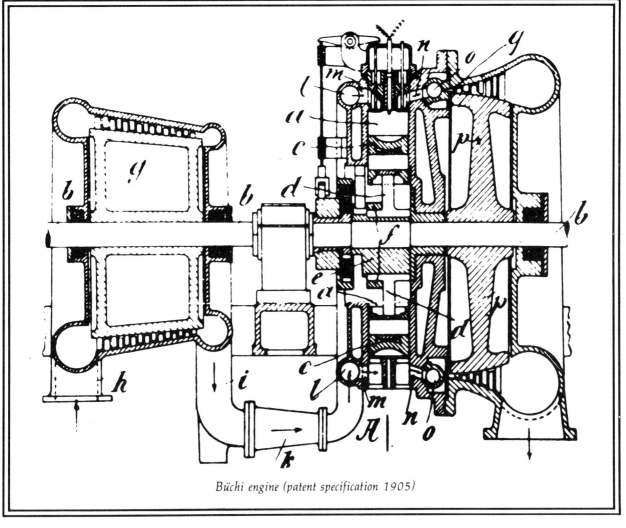

Büchi engine (patent specification 1905)

13

turbine entry, increasing back pressure in the manifold. That pressure rise could, in theory, eventually overtake the pressure in the inlet manifold.

In practice, a pressure relief valve is usually fitted to bleed excess pressure from the exhaust manifold once charge air pressure reaches a given level. The common diaphragm operated exhaust wastegate is thus a pressure differential sensing device, with a spring loaded poppet valve to bypass gas from the turbine entry once boost pressure reaches a required level.

Clearly, the speed of the turbine is the speed of the compressor. Centrifugal forces increase as the square of rotational speed but air is light stuff and in practice the compressor has to run at high speed before anything much happens in the way of significant boost. At low to medium engine speed boost will be modest, particularly as the inlet pressure build up has to carefully avoid surge. However, as revs rise pressure will start to rise disproportionately and power will climb quickly and steeply. In the worst case there will be a sudden inrush of power that the driver will find very hard to cope with. Herein lies the importance of the wastegate if a more civilised engine is desired: given the right turbocharger, the wastegate allows a desired level of manifold pressure to be achieved at medium engine speed, bleeding off the excess at higher speeds.

Power is a function of work done on the power stroke (brake mean effective pressure (b.m.e.p.) which, in effect, is an engine's torque) and engine speed. Clearly, the turbocharger increases b.m.e.p. and for greatest benefit it will be carefully matched to an engine's torque curve, with revs rather than boost used to extract maximum power. As far as possible the turbo engine will be 'tuned' via the wastegate to maintain the desired boost level constantly on a given circuit. However, on almost any road racing circuit there will be corners for which the throttle has to be backed off to the extent that there is insufficient exhaust gas energy to keep the turbine spinning fast enough to keep the compressor within its useful working range.

Opening the throttle again will not instantly speed up the rotor assembly due mainly to the inertia of the assembly. The time spent reaching useful compressor speed is known as throttle lag – an inevitable delay between pressing the throttle pedal and power arriving at the rear wheels. Harsh power delivery and throttle lag are inherent problems of exhaust gas turbo-supercharging. It is important to keep charge plumbing and exhaust primaries short to minimise lag. The entire engine and turbo system package has to be designed as an integral component and a key element of this is the plenum chamber above the inlet tracts which balances charge air prior to induction. It is very difficult to design an inlet manifold plenum chamber that will get equal flow to each port.

The turbocharged engine's geometric compression ratio is invariably lowered since a forced charge effectively increases the ratio. The turbo engine has, in effect, its compression ratio varying with boost and even if the pressurised charge is cooled cylinder temperatures will be higher than in the atmospheric engine. The piston can have a very hard time in the turbo engine. The maximum thermal loading that an engine can endure is set by the resistance of its pistons, rings, valves and valve seats to thermodynamic stress. To exceed a given level of resistance is to invite a burned valve or melted piston. Heat control is a major challenge posed by the turbo engine.

The majority of heat has to escape through the water cooling system, or out through the fins in the case of an air cooled engine. The thermal flow route is from the piston crown out to the ring belt whence the heat is transferred to the cylinder wall and thence to the coolant/fins. Early on many diesel engine manufacturers found it necessary to oil cool the piston crown.

For petrol engines, it is important to avoid heat build up in the combustion chamber, not only to avoid excessive thermodynamic stress, but also due to the heat intolerance of petrol. Controlled burning is only possible within certain limits defined by combustion chamber temperature, charge temperature and mean effective compression ratio.

Uncontrolled burning is inefficient and potentially destructive. It takes the form of detonation and pre-ignition. Detonation occurs when a portion of the mixture, usually near the exhaust valves, reaches a critical temperature and burns spontaneously, interfering with the progressive spread of the flame front. In the case of pre-ignition, a portion of the mixture ignites prior to ignition from the plug, due to hot spots in the chamber. Pre-ignition, which can follow from the occurrence of detonation, is the most serious form of uncontrolled burning: it causes a rapid rise in cylinder temperature and, sustained for more than a few seconds, is the easiest way to melt a piston crown.

Clearly, there were many pitfalls awaiting the turbocharged race engine pioneers of the Sixties. Although the supercharged racing engine had, as we have seen, been born in 1908, it was not until the mid Sixties that the turbo-supercharged spark ignition engine arrived on the race track. Supercharged racing engines had been in and out of favour over the years and when the first turbocharged road cars arrived in the early Sixties superchargers were out of fashion, and had been for some time. Consequently, although compact and dependable turbochargers were available, the turbo-supercharger still wasn't perceived as an obvious way forward for Grand Prix, Indy Car or Sports-Prototype engine development.

However, Sixties Formula One, Indianapolis and Le Mans regulations all offered supercharged engine equivalency factors based on previous experience of conventional supercharging, mainly during the interwar years. Unbeknown to the rule makers, given those factors, the potential for turbo-supercharging was in each case awesome.

AMERICAN GALLERY

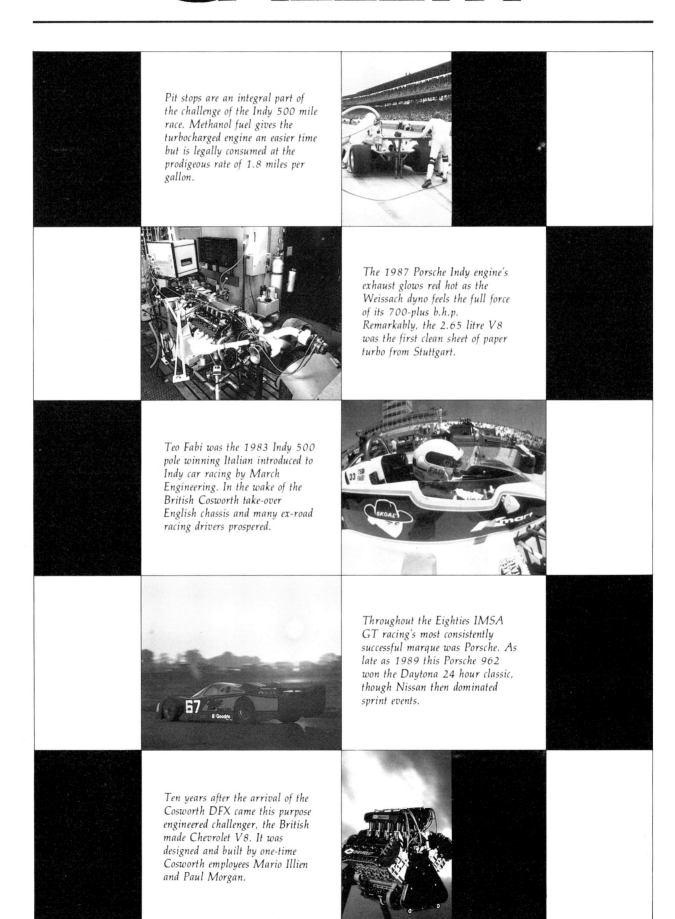

Pit stops are an integral part of the challenge of the Indy 500 mile race. Methanol fuel gives the turbocharged engine an easier time but is legally consumed at the prodigeous rate of 1.8 miles per gallon.

The 1987 Porsche Indy engine's exhaust glows red hot as the Weissach dyno feels the full force of its 700-plus b.h.p. Remarkably, the 2.65 litre V8 was the first clean sheet of paper turbo from Stuttgart.

Teo Fabi was the 1983 Indy 500 pole winning Italian introduced to Indy car racing by March Engineering. In the wake of the British Cosworth take-over English chassis and many ex-road racing drivers prospered.

Throughout the Eighties IMSA GT racing's most consistently successful marque was Porsche. As late as 1989 this Porsche 962 won the Daytona 24 hour classic, though Nissan then dominated sprint events.

Ten years after the arrival of the Cosworth DFX came this purpose engineered challenger, the British made Chevrolet V8. It was designed and built by one-time Cosworth employees Mario Illien and Paul Morgan.

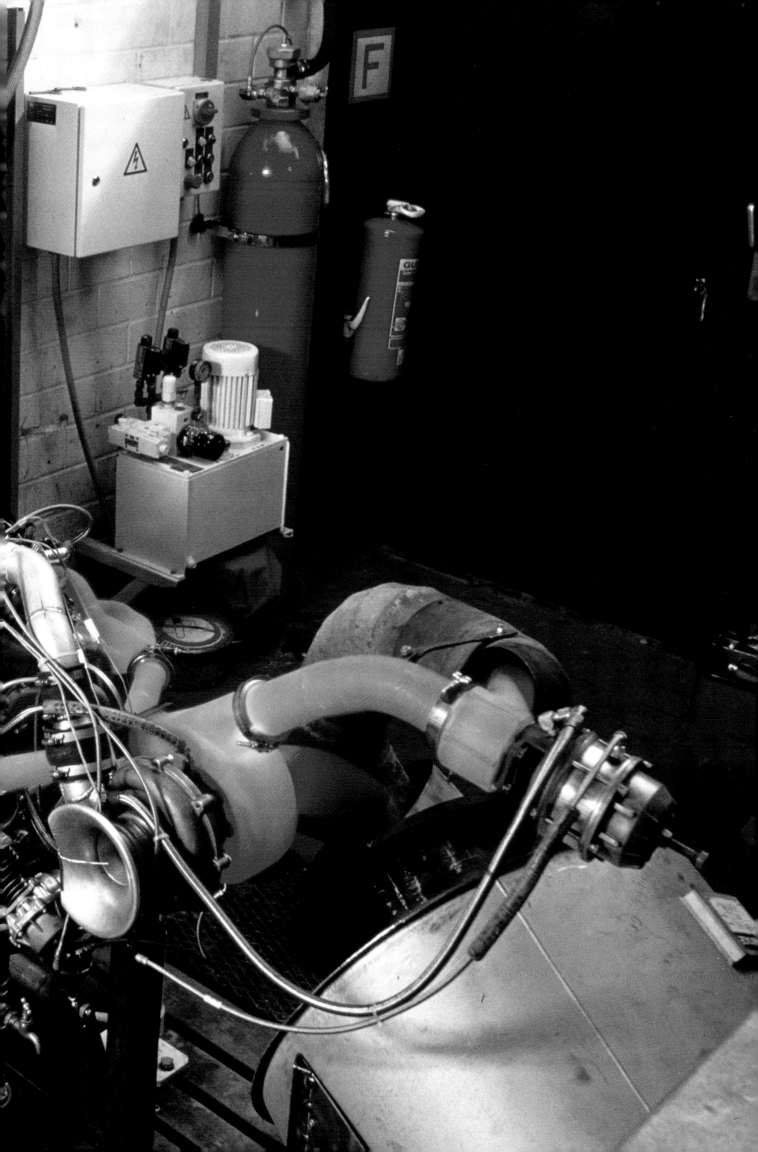

THE
SIXTIES

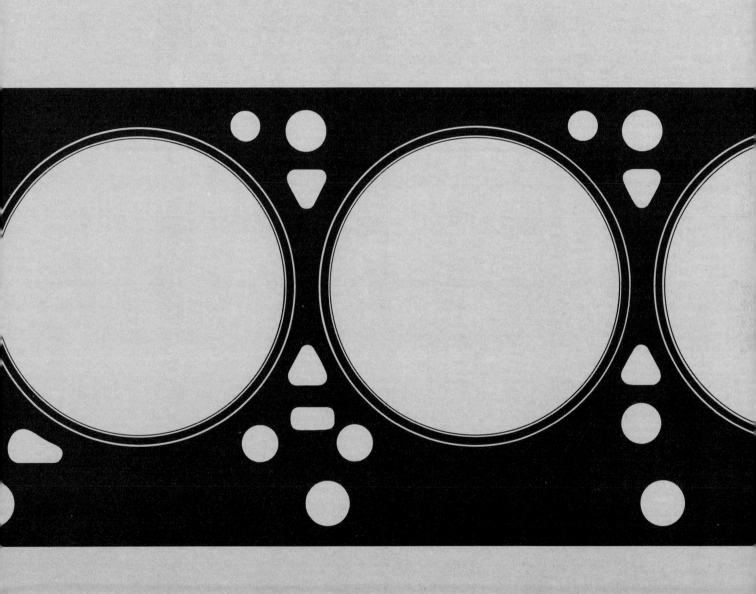

Indy Cars 1965-69

The golden age of supercharging at Indianapolis was the late Twenties. The period was dominated by two specialist car builders: Fred Duesenberg and Harry Miller. Both developed straight eights inspired by the classic d.o.h.c., four valve Peugeot racing engine. Miller, who employed Leo Goossen as designer and Fred Offenhauser as constructor, even copied the combined head and block of the European Grand Prix straight eight. Through the Twenties the authorities cut maximum displacement from 183 to 122 then 91 cubic inches but the development of supercharging saw power output heading strongly in the opposite direction...

After Chadwick supercharged racing car development had continued in Europe and blower technology arrived at The Brickyard when Mercedes entered a team of 2.0 litre, 122 cu. in. cars for the 1923 500. These cars were no faster than the same displacement, 120b.h.p. American straight eights but they set Duesenberg thinking. He had come into contact with aero engine supercharging development during the war and he had a blown car ready for the 1924 race. It won. However, Duesenberg's was a very crude supercharger installation and his car likewise showed no real performance gain over the contemporary, same displacement unblown Miller. Luck rather than speed was the key to the first blown victory, a victory that inevitably set the ball rolling.

Rapid progress in the superchargers employed and their drive mechanisms saw the 91 cu.in. (1.5 litre) supercharged cars of 1927 reach 150b.h.p. then the development of aftercooling and alcohol based fuel took power over 200b.h.p.

Aftercooling is the process of cooling the pressurised charge air prior to its arrival in the intake manifold, regaining density lost through heating and giving the cylinder an easier time. The Indy Car aftercoolers were crude air:air heat exchanger radiators while the use of alcohol further aided to cooling. Alcohol has a high latent heat of evaporation and this it helps cool the charge and internal engine parts, and it has a high octane rating – it is less heat intolerant than petrol. The most effective alcohol fuel was found to be methyl or 'wood' alcohol, which is otherwise known as methanol. The drawback of the use of methanol was markedly increased fuel consumption since it has around 50% fewer calories per unit weight than petrol.

At this point the authorities cried enough and supercharging was banned for 1930. It was not permitted again until 1937. By that stage Duesenberg was dead and Miller had gone bankrupt. Just before the Miller company went under Goossen designed a new four cylinder engine and Offenhauser bought the rights to this. Thus was born the Offenhauser Engineering Company and the legendary 'Offy' engine.

The Offy had been inspired by a four cylinder, eight valve Miller marine engine that had been converted for racing under the cost-cutting rules introduced in 1930. Like the earlier Miller straight eight the Offy had a combined iron head and block, plus an aluminium crankcase with bolt-in main bearing bulkheads. And it had four valves per cylinder, driven by twin, gear driven camshafts. It displaced 250 cu.in. – 4.1 litres – and ran, unblown, on a 95 octane benzol/petrol mix (with a 10.5:1 compression ratio) to suit the Depression-era regulations. Simple yet effective, it produced around 225b.h.p. – 55b.h.p. per litre – at 5,500r.p.m. and an example won the

1935 '500'.

Following the re-admission of superchargers in 1937, for 1938 Indianapolis switched to European Grand Prix regulations – 4.5 litres (275cu.in.) unblown, 3.0 litres (183cu.in.) blown with fuel free. This opened the door to a number of exciting supercharged engines, three of which were designed by Goossen and constructed by Offenhauser for various clients. The Offenhauser produced projects were the Sparks-Thorne in line six, the Meyer-Bowes straight eight and the Novi V8. The legendary blown Novi screamed to 8,000r.p.m. and produced over 500b.h.p. on alcohol fuel.

Although Grand Prix regulations were revised after the war, Indianapolis retained the pre-war formula. However, after the war Louis Meyer and Dale Drake bought the Offenhauser Engineering Company, allowing Fred Offenhauser to take retirement. Goossen continued to work for the company and the 1947 – '49 Indy 500 races were won by Lou Moore's lightweight, unblown 270 cu.in. Offy powered cars. Moore exploited the potential of the high – 110 – octane petrol developed for military aircraft during the war. This allowed him to run a 13.5:1 compression ratio and achieve superb fuel economy – the key to the success of his cars, along with good tyre wear. At an easy 5,000r.p.m. they were running no more than 270b.h.p.

More power was needed subsequently as the opposition got its act together and the early Fifties brought Hilborn mechanical fuel injection together with a general use of methanol, features of Indy Car racing that would continue for many years. The Hilborn injection system was simple: it consisted of a rotary pump and a metering valve. The pump was driven at engine speed and thus increased fuel pressure with increasing speed while the valve's movement was directly linked to throttle movement. One injector nozzle was positioned immediately downstream of each cylinder's throttle butterfly. Since the Indy engine operated over a limited range of speed and load and alcohol fuel is relatively insensitive to the fuel:air ratio the crude Hilborn system did just fine.

Fuel injection eliminated the breathing restriction caused by carburettors and on methanol 270 cu.in. Offy power went over 350b.h.p. at 5,500r.p.m. For qualifying, 15% nitromethane offered in excess of 400b.h.p. A downsized, injected supercharged Offy was tried but did not provide an instant performance gain and this route was not explored. In 1957 the regulations limited engines to 256cu.in. – 4.2 litres – (171 cu.in. blown) but a higher revving shorter stroke (almost square) Offy was developed to give 360b.h.p. at 6,600r.p.m. and power subsequently crept over 400b.h.p. – reaching 100b.h.p. per litre – still on straight methanol.

A figure of 100b.h.p. per litre is not very impressive given the use of methanol fuel but the Offy, although having a four valve head, was somewhat dated. It had become an Indianapolis institution by the time Ford made its big money Brickyard onslaught in the early Sixties. As such, it wasn't going to die easily. And Indy Car racers were nothing if not conservative.

The Ford engine arrived in 1963 in the form of a stock block V8 which was replaced by a purpose designed V8 race engine for 1964. The V8 configuration provided for a shorter stroke than the Offy, lifting revs while the 32 valve, four cam Ford also enjoyed more port area per cubic inch for more torque. The net result was comfortably over 110b.h.p. per litre – around 475b.h.p. at 8,2500r.p.m. on straight methanol. And there was potential to rev to 8,800r.p.m., teams disregarding the factory recommended rev limit without problem. Ford V8 performance was well beyond the reach of the similar displacement, 16 valve four cylinder engine that had been sitting so comfortably in the seat of power.

Having established its V8 as a winner Ford contracted Louis Meyer – splitting with Dale Drake – to supply it to the Indy Car world. Drake continued with the outgunned Offy. If the old engine was to have any sort of future, the only answer was to reduce displacement to 171 cu.in. – 2.8 litres – and supercharge. An option that hadn't been contemplated for over a decade. And never before had turbo-supercharging been considered for the hallowed unit.

However, a freak turbocharged diesel racing engine had run at Indianapolis in 1952. Appropriately enough, the turbocharged racing car story was started by a truck engine manufacturer. In 1950 a new 402 cu.in. 6.6 litres supercharged displacement limit had been set for diesel engines to encourage a new avenue of technical exploration. This suited the giant Cummins Engine company, a major manufacturer of truck engines which had already found good publicity sponsoring unconventional, slow but economical diesel engined Indy cars in the Thirties. Cummins had a six cylinder engine which could easily be bored to 401cu.in. and this was first fitted with a Roots-type supercharger to provide around 350b.h.p. at 4,000r.p.m. Leading chassis builder Frank Kurtis put the big, heavy power plant on track at the back of the grid.

The car was an early retirement with supercharger drive failure.

Undaunted, Cummins was back in 1952 exploiting the new generation of compact truck turbochargers. To reduce frontal area and the centre of gravity Kurtis laid the big straight six engine on its side and positioned the turbocharger ahead of it. It was one of the lowest cars the Speedway had ever seen. No wastegate was fitted and the relatively large turbocharger unit chosen provided 2.1 bar at the maximum 4,000r.p.m., for almost 400b.h.p. However, as the throttle was backed off plenum pressure dropped to 1.7 bar in the turns, throttle lag was pronounced and the car lacked acceleration off the turns.

The trick was to anticipate the awful lag, hitting the throttle early. In the hands of Freddy Agabashian the powerful if heavy new diesel car ran 139.1m.p.h. for pole position. The turbo-supercharger had arrived in dramatic fashion! Since the Cummins diesel car was heavy it was hard on its tyres but it had the potential to run through the 500 miles on one tankful. Consequently, Agabashian planned to run conservatively in an effort to make one set of tyres last the distance. Alas, he only managed 175 miles then the low set compressor intake had sucked up so much dirt that the inlet was totally clogged up, sidelining the car.

Sadly, that was the end of the diesel engine adventure and for a long while it looked to have been the end of the turbo-supercharger at Indianapolis. However, at the Brickyard conditions were favourable for turbocharging: the track was run with little variation from wide open throttle so lag was of less concern than on a road course

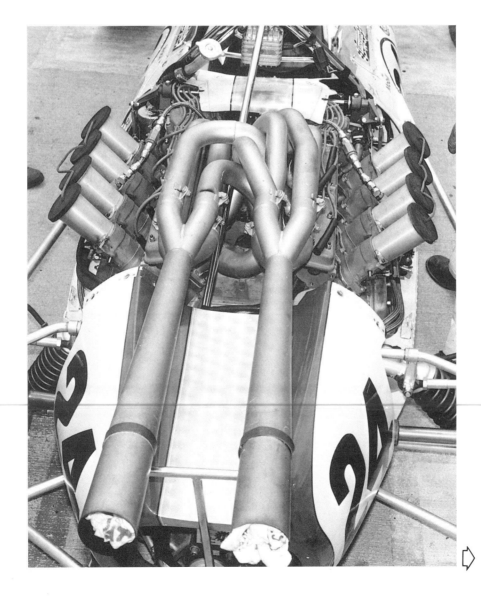

while, as we have noted, the regular methanol fuel offered a valuable internal cooling property and was less heat intolerant than petrol. Could turbocharging rather than supercharging be the saviour for the Offy?

Bob DeBisschop, an engineer with the research department of Garrett, produced the pioneering turbo Offy engine in conjunction with fuel injection manufacturer Stuart Hilborn and race engineer Herb Porter. The first installation was rigged up using one of the spare engines in Porter's 'shop' and an off-the-shelf diesel turbocharger in the summer of '65. The immediate result was over 600b.h.p. whereas the Ford V8 needed a dangerously radial methanol/nitromethane brew to push much over 500b.h.p.

The Garrett turbocharging system weighed less than 10kg. and the production turbocharger was able to run as high as 120,000r.p.m. and could pump manifold pressure well over 2.0 bar. In response to the potential demonstrated by DeBisschop, Hilborn and Porter, Dale Drake produced an updated short stroke version of his classic Offenhauser to further help counter the Ford invasion. It was the first Offy to be over square, which was intended to allow it to reach 9,000r.p.m. With a shorter stroke crankshaft came shorter con rods and a shorter block. That in turn called for a redesigned cam drive and Goossen reduced the number of gears in the drive from 13 to 10. At the same time weight was saved by casting the head/block assembly in aluminium with siamesed iron liners and bronze-based valve seat inserts.

The lightweight over square Offy was sold without induction and exhaust system, allowing Hilborn to supply a suitable turbocharger installation, together with his familiar mechanical fuel injection. Alternatively, Dick Jones of the Champion Spark Plug Racing division had produced a supercharged Offy conversion, employing a Roots blower. Jones' work had started in 1964 following the takeover by the Autolite-sparked Ford V8. However, the supercharged option could not match the potential shown by the turbo-supercharged engine.

Logically, the turbocharged Indy Car engine was designed to run a more or less constant boost pressure throughout the lap, assuring good torque coming off the high speed turns without blowing the engine apart on the straight where the engine ran higher r.p.m. and the wastegate bled the excess pressure. The 1966 turbo package included a Garrett AiResearch TE06 diesel turbocharger and a suitable wastegate. An 8.0:1 compression ratio was recommended and this original 168 cu.in. turbocharged Offenhauser was rated 625b.h.p. at 8,000r.p.m. on a modest 2.1 bar compared to 540b.h.p. at 7,800r.p.m. for the supercharged version, which was blown to 1.9 bar. The turbo engine did not waste power

driving the blower, while the 2.1 bar figure was the most considered safe (and could be run around the entire lap), although the wastegate could be adjusted to give higher power...

In fact, even 2.1 bar proved too high a manifold pressure in 1966. The simple fuel injection system hadn't yet been properly adapted to its new application and excessive heat played havoc with engine internals. The boost had to be backed off and a supercharged version was the fastest of the new generation Offy engines. Although aluminium rejects heat faster than iron, Drake subsequently switched back to the original iron block with its greater strength and better water circulation while providing additional water jacketing in the region of the exhaust valve seats. Further, water flow was stepped up 20%.

In 1967 the turbocharged Offys could run up to 2.1 bar safely. Lloyd Ruby qualified on the fourth row and finished seventh. The following year Bobby Unser put the engine into the winner's circle. By that stage the Ford engineers had joined in the game, the potential of turbo-supercharging obvious. The Indy community was as conservative as ever and manifold pressure was rarely much over 2.0 bar. There was clearly so much more to come.

Ford had commissioned special turbochargers from Schwitzer and introduced a more sophisticated fuel injection system based on Bendix aircraft equipment. On the dyno the Ford ran 2.6 bar for 650b.h.p. at 9,000r.p.m. and on the track one V8 car recorded an astonishing 214m.p.h. top speed. However, the inlet manifolding of the V8 was complicated since the inlet ports were set between inlet and exhaust camshafts and the turbocharged V8s wouldn't run clean in 1968. Ford was now the underdog, and it would stay that way...

For 1969 the displacement of overhead cam turbo engines was reduced by 9 cu.in. – to 162cu.in./2.65 litres – yet the Offy output increased, through a switch to the bigger Garrett TE067 turbocharger which could pump up to 20% more air at 80,000 rather than 100,000r.p.m. It provided a better match to the Offenhauser engine and power rose to 730b.h.p. at 8,500 r.p.m. running 2.5 bar. And lag had been reduced through the introduction of lighter turbine and compressor impellers which reduced inertia, while a squirt of extra fuel as the throttle was pressed was used to create a surge of exhaust gas to spin the rotor shaft. By the end of the Sixties turbocharger technology was well established at the Brickyard. With its wide open curves throttle lag was not of serious concern and the methanol fuel was ideal in the face of increased heat. Road racing was another matter altogether.

The engine that sparked the turbocharged racing car revolution: the Ford V8. Engine power is a function of b.m.e.p. and rotational speed. The arrival of the V8 took speed and hence power out of reach of the popular Offenhauser but turbocharging promised to keep the four alive.

1966 saw the first appearance of the turbocharged Offenhauser at the Speedway. This is Bobby Unser's Vita-Fresh sponsored machine, one of a trio of turbocars, none of which featured or finished. Just two years later Unser won the classic 500 mile race running a turbocharged Offy.

THE SEVENTIES

Can Am Cars 1972-73

The first turbocharged road racing car was seen in 1969. Clearly inspired by Unser's historic Indianapolis victory, in December 1968 BMW Technical Director Alex von Falkenhausen surprised his colleagues with a plan to turbocharge the Munich concern's contemporary 2.0 litre saloon racer. BMW knew nothing of turbocharging and its pioneering work was assisted by Michael May, the Swiss engineering genius who had run the first wing on a racing car in the mid Fifties and had later helped develop fuel injection in Formula One. The BMW 2.0 litre – two valve in line four cylinder engine had a deep, rugged monobloc and was lightly blown by a single Eberspacher turbocharger lifting power from 200 to 275b.h.p. Turbo lag was pronounced, there was no aftercooler and on pump petrol detonation was frequent. Nevertheless, the car ran against unblown models of similar displacement and it somehow hung together to win four races. Then turbocharging was outlawed for European production car racing.

The BMW exercise in turn inspired Porsche. In 1969 Porsche introduced its 5.0 litre, 12 cylinder Typ 917 sports-prototype which was developed into the 917K, the 600b.h.p.-plus projectile that dominated the World Championship for Makes in 1970 and '71. Meantime its R&D division (which contained the racing car design and development department) began studying the potential of turbocharging. In 1971 works driver Jo Siffert was supplied a 917 spyder chassis christened 917/10, still propelled by a standard engine with which to contest the unlimited capacity Can Am series. A 3.0 litre World Championship capacity limit for 1972 had turned the factory's attention towards Can Am. Although a yet more powerful engine was clearly required, the technical freedom offered by Can Am was attractive...

Turbocharging was one of two options. A major feature of the 917 engine was a central power take off and this made it quite feasible to add two cylinders at each end, producing a hefty 7.5 litre displacement. And whereas the push rod 7.0 litre Chevrolet engine that dominated Can Am was incapable of producing much over 100b.h.p. per litre (its push rod valve operation limiting maximum speed), the 917 engine in 5.0 litre guise was worth over 120b.h.p. per litre. The potential was obvious.

However, while the Porsche R&D department was starting the 16 cylinder Can Am project, it was also toying with the possibility of turbocharging the 917 engine. Early in 1970 it had started testing a turbocharged Typ 910 2.0 litre engine and that soon gave way to experiments with a 4.5 litre 12 cylinder 917 engine. Thankfully, Can Am races allowed the use of high octane racing fuel. A 1500b.h.p. flash reading helped shelve the 16 cylinder project with only five engines built. It was clear that the central drive made the 7.5 litre derivative workable but Porsche saw more power, more long term development potential and an important relevance to future road car projects from the turbocharged alternative. There was also the question of flag waving for Porsche's growing R&D department, which was an increasingly important source of revenue for the company.

The R&D department was based in a new giant complex at Weissach, out in the countryside well away from the Stuttgart factory and undertook research work on behalf of many outside clients as well as the factory. Weissach was run by Helmuth Bott while Hans Mezger headed the racing car design group – the Konstruktion Rennfahrzeuge – and responsible for development of the Can Am engine and chassis were, respectively, Valentine Schaffer and Helmut Flegl. Flegl's car development team reported to Racing Manager Peter Falk. His aim was to see a turbocharged version of the 12 cylinder 917 engine prepared in time for the 1972 Can Am Championship.

Whereas the 1970 and '71 World Championship for Makes campaigns had been run by JW Automotive, the new Can Am programme was to be entrusted to Penske Racing, the highly successful Philadelphia team run by Roger Penske. Penske was contracted to run a single car for Mark Donohue. A qualified engineer, Donohue had won the 1967 and '68 American Road Racing Championships, and the '68, '69 and '71 Trans Am Championships with Penske. In 1971 he dominated the Indy 500 before retiring. Soon afterwards, accompanied by Penske's engineer Don Cox, he had started flying regularly to Weissach to test the emerging Can Am version of the 917.

The 917 engine had abandoned Porsche's traditional boxer engine layout for a 180 degree V12 configuration to reduce power sapping inner compression and turbulence. It consequently ran a six pin rather than 12 pin crankshaft. Each pin was phased at 120 degrees from its neighbour – the crankshaft configuration employed an in line six – which ensured good balance. It had been necessary to retain a flat engine configuration since, for political reasons, Porsche had found itself continuing to exploit its traditional air cooling. The air had to be supplied by a fan which sapped a little power. However, drag caused by pushing a water radiator through the air did not have to be overcome. The serious drawback of air cooling was a restriction to two valves per cylinder head – four valves would not have left room for adequate cooling fins. Further, the fins around the cylinders caused the cylinders to have to be widely spaced. That in turn led to a longer crankshaft. The length of the crankshaft required for an air cooled 12 cylinder engine was such that Porsche calculations had suggested torsional vibration could be a serious problem. It was in view of the danger identified by Porsche that Mezger's long shaft had its power take off gear situated at the centre.

Given air cooling, the cooling function of the oil system was important. Mezger estimates that the 180 degree V12 was 15 – 20% oil cooled in normally aspirated form. Cooling air was supplied by a single centrally located horizontal fan whereas the boxer engines had always run an upright fan at the front of the engine. In fact, the 917 engine had borrowed reciprocating parts from the earlier 3.0 litre Typ 908 boxer engine to save time and expense. Indeed, even the cylinders (individually detachable from the crankcase) and heads were from the superseded boxer.

The cylinders were consequently aluminium with chrome plated bores at the outset but in 1971 Porsche had switched to a nickel-silicon carbide coating developed by piston supplier Mahle primarily for the NSU Wankel engine. This so-called Nikasil coating, unlike chrome plating was not in any danger of lifting and worked well with aluminium, offering excellent friction characteristics. And alloy pistons running in Nikasil liners were appropriate for a turbo engine, tight clearance avoiding intense combustion 'torching down' the gap between piston and bore, while good conductivity helped get heat out to the fins.

Of further benefit to the adaptation to turbocharging was a piston cooling option developed by Mezger from the outset. This took the form of oil jets spraying the piston crown from underneath. Unblown, the 917 engine could be run without such sprays but fitting 1mm. diameter jets tapping 5 – 10% of total oil flow through the engine had reduced piston crown temperature by 30 – 35 degrees centigrade. That allowed an 0.5:1 higher compression ratio to be run.

The 917 engine had a classic two valve (wide angle) hemispherical head and domed piston (the so called 'orange peel' chamber) and twin plug ignition and could produce 120b.h.p. per litre unblown. Compared to a four valve pent roof chamber, an orange peel chamber gave a high surface: volume ratio and caused relatively long flame travel which increased susceptibility to detonation and discouraged the spread of the sort of turbulence needed for good combustion. The 917 had a slightly narrower valve angle than the earlier boxers for a more compact chamber, and still had an angle of 65 degrees included.

The 917's unusual crankshaft ran in plain bearings supported by a vertically-split crankcase. It was turned by robust H-section forged titanium con rods. The short skirted piston carried Goetze rings and its spherical crown had valve clearance notches. Between head and cylinder was an O-ring gasket, allowing metal to metal contact to provide good heat transfer. The head was equipped with cast iron valve seat inserts and cast iron valve guides. The valves were of nimonic steel and were hollow and sodium filled to aid heat dissipation.

The lefthand inlet camshaft drove a 12-plunger injection pump designed and produced by Bosch. The fuel quantity was controlled by a three-dimensional cam which in turn was responded to the position of the throttle slides and engine revolutions. The injection nozzle was mounted as high as possible in a tall g.r.p. induction funnel, injecting downstream. The funnel was attached to the manifold, which carried throttle slides. Positioning the injection nozzle high kept the process of atomisation cool for a homogeneous mixture, and to avoid the danger of accumulation of fuel above the throttle slides on over-run, the three-dimensional cam (which continued to inject the quantity required for idle even with the throttle shut) interrupted the fuel supply at engine speeds in excess of 4000 r.p.m. when the throttle was shut.

Bosch supplied the CD ignition system while the dry sump lubrication system featured seven pumps and a large, 30 litre oil tank in recognition of its role in helping cool the engine. Unblown, the 917 engine ran a 10.5:1 compression ratio as standard and in 1970 a 4.4mm. longer stroke crankshaft and a 1mm. bigger bore gave a displacement of 4.9 rather than 4.5 litres while in 1971 an 86.5mm. bore gave a full 5.0 litres, the engine then producing 630b.h.p. at its 8,400r.p.m. safe maximum.

To produce the first turbocharged version, Schaffer took a 4.5 litre engine, changed the piston to drop the compression ratio to 6.5:1 and reduced inlet and exhaust valve overlap by using an exhaust cam for both valves. It was then a case of producing a new exhaust manifold to lead each bank's exhaust to the turbocharger, and suitable plumbing to feed the compressed charge air to the twelve vertical inlet stacks. The charge air feed pipe was split to a separate pressure-balancing plenum chamber above each row of six stacks. The turbocharger employed was a standard Eberspacher diesel engine model.

This test engine started running on the bench early in 1971 and the decision was soon taken to employ a separate turbocharger for each bank of cylinders. Using two smaller turbochargers reduced inertia, cutting lag. The twin Eberspacher units ran up to 90,000r.p.m. on ball bearings and could deliver a quoted 0.55kg. of charge air per second at a temperature of 150 degrees centigrade.

Exhaust temperature went as high as 850 degrees and while the compressor housing and wheel were aluminium, the Eberspacher turbine assemble was fashioned from high temperature steel. The two induction systems shared a common wastegate, with a crossover pipe to equalise pressure on each side. The wastegate was supplied by Garrett and was of the usual diaphragm and spring type.

The early dyno tests suggested that durability wasn't the best feature of the Can Am turbo but as Schaffer proceeded things gradually improved. For example, a problem of exhaust valves tending to seize in their guide was solved by shortening the guide and modifying and chrome plating the valve stem. It didn't, however, otherwise prove necessary to modify the heads.

By December of 1971 Schaffer had improved durability to the point at which the engine was able to survive an eight hour full power run. However, the real problems were to be found on the track. Part of the difficulty Porsche faced could be traced to an engine fire in the middle of '71 in the engine test cell area at Weissach which had upset the best part of three months development. Lack of development saw the challenge of 'driveability' still to be overcome.

The extent of the problem had been made clear when test driver Willi Kauhsen first tried the prototype turbocharged 917/10 at Weissach early in the summer of '71. It had been a traumatic experience for Kauhsen. Flegl recalls: 'Kauhsen was testing a 917L, the 917/20 and the turbo engine at that time. At first the turbo took an hour to start! And when it eventually started it went slowly, then suddenly exploded – there was nothing in the middle. And there was long, long turbo lag – unacceptable'.

Bit by bit Kauhsen was able to bring the difficult turbocar's times down but by the end of the year he was only lapping two tenths faster than Donohue's best in a normally aspirated chassis development car. Siffert had also experienced the on – off temperament of the engine in tests at Weissach and Hockenheim and like Kauhsen had found the engine tending to run on after the throttle had been lifted. That had caused some hairy moments!

By the end of the year Schaffer had moulded the turbo engine's final mechanical configuration. In addition to the revised pistons and cams, cooling capacity had been increased by exchanging the bevel gears in the fan drive so that the fan turned at 1.2 times engine speed. The ignition timing was fixed at 22 degrees b.t.d.c. To stop the engine running on as fuel spilled from the injectors even after the pump had been cut, the injectors were repositioned lower down and close to new butterfly throttle valves. Slide valves suffer friction problems in the face of heavily pressurised air.

Donohue's introduction to turbocharged road racing came in late January at the Road Atlanta circuit. After towing the first turbo car sent out to Penske to get it started, Donohue found the task of circumnavigating the track near impossible due to the all – or – nothing syndrome that had bugged Kauhsen and Siffert. Eventually, driving on the ignition switch, an impeller failed. Pieces flew into Penske's sole test engine, destroying it.

Another turbo engine was supplied in March and Schaffer and Flegl flew out with it. Still the car proved difficult to drive and Donohue went back to Weissach with the Porsche engineers. Like Kauhsen, he found it hard to better his normally aspirated lap times on the test track and he and Penske took the view that early Can Am races should be skipped while efforts continued to make the turbo car more driveable.

Then came the breakthrough. So far the Bosch injection pump had been sensitive only to engine speed and load – throttle opening. An additional control was now fitted, responding to boost. Flegl: 'With a normally aspirated car the injection system had responded to revs and throttle position – we were used to working with those parameters. Now we had a third, boost and we had to learn how to work with it.

'Right from the first moment the setting of the pump

had been correct for high boost. Intermediate boost, low boost had been incorrect. We now had to run different settings on the dyno, then all the knowledge had to be put into the injection pump. It took two or three months to produce a completely new system, with the pump about right.

'Donohue got into the car, left the pits, put the throttle down and the engine started to run – before that he'd had something but it hadn't really corresponded to the throttle. Programming the pump properly was the breakthrough'.

With the addition of some more valving, the exciting new engine was now ready to race. One butterfly valve was put on each plenum, linked to the throttle and designed to bleed air out when the throttles were closed, in order to reduce the back pressure faced by the impeller. In addition, four suction operated valves were located on top of each plenum to ensure there wasn't a vacuum in the induction system while the turbos were spooling up. The most significant decision at this point was to use a 5.0 litre engine as the base for the units sent out to Penske. Of the three supplied by Weissach for the 1972 season, maximum power was reportedly in the range 880 – 920b.h.p. according to the boost setting which was adjustable in the range 1.3 – 1.4 bar gauge (2.3 – 2.4 bar absolute). Maximum boost was attained in the region of 5,000 – 5,500r.p.m.

The Can Am series commenced at Mosport Park in June with the works McLaren-Chevrolets hot favourite after years of domination. However, Donohue won pole and led the first 18 laps. Then a pressure relief valve stuck and the engine went sick. Three laps were lost. However, only one McLaren finished and Donohue clawed his way back to second. Alas, testing for the second round at Road Atlanta, Donohue crashed, wrecked the car and put himself on the sidelines with a damaged knee. The accident had been caused by improper fixing of the tail section, which had blown off with disastrous results. Donohue's car was replaced by the team's test car which was driven by George Follmer. Follmer found better sorted McLarens at Road Atlanta and was content to split them on the grid as he played himself in. He got ahead in the race but couldn't shake the orange cars off. However, one retired, the other crashed and Porsche had its first factory Can Am triumph.

The Porsche hierarchy flew out to see more of the same at Watkins Glen but Follmer didn't seem able to get to grips with the car on this circuit. After losing time in the pits he finished an uninspired fifth. Following testing, at Mid Ohio Follmer put Porsche back on top, then at Road America the advance was even more pronounced. It was now clear that while the McLaren-Chevrolet was near the limit of its potential the 917/10 had a long way to go. Making life more difficult for the hard pressed McLaren team, Donohue was ready to return to the cockpit and Penske built a second car. However, at Donnybrook both fell by the wayside. As did both McLarens. Victory went to a McLaren privateer. Then came Edmonton and Donohue's first win. Follmer salvaged third, having suffered a puncture. Next came Laguna Seca and Donohue led most of the race before letting Follmer through to clinch the Can Am title.

Although, faced with little profit potential, McLaren withdrew its opposition, there were many improvements that Flegl and Donohue wanted to incorporate to make the Can Am Porsche quicker for 1973. The most obvious improvement for the new car was a 5.4 litre engine. This displacement had been developed for 'atmo' customer Group 7 cars via a stretch of the bore size from the 5.0 litre's 86.8mm. to 90mm. This significantly reduced the head/cylinder contact surface area and that was not in the best interest of a turbo engine. Nevertheless, by mid '72 Schaffer had started work on a 5.4 litre turbo. He created a truly awesome engine – with a 90mm. bore and a 70.4mm. stroke it had a capacity of 5374cc.

Again the cylinders were Nikasil and again the compression ratio was 6.5:1. The cams remained the same but the ignition timing was slightly altered, to 20 degrees b.t.d.c. Schaffer also simplified the induction system, eliminating the extra valves designed to reduce impeller back pressure and the section valves, a move made possible through better matching of turbocharger to engine. Pressurised at 2.3 bar absolute, the 5.4 litre engine was rated 1,100b.h.p. at 7,800r.p.m. and a cockpit control was introduced to allow Donohue to adjust the boost level via the wastegate setting, in the unlikely event of him challenged by other cars...

But, in spite of the engine's output, when Donohue tried it in his late season, he cut his Weissach lap time by only 0.5 seconds. It was clear that chassis advances were required to match the power. The 917/10 enjoyed a reasonable amount of downforce but more could and, with the extra power, had to be exploited. Additionally, there was the call for a longer wheelbase and these factors were accounted for by the so called 917/30 raced by Donohue in 1973, which had a 200mm. longer wheelbase, a longer tail and a reshaped body form.

The longer wheelbase allowed fuel tankage to be increased from 325 to 350 litres. Even so, Flegl and Schaffer felt this was marginal for 200 mile races, given the thirst of the 5.4 litre engine. Consequently, additional cells were fitted taking total capacity to 400 litres.

The '73 Can Am posed only one question: how superior would the 917/30 prove over the 917/10s Porsche sold to customer teams? At Mosport Donohue hit a backmarker and consequently finished well down. The race was won by a 917/10. Road Atlanta was run as a two part race. Donohue easily won part one but in part two a fuel leak cost two laps: Follmer's private 917/10 won. And at Watkins Glen Donohue crashed in practice. However, the back up car went on to victory. The only other trauma was a late engine change at Laguna Seca. Donohue won all the remaining races.

Having seen Donohue walk the title, the SCCA announced a very stiff fuel ration for '74. Stiff enough to strangle the Porsche turbo engine. The Penske contract consequently ended a year early. Nevertheless, one car remained at Philadelphia and as a strictly private entry this was run in the '74 Mid Ohio Can Am race. Donohue had found the best mileage at Mid Ohio. With the champion having gone into retirement Redman took the controls and with the boost well down he gave the pace making Shadow-Chevrolets something to think about. Only tyre problems cost victory.

In Europe, the turbocar lived on in the German based Interseries, where it had reigned supreme since its introduction in mid '72. The factory lent the original 917/30 development car, with wheelbase set as standard 917/10 and 917/10 bodywork, to Herbie Muller and using a 4.5 litre turbo engine he won the '74 title. That was no great feat.

The only moment of glory left for the 917 turbo came in '75 when Penske dusted off his '30 chassis for a closed circuit speed record attempt at the high banked Talladega oval. Donohue was out of retirement and at the wheel. Alas, he blew one engine after another around the 2.66 mile track chasing AJ Foyt's 217.854m.p.h. record, set in an Indy Car. Constant high boost running caused detonation but the introduction of aftercooling did the trick: 221.120m.p.h.

The technical freedom offered by the Can Am Championship gave turbocharging a chance to take a foothold in the road racing sphere. Porsche, ever keen to exploit new technology, introduced the turbocharged sports-racer, these fabulous 5.0 litre 917/10s of 1972.

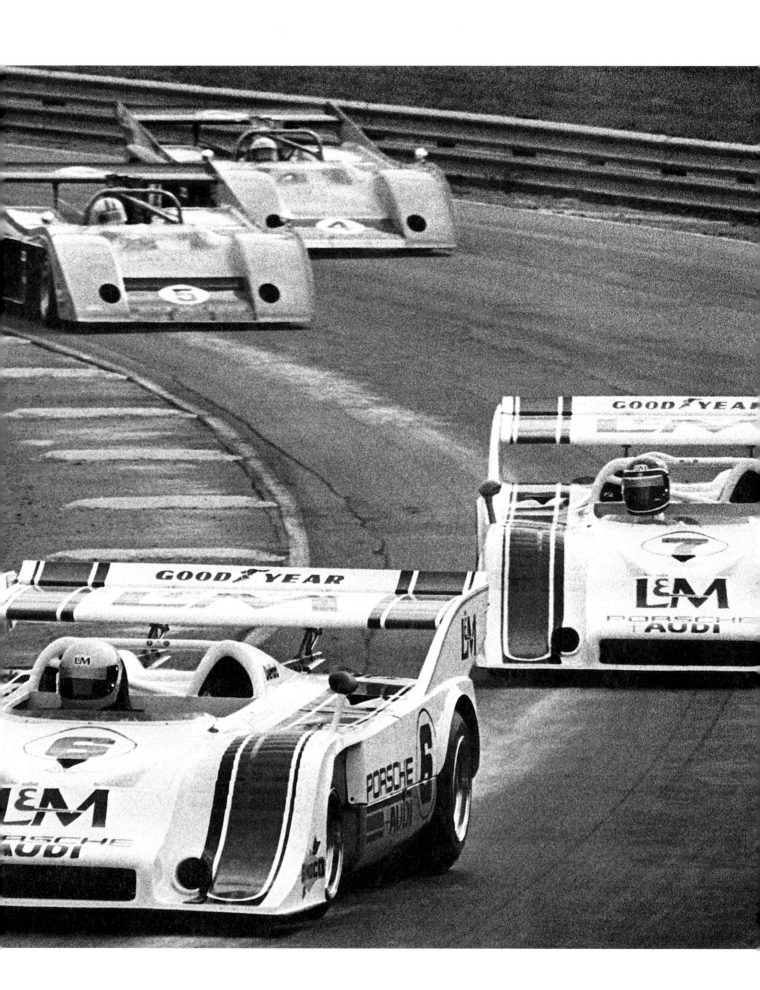

Prototypes 1974

While Porsche was active in Can Am, its former playground the World Championship for Makes was in decline. However, plans were hatching for a switch to a new Group 5 category catering for radically modified production cars, retaining little more than the engine block, the engine position and the silhouette of the base model. Bott had played an important role in the development of the six cylinder boxer engined 911 road car as a GT racer and he was keen to see it further developed into a turbocharged silhouette racer benefiting from the lessons of the Can Am programme. The new category was slated for introduction in '75 so in '74 Porsche entered an experimental turbocharged derivative of its Carrera RSR GT racer in World Championship for Makes races, exploiting the freedom of Group 6 Prototype regulations.

Porsche had started serious turbo development on the 911's Typ 901 six cylinder boxer engine in 1973. The engine had come a long way from the original road car unit introduced in the mid Sixties. The original Typ 901 engine displaced 1991cc (80 x 66 mm.) and had individual aluminium heads on individual Biral cylinder barrels bolted either side of an aluminium crankcase cum sump that split vertically into symmetrical halves. Biral was a combination of an iron liner in an aluminium sleeve, the latter forming the cooling fins. The separate heads on each side were joined by a magnesium cam box that carried a s.o.h.c. chain driven off the front end from a layshaft running under the relatively high mounted crankshaft and geared to it. The short layshaft was supported by two bearings and a shaft was screwed into the back of it to drive the oil pump which was situated at the back of the centrally scavenged sump.

Each camshaft actuated two valves per cylinder through rockers to allow the valves to be disposed either side of the cylinder axis in a hemispherical combustion chamber. The piston crown was domed to match (with light valve clearance notches) forming the 'orange peel' chamber. Ignition was via a single plug per cylinder while each cylinder was fed through its own Solex carburettor. The inlet manifold fed down into the head with the exhaust tucked underneath the engine.

Conventional reciprocating parts drove an eight bearing steel crankshaft, each con rod having its own pin and there being an additional bearing to steady the layshaft drive gear and to provide an oil feed to the crankshaft. The 901's six-pin crankshaft allowed adjacent crankpins to be set at 180 degrees to one another so that opposite pistons would 'box' towards and away from each other. On the nose of the crankshaft was a pulley which drove the belt powering the fan which had the alternator mounted in its hub. The fan was vertically mounted ahead of the cylinders with g.r.p. ducting to direct air to the barrels and the generously finned heads, VW Beetle style.

The Porsche flat six was designed to be rugged and to allow for future capacity increases. As early as 1966 a supertuned derivative was powering the marque's Sports-Prototype racer, the 2.0 litre Carrera 6. This featured chrome plated bores allowing all-aluminium cylinders and also had a lightweight magnesium crankcase, as later used for 911 road cars. Its stock heads were ported and were fitted with larger valves while it also had a higher compression ratio (10.3:1), forged pistons and titanium con rods. With a tuned exhaust, two plugs per cylinder

and high pressure mechanical injection (from a six plunger Bosch pump) it produced 220b.h.p.

Although the six cylinder Sports-Prototypes had soon given way to larger capacity eight then twelve cylinder contenders turbocharging could and would give the Typ 901 engine a new lease of life in the international endurance racing arena. As we have seen, the twelve cylinder Typ 917 had abandoned the boxer layout for improved power potential. A boxer six is easy to balance and fires on cylinders in alternate banks so advantage can be taken of pressure wave tuning principles. However, the major drawback is excessive pressure and turbulence in the crankcase, sapping power. With turbocharging the exhaust tuning potential was less important and – significantly – so was the adverse effect of excessive crankcase windage. With forced induction, extracting adequate power would not be challenging – the Can Am experience had shown that – and the smooth running nature of the boxer unit was ideal for endurance racing.

The 901 'ATL' (Auspuff Turbolader) engine which surfaced in 1974 displaced 2142cc. to suit existing 3.0 litre Group 6 Prototype regulations. Like the early Seventies' atmospheric RSR/Carrera RSR 2.7 – 3.0 litre GT racing versions of the 901 engine the ATL engine had Nikasil cylinders bolted to its magnesium crankcase. It likewise adopted a Bosch CD system to fire twin plugs but otherwise retained the characteristics of the Carrera 6 engine of 1966 and even had the same 66mm. stroke steel crank, and borrowed Carrera 6 polished titanium con rods.

Indeed, the Alfing-produced crank was taken from a production 911. Its 66mm. stroke was married to a new 83mm. bore size to produce a capacity just 1cc. under the maximum permissible, given the FIA's 1.4 times Group 6 turbo equivalency factor. With no water passages in the head there was less of a sealing problem so Porsche had been able to employ a lapped head joint without any gasket or O-ring. However, one of the most obvious concessions to turbocharging was the fitting of a cylinder head O-ring seal. Also fitted were sodium cooled valves, Nimonic on the exhaust side, titanium for the inlet. The exhaust valve was from the 917 with a diameter of 40.5mm. while the 47mm. inlet valve was sized after the Carrera 6. There was less valve overlap and the softer camshafts were carried in four bearing racing cam carriers, rather than three bearing production versions. The camshafts were still driven by the production double row chain system.

The output of the belt driven vertical fan was stepped up and to further assist cooling the oil circulation was increased and this necessitated the use of a higher flow oil pump and an oil cooler from the 917. Bosch mechanical injection was again employed – a six cylinder version of that run on the 917 – with the pump again made sensitive to boost pressure as well as throttle opening and revs. However, the pump had enlarged cylinder bores for a greater flow capacity.

In general terms the turbocharger system was similar to that of one bank of the 12 cylinder engine and again the compression ratio was lowered to 6.5:1, Schaffer installing a thick crown flat top piston to improve the combustion chamber shape. A Garrett wastegate was still employed, again with a cockpit adjustable boost facility. Up to 2.4 bar pressure was felt in a single central plenum thanks to a single Kuhnle, Kopp & Kausch (KKK) turbocharger – German company KKK had bought the assets of Eberspacher. The plenum feed to the inlet tracts was balanced by crosspipes linking opposite tracts, each containing a throttle controlled pressure relief valve, opening when the throttle was shut to bleed off excess pressure. In the inlet tract, a butterfly valve was high mounted while the single injector was mounted low, close to the head.

The turbo torque was fed through a production based Typ 915 five speed gearbox equipped with strengthened sideplates. Nevertheless, this was the weak link in the drivetrain, which employed only a single plate clutch yet 917-derived racing driveshafts. The turbo boxer ran a heavily modified 911 chassis, retaining a production floor pan and a steel body shell. However, an aluminium roll cage added a significant amount of torsional rigidity. At the back, an aluminium sub frame carried the drivetrain, with the engine still overhung behind the rear axle line. That was clearly a major disadvantage, as was the inherently high centre of gravity and the production length short wheelbase. The front – rear weight distribution was not far off 30 – 70. This experimental machine was far from a pure Group 6 prototype.

The suspension was heavily modified but retained MacPherson struts at the front while the rims were 15' diameter, 10.5' wide at the front, 17' wide at the rear where the arches were flared radically. These were g.r.p., as were the doors and lids and the machine weighed in at 825kg – some 75kg. more than a real Group 6 machine. It first ran in public at Paul Ricard in December '73 and was back again in February '74 as the engineers sought to counter lift at the front and to find useful rear downforce. A solution was found in a front air dam with a splitter lip at its base plus a rear wing, which was outrigged on a tubular frame.

The wing looked unsightly and for promotional reasons the styling department produced an alternative version that sat behind and just below the rear window, over the engine compartment on flares extending back from the rear arches. From an aerodynamic point of view it was an inefficient location (stylists are not race engineers) and the race team did the best it could to subtly rework the rear window to feed air down to the compromise wing with the minimum of turbulence.

The race car that emerged in March had its fuel tank repositioned from the nose to the cabin, where it sat on the passenger side over the centre of gravity, ensuring that it did not upset weight distribution as it emptied. This left just the battery, oil tank and fire extinguishers in the nose and weight distribution was now a pure 30 – 70. Faced with a lumbering chassis and increasing turbo power, Porsche logically was putting a premium on traction.

On the engine front, the major development was an air:air aftercooler. Mezger noted that: 'experiences from turbocharging had shown that the performance of a turbocharged engine is limited by overheating the pistons, valves, cylinder head and so forth, rather than by mechanical difficulties. By providing the six cylinder engine with an air:air aftercooler the engine component temperatures decreased, and the charge temperature fell from 150 degrees to approximately 75 degrees centigrade'.

The 30 – 70 weight distribution, aftercooled car with its 'designer' wing was rolled out for the Le Mans test weekend in March. It was a difficult time: the machine lapped only 5% faster than the '73 3.0 litre atmospheric Carrera RSR and the outing was plagued: two engines, a turbocharger and a clutch failed. Post-Le Mans there was a modified aftercooler and a simplified charge plumbing system for greater efficiency and Porsche went racing with a 'Phase II' engine rated 470b.h.p. when pressurised to 2.4 bar. In qualifying the boost gauge went well over 1.4 and power exceeded 500b.h.p. Whereas the Can Am engine had only just managed 200b.h.p. per litre, the '74 ATL was good for 250b.h.p. per litre in its aftercooled guise.

A 3.0 litre atmospheric Sports-Prototype produced in the region of 450 – 500b.h.p. so Porsche had a competitive power level. Clearly, though, it had throttle lag to overcome and was badly handicapped in the chassis department. The unwieldy short wheelbase dragster finished fifth at Monza then third at Spa Francorchamps. From the 'Ring onwards two cars were run and sixth and seventh places were collected on home soil. Next came Imola where a new version of the engine appeared, this equipped with a horizontal fan for improved cooling. The fan was now driven through the usual belt then a pair of shafts connected via bevel gears. In this case the alternator was mounted on its own bracket and had its own drivebelt. The new engine was known as Phase III. Alas, both the Phase II and the Phase III entry retired in Italy.

For Le Mans the team again had one Phase III, one older car. The horizontal fan was now fed air from NACA ducts set into the rear quarter windows. The Phase II car ran slightly higher boost and threw a rod after six hours. The Phase III car came home second with fifth gear stripped. Although the chassis technology cost competitive speed, reliability was 24 hour solid at the right boost level. After Le Mans there was another second, at Watkins Glen, again a tribute to reliability rather than speed. However, there was more boost to come with development. In 1974 Porsche had showed that a 2.1 litre turbo engine (in the right chassis) could provide a very competitive and reliable power level for Group 6 Prototype Competition...

The first turbocharged racing engine seen in European competition was this fan cooled boxer six inspired by the VW Beetle. Professor Porsche designed the Beetle, his son Ferry created the flat six Porsche 911 and saw a 2.1 litre version turbocharged for '74 Group Six races.

It didn't look like a sports-racing car: the 1974 Porsche Group Six contender was based firmly on a production 911 chassis. It wasn't intended to challenge pure 3.0 litre spyders for outright speed – it was a test bed for the new 2.1 litre turbo race engine from Stuttgart.

Indy Cars 1970-79

While development of the Offy turbo was going from strength to strength, in 1970 Ford abruptly pulled out of racing. Meyer then retired and Foyt took over the V8 project. However, the V8 wasn't capable of sustaining high boost, possibly due to its dry liner construction. As the Offy users pushed boost levels ever higher, the region above 2.5 bar absolute was found to be dangerous territory for the Ford while the complex inlet manifolding didn't help and might have been the root of the problems.

Over the years '69 – '73 Offy race boost climbed steadily (and the larger TE069 turbocharger replaced the TE067) and revs exceeded 9,000 as Drake introduced an even shorter stroke. Race power topped the 800b.h.p. mark – it was then in the region of 200b.h.p. per litre, or around 70b.h.p. per litre per bar boost given a typical plenum pressure of approximately 2.8 bar absolute. Maximum pressure was now topping 3.5 bar absolute in qualifying taking power over 1000b.h.p. and intensive work on pistons and valves was proving necessary. The fuel injection system had been developed with additional valving and twin injectors, one each side of the butterfly, but was still rather crude and aftercoolers were banned. Thankfully, there was tonic in the fuel tank: given pump petrol it would have been much, much harder to hold the Offy together at such pressures.

In 1974 Indy Cars were forced to qualify with a modified bleed valve from a jet engine restricting plenum pressure to 80 inches of mercury – approximately 2.7 bar absolute. The day of the 1000b.h.p. Offenhauser was over. Further, the venerable Offy now found itself at a disadvantage: at 80 in. Hg. the Ford V8 produced around 5% more power. The larger breathing area and higher r.p.m. potential of the eight cylinder engine was once again crucial. A V8 had to be the way to go under 80 in. due to its higher revs while the better heat dissipation of its smaller piston crown was important since fuel was now in limited supply, and thus could not be used liberally to assist cooling. Race fuel had been limited to 280 US gallons in the wake of the fuel crisis that was sweeping the western world. The Ford V8 produced around 820b.h.p. at 9,600r.p.m. as against 770b.h.p. at 9,000r.p.m. for the Offy, and the Ford offered marginally better fuel consumption.

Foyt was on pole for the 1974 500, emphasising the renewed superiority of the Ford V8 tended by his engine man Howard Gilbert. Meanwhile, Pat Patrick's engine man George Bignotti had been playing with a larger Garrett turbocharger, the T18, which was capable of higher flow and could take plenum pressure over 4.0 bar. The T18 had been tried by Penske in '73 but had not been employed since the team was warned that if it qualified with the T18 it would have to race with it. The T18's higher flow was at the expense of response and fuel consumption.

Bignotti heard that Penske had discovered something rather interesting. The T18 could be used to overpower the new bleed valve – the valve didn't flow enough to fully counter its greater capacity. Even with the mandatory valve blown fully open the T18 could push plenum pressure to over 90 in. Hg. That was worth a bonus of 100b.h.p. or so. Sure enough, Bignotti saw Dallenbach onto the front row. Then he switched back to the TE069. Other competitors users were not amused, nor were Speedway officials. Dallenbach was forced to race the big turbo, but in any case retired early.

Although the Offenhauser runners were now playing the underdog, moves were afoot to improve the classic engine. Sadly, Goossen had died in 1973. At the time he had been working on a revised head, inspired by Art Sparks, the engineer behind the Sparks-Thorne supercharged six. Sparks was apparently influenced by the advice of German piston manufacturer Mahle, supplier to Porsche and other European engine producers. Certainly, Sparks' proposal followed European four valve head philosophy. In essence, Sparks wanted an included valve angle narrowed from 72 degrees to 44 degrees for a shallow pent roof chamber to run with an almost flat piston crown and split rather than siamesed porting to each pair of valves.

Clearly, any project to improve the Offy took on a new significance with the 80 in. Hg. limit. Pat Patrick was an enthusiast for the engine and funded a continuation of Goossen's work, this carried out by German designer Hans Hermann, assisted by Bignotti. Sure enough, the so called Sparks-Goossen head added the best part of 50b.h.p., at 80 in. Hg. putting the Ford engine within reach. Less spark advance was necessary, suggesting better combustion (as would be expected) while fuel economy and throttle response were improved. Foyt had to overcome much more opposition in winning pole in '75.

The fact that the old four cylinder engine could get so close under conditions of restricted boost hinted at the truth: the Ford engine was not an optimum design. It was lagging behind contemporary European four valve engine design, it was top heavy, it was excessively wide and it had to be run semi-stressed. Over in Europe a newer, much more advanced Ford-badged V8 engine was the mainstay of Grand Prix teams and already the Vels Parnelli Jones team was looking to convert it for Indy car racing. In time the Cosworth Ford V8 would overthrow the Indy car establishment, meanwhile Drake had more to come from the Offy...

For 1976 Hermann drew a tighter, 38 degrees included angle to run with a flat top piston and further revised the porting, which was still siamesed since this was found to work well for the blown engine but now featured smaller passages for higher gas velocity which helped throttle response and fuel economy. The so called 'Drake Offy' produced a marginal improvement over the Sparks-Goossen Offy when it arrived in 1976. However, it was not fully developed. By 1977 the leading Indy Car runners were switching to the Cosworth Ford V8.

The Cosworth engine was freely available, powerful and dependable and good value for money. It was proven in the Grand Prix arena, and given restricted boost eight cylinders had to be the way to go at the Brickyard. Indeed, in 1977 design work was started on a Drake V8 engine with belt driven cams, part financed by Patrick. Dyno and track tests led to a switch to a Cosworth-style gear drive, then the project fizzled out and Drake went out of business. Never properly developed, the Drake V8 never qualified for a race. As we shall see, by the end of 1978 Cosworth's Indy Car DFV-derivative was so well developed that there wasn't a market for an alternative engine that offered no obvious performance gain...

The Cosworth engine had been under development as a Grand Prix engine for over a decade. An all aluminium, d.o.h.c. four valve engine, it ran a 38 degree included valve angle with a flat top piston. Cosworth didn't invent the narrow angle pent roof chamber but had championed the concept to great effect with the famous V8 designed by Keith Duckworth. The Ford-badged DFV was a new generation four valve racing engine, exploiting technology more advanced than that of the Offy and Ford Indy engines.

The Cosworth DFV's wet linered block extended from the decks to the centreline of the crankshaft, the lower half of the crankcase being integral with the sump casting. That casting formed three of the five main bearing caps: front, rear and centre. Each of those bearings was flanked by the major studs that tied the bottom end together while the two intermediate bearings were the thrust bearings and their conventional caps were each secured by four bolts. Originally, in 1967, the sump casting had formed all five caps but significant reductions in pumping and windage losses had been achieved by the switch to separate intermediates.

The DFV ran iron liners located by a flange at the top with two O-rings to seal the bottom which was free to expand. Sealing between head and block was by bronze sealing joint. The fact that there was no conventional gasket reflected a fundamental principle of Cosworth race engine design, as explained to the author by Chief Racing Engine Designer Geoff Goddard.

Cosworth considers primarily strain rather than stress. It was known, and accepted that the DFV block weaved 22 thou'. Goddard gives the graphic example of a con rod: 'there are 12 tons going down a rod so it gets slightly shorter. Then seven tons go up the rod, so it gets slightly longer'.

All the mechanicals are affected. Big ends change shape, while a head moves up something like 11 thou' – 'so there is no chance of a head gasket working, so we don't have a gasket!' Goddard explains: 'the whole engine is designed as an elastic device'. Given that philosophy, clearly an all aluminium engine is preferred over the rigidity of iron.

Through the DFV Cosworth had pioneered the concept of mounting the engine so as to act as a member of the chassis. Particularly ingenious were its top front mounts which linked the magnesium cam covers to the monocoque. Triangular, angled brackets, these gave total rigidity in the planes in which it was needed while still flexing to accommodate the expansion and contraction of the whole engine under heat.

The DFV had been designed to be as compact as possible to further assist the chassis designer and its crankshaft had been mounted as low as possible to keep the centre of gravity low. It was a 90 degree V8, of course, with a flat plane crankshaft for tuning potential and this gave the engine its reputation as a bone shaker.

The configuration suffers an inherent secondary imbalance which manifolds itself as side to side shake along the crankshaft.

The DFV was gear driven off the front end and early in its long life the DFV had suffered numerous gear breakages as the torsionals were amplified on their way up through the gear train. Duckworth had faced a major headache. He had eventually cured the problem by mounting the second of two intermediate compound drive gears on a hub which incorporated 12 miniature quill shafts. Those shafts acted as torsion bars that allowed some angular movement of the gears and quietened the heavy vibration sent up the drive train. That had been a major breakthrough in the quest for reliability and higher revs.

The DFV's crankshaft was a Nitrided steel in house forging with eight extended counterbalance webs and plenty of journal overlap for stiffness. A steel flywheel to match a traditional AP 7 1/4 inch clutch was attached at the back by eight bolts while the power take off at the front was keyed onto the shaft. During its middle age the DFV had been equipped with an internally modified crankshaft having a single central drilling with short lateral feed passages from the main bearing annuluses. Since the feed passages were shorter the effective centrifugal force against which the oil had to enter the shaft was lessened and the engine oil pressure could be significantly reduced. Indeed it had been reduced from the region of 85lb. to 50lb.

The crankshaft and steel camshafts each ran in five plain bearings supplied by Vandervell. The camshafts were again in house productions as were the pistons, which were forged in a plant acquired from Hepworth and Grandage. Three rings sat above a conventional, fully floating steel gudgeon pin, retained by circlips in the normal manner. The gudgeon pin ran in a bush in an I-section forged steel con rod. This was a vacuum remelted fat forging that was reckoned to be virtually equivalent to machining from solid. The rods were retained by two bolt caps. Plain bearings were run throughout the engine, supplied by Vandervell.

Retained by ten major studs, the DFV head accommodated four large valves and a central plug and had bronze based seats. The valves were conventional steel items closed by dual interference springs supplied by Schmitthelm which were secured by a split retainer and a top cap, in a conventional manner. The valve was operated through a steel bucket tappet which sat in the detachable cam carrier cum tappet block.

The cam carrier was attached by ten pairs of studs which passed through the camshaft bearing caps and the magnesium cam cover. At the end of the cam carrier was

a housing for each camshaft drive gear. The camshaft drive gear was bolted to the camshaft with provision for timing adjustment. The two camshafts were driven by a gear mounted centrally on the head. That gear ran on a roller bearing carried by a steel pin which protruded from the front of the aluminium casting.

The gear on the head was driven from a central gear train via an intermediate gear. The intermediate gear was driven from either the front or the back of a compound three-row gear at the top of the central drive train, the gear at the front driving the lefthand bank. The middle gear of this top compound gear was the largest and was driven by a two-row compound gear below, of which the front gear meshed with the crankshaft gear underneath.

The miniature quill shaft-dampened top compound gear not only drove each bank's intermediate gear but also powered a quill shaft running behind it, down the centre of the vee, and a pulley attached to the front of it. The quill shaft took power to a small central gearbox which powered the metering unit, distributor and alternator, mounted as one unit in the centre of the vee. The pulley drove a belt that took power to the pumps mounted each side of the sump, this arrangement keeping the front of the engine flat to benefit chassis installation.

Lucas supplied the metering unit, which was of the shuttle type driven at engine speed with a purely mechanical linkage to the throttle and fed fuel at constant pressure. The throttle slides were linked by a finely adjustable rod to a carefully contoured cam which in turn controlled exactly how far the shuttle – a free floating piston – could move. Shuttle operation combined with rotation of its cylinder sent a timed shot of fuel to the appropriate injector, a single injector being located in each cylinder's inlet trumpet.

Each bank's trumpets were bolted to a common slide throttle manifold. Below each cylinder's slide the manifold formed a short inlet tract which bolted to the top of the respective port. Inlet and exhaust ports were split below the manifold and between the port flange and each inlet tract was a 1/8th inch thick Tufnel spacer which acted as a seal and as a barrier to heat flow from head to manifold.

Born in 1967 producing around 400b.h.p. at 8,500r.p.m., a very impressive figure for the day, Cosworth's pioneering four valve 3.0 litre Grand Prix engine had been developed to run to 11,000r.p.m. and to produce over 450b.h.p. by the mid Seventies. Running an 11.0:1 compression ratio, its dimensions remained 85.67 × 64.8mm. for a 3.0 litre (183 cu.in.) displacement.

As we have seen, key developments had included the introduction of a cushioned second compound gear and the switch to separate intermediate main bearing caps. There had also been valve spring improvements, which allowed higher r.p.m. Other important improvements had been a 4 into 1 rather than 4 into 2 into 1 exhaust system and oil system modifications (including the aforementioned low pressure crankshaft) as well as head, camshaft and manifold development. Of course, there had been many other subtle changes to the 1967 specification as Cosworth had pushed the frontiers of four valve race engine technology forward. Generally power had gone up in 20b.h.p. increments and the DFV had always had the measure of its Formula One opposition.

The Vels Parnelli Jones team that introduced the DFV to the Indy Car world ran Offy engines which it found

◁

A. J. Foyt was one of the great characters of Seventies Indy Car racing. Throughout the decade the world of Indy racers was turbocharged. Foyt exploited the Ford V8 after the withdrawal of the factory and found an advantage until others replied with a turbocharged Cosworth V8 engine.

less than reliable and like everyone else at Indianapolis in May '74 looked enviously at Foyt's V8, while appreciating the limitations of the American design. In comparison, Cosworth's no compromise race engine was much more attractive. And converting it to a 2.65 litre displacement would be a relatively straightforward operation, though the introduction of turbocharging and methanol fuel added complications. Clearly, however, it was an operation that ought to pay dividends. After the '74 Indy 500 the Vels Parnelli Jones team started construction of a Formula One car propelled by a Cosworth DFV and also set aside a team to develop an Indy Car version of the DFV.

Larry Slutter and Chickie Hiroshima were given the task of creating an Indy engine from the DFV at VPJ's Los Angeles base and dyno testing commenced in the autumn of '74. The conversion work entailed the local production of a a 57.3mm. crankshaft: this, combined with the standard 85.67mm. DFV bore gave a displacement of 2645.0cc. The compression ratio was set at 8.5:1 and VPJ had to produce new pistons, gudgeon pins, con rods and camshafts while turbocharging further called for an increased water flow and new a new head sealing method. The rate of flow from the pump was stepped up and the traditional Cooper ring seal was replaced by the bronze sealing joint subsequently adopted by the DFV.

While a suitable Garrett turbocharger was readily available, Slutter and Hiroshima had to devise an appropriate exhaust and charge plumbing system, with a new inlet manifold to accept butterfly rather than slide throttles. Further, the use of methanol required a new fuel injection system to handle the increased flow and VPJ employed the same Hilborn constant flow mechanical system used on the Offenhauser. This was less sophisticated than the Lucas system it replaced.

Early tests were encouraging: on 80ins. the engine produced in the region of 750b.h.p. at around 9,000r.p.m. However, it was difficult to get suitable forged pistons produced locally – this was still a private effort – and while the water flow rate had been doubled there was still a severe exhaust valve cooling problem. Head life expectancy was short when the engine took to the track, during Indianapolis qualifying in May 1975. It was only run in a back up car: the first race came at Phoenix. Al Unser Snr. put the Parnelli-Cosworth on pole position and the writing was on the wall.

The '75 Parnelli chassis was somewhat lacking but for '76 a new English designer John Barnard got the package right, power was now in excess of 800b.h.p. at 9,000r.p.m. and Unser Snr. won the Pocono 500. The effort was subsequently assisted more directly by Cosworth and a modified head was supplied. This had the exhaust valves on the same centres as the inlet valves for larger water passages and an upgraded bronze based valve seat alloy. The Interscope team became the second Cosworth runner in late '76 and for '77 McLaren and Penske joined the ranks. Cosworth set up a base in Los Angeles and employed Slutter to run it.

That base was a marketing outlet and rebuild facility: development work was carried out at Northampton. However, the engine retained as many American parts as possible, including a Moldex crankshaft, Carillo rods, and so forth. This was political reasoning – the characteristic parochialism of the Indy Car ruling body was the greatest threat to the clearly superior new engine. Indeed, on 80 in. Hg. the Cosworth DFX, as the engine was known, proved capable of 1000b.h.p. as the compression ratio was pushed higher in 1978. That was 377b.h.p. per litre or 140b.h.p. per litre per bar boost at 2.7 bar absolute.

While the Offy had fought a stern rearguard action with the Sparks-Goossen and Drake-Offy versions, it couldn't overcome its lack of revs. Foyt's old V8 went out gloriously winning Indianapolis in '77. But Sneva's Penske run Cosworth-McLaren won the '77 National title and by 1978 Cosworth was in charge at the Brickyard. It stayed in charge all the way into the Eighties.

 Seventies Indy Cars were confined to a single turbocharger, invariably this unit supplied by the Japanese company IHI. The heavy lump was mounted low over the transaxle. Note the merging of the Cosworth V8 left and right bank pipes ahead of the turbine inlet and wastegate.

Prototypes 1975-79

Based on what it was learning with its experimental turbocharged Carrera RSR in Group 6 competition, in 1974 Porsche set about development of a larger capacity 'silhouette' car to suit the forthcoming Group 5. The new category, however, got off to a shaky start. Aside from Porsche there was little interest from major manufacturers and the specialist constructors – the backbone of international racing – were automatically excluded. Group 5 was postponed until 1976 and Falk's factory team took a year off.

Of course, 3.0 litre Prototype racing lived on in 1975 and a number of Porsche privateers continued to campaign old 908/3 spyder models in the World Championship for Makes. Porsche agreed to sell them ATL engines, while warning that the 908/3 transaxle was not really man enough for the job. Nevertheless, three cars were converted to '908/4' specification. The conversion work involved some systems modification since the engine was now in the right place, ahead of the rear axle line. Porsche also assisted with body revisions: a reprofiled nose and a 917/10-type tail.

The single-car Joest and Dannersberger teams contested eight rounds of the '75 World Championship of Makes with a degree of back door support from the factory. Between them, they scored in all but one event and Joest's car finished second at Dijon and at Monza. With a good string of placings, Porsche finished second overall in the title chase to a team of works supported Alfa Romeo T33/TT3s run by Willi Kauhsen, profiting from the unreliability of a new Renault turbocar.

Heart of the Renault challenger was a V6 engine designed as a 2.0 litre normally aspirated unit in 1972 by Francois Castaing of Renault Gordini. The V6 had been born of a meeting of Castaing's bosses Christian Martin (member of the main board), Jean Terramorsi (director of Gordini, Renault's competition and high performance engine wing) and Claude Haardt (manager of the Usine Amedee Gordini at Viry Chatillon, just south of Paris) with Francois Guiter of Elf. The State owned petroleum company was actively supporting the competition programme run by Jean Redele's *Automobiles Alpine* concern at Dieppe. Alpine based its cars around Renault engines and on its behalf Elf was keen to support a new Renault race engine.

Renault agreed that Gordini should produce a 2.0 litre unit following the general architecture of the 2.0 litre V6 'PRV' road engine that was under development as a joint project between Peugeot, Renault and Volvo (hence PRV). Castaing had his 90 degree vee, d.o.h.c., four valve V6 running on the bench by the end of the year. Meanwhile, and in no connection with that work, Alpine's engine preparation chief Bernard Dudot was exploring the potential of turbocharging. Up at Dieppe he had prepared a single Holset blown Alpine 1600 rally car which promptly won the '72 Criterium des Cevennes. It was, says Dudot: 'a small test; a simple installation with no wastegate and no special injection adaptation. We were simply trying to find a way to increase the power of a limited capacity rally engine'.

Castaing's V6 was unveiled by Renault in January 1973, named the Gordini CH1 in tribute to Claude Haardt who had been killed testing a Renault propelled powerboat. It was destined for the European 2.0 litre sportscar series, powering an Elf sponsored Alpine prototype. Although the first season was not a success,

that didn't stop Terramorsi and Guiter aspiring to 3.0 litre honours via the turbo route. The Porsche Can Am programme had been closely watched...

Before 1973 was out Dudot had been recruited by Gordini and had been dispatched to California to further investigate turbocharging, and to look at supercharging, the other alternative. 'I went to California with no idea of the technical choice. I visited a lot of small companies, and also Garrett, the biggest turbocharger company. At the same time I had a look at the Porsche Can Am car. At the end the choice was turbocharging – it was the most efficient solution', he told the author.

In 1974, exploiting a reliable 305b.h.p. at 10,800r.p.m., the 2.0 litre Renault-Alpine A441 was fast enough to dominate the European title chase. Meanwhile, Dudot and fellow Gordini engineer Jean-Pierre Boudy had further developed the turbocharged 1600cc. in line four to extend their knowledge. Dudot recalls that at this stage he didn't believe it would be possible to do a competitive 1.5 litre turbocharged Grand Prix engine. Nevertheless, Gordini and Elf were already toying with the idea of a radical Grand Prix engine, perhaps a 3.0 litre W9 or a 1.5 litre V6 turbo?

Already, in May '74 Dudot and Boudy had turned to the V6 with intent to produce a turbocharged 2.0 litre sportscar engine. Dudot recalls: 'we had taken the bull by the horns and we worked like idiots. By the beginning of 1975 we had tested our engine for the first time. Jabouille was in despair – he dared not tell us the thing was undriveable'. In fact, Jabouille later likened its throttle response to pushing a button to call a lift...

Dudot and Boudy persevered and found improvement, mainly through adaptation of the turbocharger; in particular the size of the turbine and compressor housings. Their CH1 was blown by a single Garrett turbocharger, using standard production equipment intended for diesel engine application. The block ran non-standard pistons to lower the compression ratio and had improved lubrication, improved water flow around the heads to cool the exhaust valve seats and sodium filled exhaust valves. The fuel injection system incorporated a Bosch Kugelfischer metering unit similar to that run by Porsche and this was equipped with a pneumatically controlled 3D cam to adjust flow to match boost pressure, as well as throttle opening.

The improved engine slotted into a suitably modified Alpine A441 to contest the 1975 World Championship for Makes. The debut race at Mugello brought victory but the balance of the season was a disaster, allowing the Kauhsen Alfa Romeo team to mop up the spoils. Learning hard was the name of the game and Renault would be back...

Although for 1976 the spotlight swung upon silhouette cars, given the low interest in the new Group 5 category the CSI created a parallel 'World Sportscar Championship' for Group 6 Prototypes, to which Renault immediately committed itself. In '75 Le Mans had stepped outside World Championship racing and it remained outside, open to all comers and potentially a battleground for real racing cars. Prototypes continued to be confined to the established Group 6 capacity limits but promised to be swifter than the larger capacity but heavier, clumsy-chassied silhouette cars. Although committed to Group 5 racing, in September of '85 Porsche made the late decision to build its own Group 6 turbo car. The battle of the turbocharged Prototypes was shaping up: Porsche flat 6 versus Renault V6.

Renault, assisted by Garrett, was now dedicated to both Prototype and Formula One turbo engine development. At Viry Chatillon Boudy had already started working on a reduced stroke 1500cc. Formula One version, this commissioned by Tyrrell sponsor Elf for evaluation purposes. Renault took over Alpine and incorporated its competition activities with those of Gordini, creating 'Renault Sport' under the direction of Mangenot and the management of Gerard Larrousse, Terramorsi having been forced to stand down due to ill health. Castaing was Technical Director of the Viry Chatillon based operation, which was liaising closely with Garrett, Elf and Michelin.

Early in 1976 the EF1 Formula One engine was tested on Michelin's Ladoux test track in a *Laboratoire* Alpine single seater. Meanwhile, Dudot's sports-prototype team was wheeling out its improving Group 6 challenger. The semi-monocoque chassis car ran on Michelin radials and the turbocharged adventure was proving a challenge for Michelin as well as Renault Sport. Tyre problems had badly compromised the '75 effort. At least the chassis was close to the 700kg. weight limit, while the 2.0 litre engine was now rated 500b.h.p. pressurised to 2.0 bar through an air:air aftercooler. It ran iron liners in an iron block and was designed to be run fully stressed.

The CH1's iron block was closed by alloy heads and an alloy lower crankcase that supported the main bearings. The heads carried separate cam carriers with cam bearing caps formed by the cam cover. Block/head sealing was achieved via a composite metallic gasket for gas sealing with Viton ring seals for oil and water passages.

The crankshaft, incorporating extended balance webs, was machined from solid and nitrided and rotated in Glyco bearings. The smooth running unit required no vibration damper. The camshaft drive was taken off the front of the crank, a gear on its nose driving a gear either side, one per bank. The drive was then transferred via external toothed belt, the belt looping down around a lower crankcase mounted pulley on its own side. The low set pulleys drove oil and water pumps neatly tucked, Cosworth style, either side of the crankcase.

The crankshaft was turned by nitrided steel con rods through plain big end bearings secured by two high tensile steel bolts. Steel gudgeon pins were free floating in the three ring pistons, which were flat topped. The combustion chamber was of the Cosworth-style narrow angle shallow pent roof type with a gap between the piston and the top of the liner lowering the compression ratio. The inlet valves were at 10 degrees from the cylinder axis, the exhaust valves at 11.5 degrees. The sodium filled valves were closed by conventional coaxial springs and were operated by steel bucket tappets housed in the cam carrier. The inlet tracts were siamesed, unlike the exhaust tracts.

Lubrication was dry sump while water circulation was ensured by a centrifugal pump for each cylinder bank. Drives for the alternator, distributor and the Kugelfischer metering unit, all located within the central valley of the block were taken off the camshafts via short toothed belts.

Clearly, the water cooled 90 degree vee CH1 turbo engine was a lot more conventional than the rival Porsche six cylinder with its air cooled boxer layout. The so called Porsche 936 Group 6 car was essentially a development of the 917 Can Am project, with the 2.1 litre boxer turbo from the 1974 911 Carrera replacing the formidable 5.4 litre V12 turbo. The Phase III engine was further developed to produce 520b.h.p. at 8,000r.p.m. on 2.4 bar absolute for championship races, the new World Sportscar series comprising relatively short events. The single KKK turbo now blew through twin air:air aftercoolers to an individual plenum chamber for each bank. Due to the short length of the unit a long spacer had to be inserted between it and the gearbox to keep it far enough ahead of the rear axle line for good weight distribution. A 2400mm. wheelbase was chosen as a compromise between the traditional 2300mm. 917 coupe wheelbase and the 2500mm. of the 917/30.

Generally, the 936 chassis was adapted from the 917 Can Am spaceframe spyders and employed the brakes developed for the Can Am programme. Early in the career of the Can Am car the normal racing brakes had shown temperature problems since the driver still had his left foot on the pedal as the left foot brought the throttle in early to spool up the turbos. Pad and fluid temperatures had been running high and in response Porsche developed its own four pot calipers with finned bodies the better to dissipate heat. In the 936 chassis the boxer engine was run for the first time semi stressed, the compact engine quite capable of accepting chassis loads. This move increased torsional rigidity by 28%. The 2400mm. wheelbase allowed the driver to be inclined more than usual to help keep the body profile low. However, the lines of the g.r.p. body were typical Porsche spyder and the car ran a long tail with lateral fin-supported wing above, 917/30-style. The Alpine Renault spyder had similar aerodynamics.

Porsche faced Renault for the first time at the Nurburgring, in a 250km. race for which only a single 936 entry was made, facing two A441s. There was controversy in the scrutineering bay: the 936 had been developed to run on Goodyear tyres of 16" width fitting 15" wide rear rims whereas the Renault ran 17.5" Michelins on 16" wide rims. Was the maximum wheel width ruling applicable to rim or tyre? The FIA ruled in favour of Renault, and also legalised the larger rear wing of the Alpine, again to Porsche's surprise. Nevertheless, the French two car team eliminated itself at the first corner! The 936 then commanded the race, until its throttle stuck. Joest's 908/4 saved the day...

Porsche tackled round two, a four hour race at Monza, with suitable chassis revisions and the single entry for Ickx/Mass dominated the event. That was the start of a winning streak. Ickx/Mass also took the Imola and Dijon 500kms., Mass/Stommelen took the Enna four hours, Ickx alone the Mosport 200 miles (behind two non-championship Can Am cars) and Mass alone the Salzburgring 300kms. Nevertheless, the French cars were often just about as fast as the 936, sometimes a little faster; Alpine Renault didn't get its World Championship act together.

For the non championship Le Mans race Porsche increased its strength to two cars and introduced a new tail section sporting a prominent air box. Feeding air to the fan and aftercoolers (a NACA duct further back fed the compressor), the air box cost 200r.p.m. but lowered cylinder wall temperatures which had been worryingly high on occasion. There were other modifications aimed at lower drag, yet the single car entered by Alpine Renault lapped six seconds faster in qualifying. However, this year Renault realistically was looking for experience rather than a win. After all, this was its first 24 hour turbo race. Sure enough, the A441 had less impressive pace come the weekend, and it was soon set back by an electrical fault. Then it developed a high engine temperature and later it suffered detonation caused by the strain of running the three and a half mile long Mulsanne straight. Nevertheless, Le Mans project manager Dudot reported that he felt sure he had the basis of a future winner.

Aside from Renault's single car, the works Porsche prototypes had no real opposition: as anticipated, even the factory Group 5 runners were less competitive than the Group 6 turbo cars. Porsche's second prototype (running without the new air box) failed Joest/Barth, a driveshaft breaking soon after the car had left the pits with an obvious engine malady. Its departure left the Ickx/van Lennep car over 100 miles ahead of a mixed bag of runners as Sunday lunchtime approached. Then a crack appeared in the exhaust system, running from the engine to the turbocharger. Replacing the red hot system took over half an hour but the car still won by a handsome 11 lap margin.

Soon after that historic occasion Renault President Bernard Hanon gave the go ahead for the first turbocharged Grand Prix car. At the same time he dictated that Renault Sport must pursue its challenging Le Mans programme to a successful conclusion. Sadly, soon after Hanon's historic decision Terramorsi died, not having had a chance to see Le Mans conquered, or to hear Renault bring a distinctive new exhaust note to the Formula One scene. But his aspirations continued to unfold and on September 16 an in-house Formula One racing team was consolidated at Viry Chatillon, leaving Alpine's Dieppe factory as the base for the Le Mans operation.

The first half of '77 saw the prototype Renault Grand Prix car test and the Alpine Renault prototype readied specifically for Le Mans. This year both Renault and Porsche shunned the World Sportscar Championship to concentrate upon Le Mans. Both looked to more specialised aerodynamics while the Porsche engine was also significantly modified, following contemporary Group 5 practice. Thus, twin KKK turbochargers were fitted, each feeding one bank of cylinders and linked via a common wastegate. This improved response, and 24 hour power of 540b.h.p. was claimed. Running familiar Dunlops, the uprated 936s (chassis 001 and 002 as in 1976) ran the Mulsanne 15m.p.h. faster at 215m.p.h. and were around seven seconds a lap quicker. Nevertheless, Renault's Michelin radial shod challenger claimed pole position. In fact, Alpine Renault took the two best qualifying times and put its two back up cars ahead of the second 936. Renault was also supplying engines to the Mirage team to help bolster its chances, and had tested extensively at Paul Ricard.

The 936s driven by Ickx/Pescarolo and Barth/Haywood raced the lead Renault in the early stages, then the Barth/Haywood car lost almost half an hour while a new fuel injection pump was fitted. And soon the sister car lost a con rod due to a manufacturing fault, just while it was being lapped by the leader...

With the home team one – two – three and the surviving works Porsche in 41st. position things looked bad for Porsche. However, instructed to drive as a win or bust effort, Ickx switched to 936-001 and by midnight the car was up to fourth position. It was stirring stuff. Before half distance two of the French cars ahead had stumbled, but the charging 936 was still half a dozen laps adrift in second place. Then at 9.00am. the leader broke! Piston failure had robbed the hopes of the home team. Piston failure, however, almost knocked out the surviving 936. With only 45 minutes to run it was also hit by the disease and had to limp home to win...

Soon afterwards, Renault's RS01 Formula One car made its famous race debut at Silverstone . Bugged by problems, the pioneering Renault Grand Prix programme continued into '78 with a single car for Jabouille while three Group 6 cars were prepared for Le Mans. These were backed up by two Renault propelled Mirages. Renault couldn't accept defeat at Le Mans – this was a matter of national pride. It tested extensively, including running on GM's high speed Ohio proving ground which offered a longer straight than Paul Ricard, its regular test venue. Overall, in excess of 10,000 miles running went into the '78 programme and some 30 engine changes were instigated. Probably the most significant was greater piston thickness above the crankpin, allowed by a higher block. This was thought to be the answer to the '77 piston failures. Alpine chassis modifications included an optional 'bubble' over the cockpit which improved top speed but left the driver hot and somewhat claustrophobic in spite of a slot in the front of it.

Porsche counter-attacked with three cars, two propelled by a new four valve engine. The four valve Porsche flat six race engine had been born back in 1976 when Hans Mezger sat down to design a new, more exotic derivative of the turbocharged boxer. In fact, he drew a gear driven four valve engine in five possible displacements ranging from 1.4 to 3.2 litres, the larger versions for Group 5 cars.

The new (individual) four valve water cooled heads were welded to the cylinder barrels, overcoming any potential gasket problem. Two valve heads could not have been welded in place since it would then have been impossible to insert the valves. The new (single central plug) head featured a narrow valve angle (30 degrees included) and was run together with flat top pistons. The inlet valve was set at 14 degrees from the cylinder axis, the exhaust at 16 degrees.

The cylinders were still Nikasil and the production aluminium crankcase was retained, although with provision for larger main bearings and larger crankpins. A new magnesium cam box carried twin camshafts per bank which actuated the valves through conventional steel bucket tappets. The revised turbo engine was designed for 9,000r.p.m. operation and was gear rather than chain driven. In effect, two intermediate gears replaced each chain. Since it now cooled only the cylinder barrels, the fan was again vertical, as usual belt driven off the nose of the crank. It was smaller in diameter, absorbing far less power, and with all its output directed on the cylinders these ran cooler. Again the alternator was mounted on its own bracket and was belt driven from the fan drive pulley.

Each bank of heads had its own water cooling system with the pump driven off the front of the respective exhaust cam. The CD trigger was now mounted on the rear of the righthand intake camshaft rather than the crankshaft for less vibration while the distributor was positioned symmetrically on the opposite bank. The twin turbo engine ran a 7.0:1 compression ratio and in 2.1 litre Group 6 (Typ 935/73) form was reckoned initially to produce the 580b.h.p./8,500r.p.m. at 2.5 bar absolute and 625b.h.p. in qualifying pumping 2.7 bar. It had a special crank to provide a stroke of only 60mm. which left the generous bore of 87mm. (for 2140.0cc.) with plenty of room for the four valves. The water radiators were positioned just ahead of the rear wheels and were fed via NACA ducts in the flanks.

The 936/78 had a body adapted from the 936/77 with only mild modifications and the prototype chassis was an uprated 936/76. This was joined by a brand new '78 chassis which took pole position at Le Mans. However, in the race it was clear that Renault had the better pace. And team leader Ickx was soon in the pits for fuel system adjustments. Come Sunday evening and the lead car lost 45 minutes due to a stripped fifth gear. And while it was stationary the older chassis car suffered a turbo failure. That cost only 10 minutes and Ickx transfered to join Wollek and Barth in the car, which went on to finish second – to the sole surviving Alpine Renault. This car also stripped fifth gear, late in the race, but in any case would not have beaten the French machine. The sister four valve car eventually crashed in Mass' hands but the back up two valve car was driven by Haywood/Gregg/Joest and finished third. In 1978 it was clear that Renault had the stronger Le Mans challenger. Having won Le Mans, Renault quit Group 6 to concentrate upon Formula One while Porsche looked to an Indy Car programme, though Essex petroleum persuaded it to field two cars at Le Mans in '79. Neither finished...

Grand Prix Cars 77-79

As we have seen, Bernard Hanon gave the go-ahead for the first turbocharged Grand Prix car of the mid engine era in 1976. Renault's Managing Director saw the benefit to his giant corporation in terms of image, publicity, technical spin-off and sheer inspiration for all its engineers. On the other hand, with the turbocharging of road racing engines a relatively unexplored science, the programme was nothing if not ambitious. And there was that additional burden for its bold advocates, Hanon's dictate that Renault Sport, the marque's new competition wing directed by Max Mangenot, must simultaneously pursue its similarly challenging Le Mans programme to a successful conclusion.

Developed initially by Boudy, the original reduced stroke 1500cc. Formula One engine had been commissioned by Elf, which in late '74 had ordered two so called 'EF1' engines for evaluation purposes.

The first EF1 was fired up on the bench on July 23 1975. The second was measured at 360b.h.p. during a test of August 8. Dudot says: 'we very quickly reached 500b.h.p., using 2.5 bar boost'. On November 18 the engine was track tested in an A441 prototype at Paul Ricard. However, its development was being bugged by failures stemming from the fact that the production based Garrett turbocharger was not up to the strain of the 500b.h.p. output necessary to match 3.0 litre normally aspirated engines.

On March 23 1976 the EF1 was tested on Michelin's Ladoux test track in a *Laboratoire* Alpine single seater. Engine testing included evaluation of an alternative 80mm. bore EF1, without definite conclusion. Boudy stuck with the regular 86mm. bore.

On December 18 Ken Tyrrell, hedging his bets, signed an option for the supply of the EF1 from 1977 until the end of the decade. Tyrrell designer Maurice Philippe began work on a six wheeler Renault design while production of Renault's own Formula One car had already begun following Tyrrell's reluctance to commit for the 1976 season. Following wind tunnel tests of a straightforward four wheel chassis at St Cyr, construction of the aluminium monocoque Renault RS01 commenced in January 1977.

The first half of '77 saw the heavy (iron block, turbo laden), radial shod Renault Grand Prix car test and the Renault Le Mans car fail again to beat Porsche due to piston failure. The RS01 made its race debut at Silverstone in mid July: Jabouille qualified 21st and retired when the induction manifold split. In any case, the car would have run out of fuel. Tyrrell was meanwhile concentrating all effort on his regular Cosworth car...

Renault Sport took a deep breath for further development, then tackled four more '77 Grands Prix. Blown at 2.7/2.8 bar whereas the Le Mans engine was run at 2.0 bar, the car continued to lack speed and reliability. Come the end of the season and Tyrrell let his option lapse.

The Renault Grand Prix programme continued into '78 with a single car for Jabouille and a high at Kyalami, where the altitude helped secure sixth fastest qualifying time. There was little else to report until mid June when, having won Le Mans, Renault Sport could close the resource-sapping Sports-Prototype department, increasing the size of the Viry Chatillon workforce from 136 to 176.

With Le Mans out of the way an air:water aftercooler was brought into play. With the previous air:air after-

cooler charge temperature had varied with ambient temperature – since the pneumatic control over the metering unit was sensitive only to pressure, it had been fooled as charge density varied with charge temperature. The mixture had been liable to become over-rich, sometimes diluting the oil film in the cylinder to a disastrous degree. The air:water aftercooler provided a steadier charge temperature thanks to better low speed cooling and a decrease of peak temperatures, and helped improve throttle response.

Toyed with at Monaco, the air:water cooler became standard equipment from the Austrian Grand Prix, in which Jabouille was a splendid third quickest. Monza saw the RS01 fastest in a straight line, though throttle lag, excess weight and lack of dependability were still hurdles to be overcome. Nevertheless, the *Regie* collected three World Championship points at Watkins Glen in October.

Renault Sport ran two cars in '79, Jabouille joined by Arnoux, at first in the RS01 design which took pole at Kyalami this time around. Then came the RS10 ground effect design master minded by Michel Tetu, who had joined in 1976 from the Alfa Romeo Autodelta prototype team, having previously worked on Ligier GT cars. The Tetu chassis proved effective and for Monaco was equipped with a twin turbo engine, the pair of smaller, lighter turbos (one per bank) offering faster response and a wider power band. As Garrett had wanted an understandably long lead time to develop the new hardware, Castaing had turned to Porsche twin turbo supplier KKK. He had also improved the induction system, and had introduced oil jets to spray the underside of the piston for the first time, reducing crown temperature. Thermal problems affecting pistons and rings had been a major headache.

'At the start', says Dudot, 'the engine was a new problem for the sub contractors. For the piston and ring suppliers, the temperature was so high it was beyond their experience of other engines. For example, we tried many new solutions to decrease the temperature of the piston. Mahle had no experience of oil circulation in such a small bore piston. It eventually developed the oil gallery piston, which it then could make for everyone...'

The oil gallery piston set a circular oil channel in the top of the piston, just below the crown. Two holes were provided: oil was sprayed into one hole, circulated around the channel via the so called 'cocktail shaker' effect then escaped via the second hole. Run as high as 3.0 bar, the 7.0:1 compression ratio twin turbo engine was officially rated at over 600b.h.p. with a maximum of 11,000r.p.m., enjoying a significant power advantage over 3.0 litre normally aspirated engines. However, weight, turbo lag and reliability still left scope for improvement. Piston failures continued, this time due to inadequate charge cooling which demanded two stage aftercoolers incorporating a primary air:water matrix and a secondary air:air matrix. There was also a valve spring problem caused by the savage cams necessary to get the required valve opening which was tackled in conjunction with supplier Schmitthelm.

Michelin was on a steep learning curve too, its radial Formula One tyres not yet consistently competitive. And the weight handicap was around 30kg., which put a burden on brakes, in particular, due to the lack of engine braking, while the impressive torque of the twin turbo 'EF2' was unkind to the transmission. Nevertheless, victory came in 1979, at a memorable French Grand Prix.

Renault brought exhaust gas turbo-supercharging to the pinnacle of motor racing – the Formula One World Championship – at Silverstone in July 1977 (lower photograph). By 1979 (above) the marque, having succeeded at Le Mans, was putting all effort into a two-car Grand Prix team.

The Renault Formula One turbo engine of 1977 was equipped with a water/air aftercooler which ensured a steady charge temperature. A simple central plenum served both banks of the V6 engine. From 1.5 litres power was in excess of 550b.h.p. without undue thermal stress.

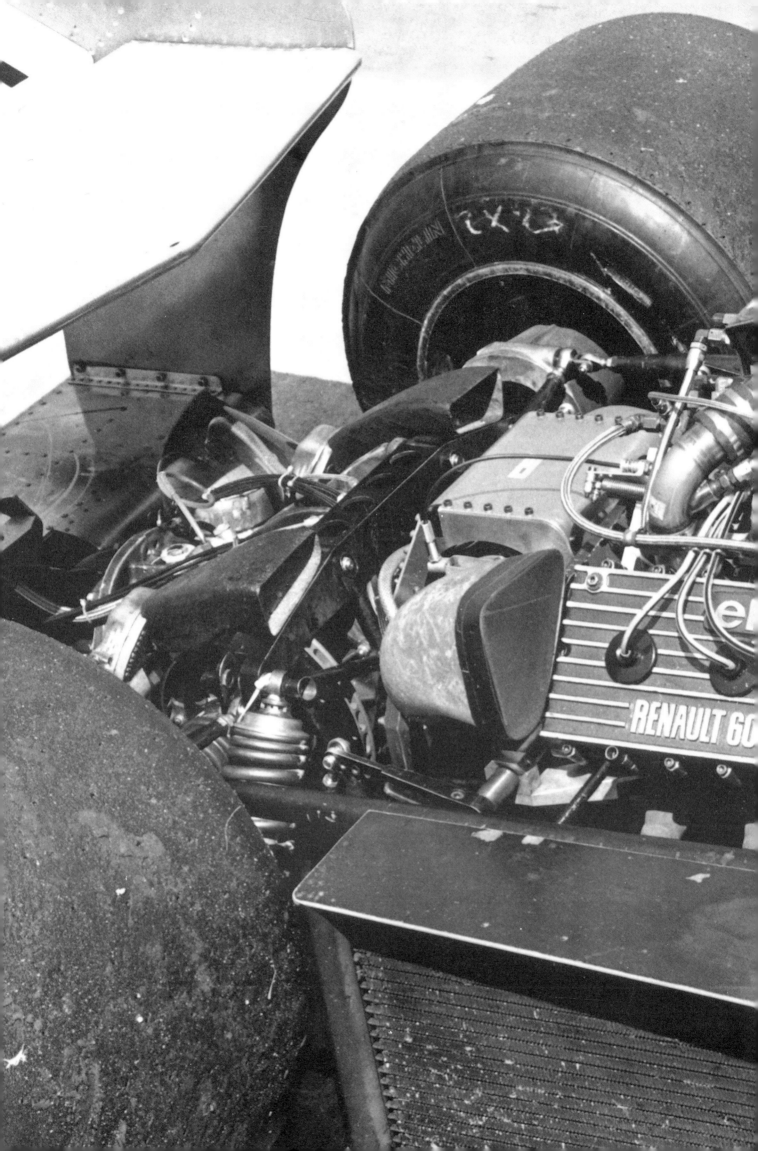

THE
EIGHTIES

THE EIGHTIES GALLERY

In 1987 Lotus joined Williams in the Honda turbo camp. The team introduced the advanced computer-controlled 'Active' suspension system which excelled here in the bumpy Monte Carlo streets, Senna winning.

In 1987 4 bar Honda turbo engine tightly packaged in the Lotus Active suspension 99T. In spite of the boost control pop-off valve the V6 engine produced in excess of 1000b.h.p. running to over 13,000r.p.m.

The involvement of major manufacturers took Group C success out of reach of small builders such as the WM Le Mans team. Consequently WM produced this low drag special aimed purely at exceeding 400k.p.h.

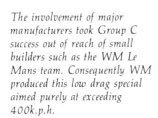

Sparks fly from the Williams-Honda, the car that dominated so many 1986 and '87 World Championship races in the hands of Mansell and Piquet. A titanium gearbox skid plate produces the firework display.

Ferrari replied to Honda's devastating 1988 2.5 bar turbo engine with this year-old iron block V6. It couldn't quite match the Honda for r.p.m. or power and Ferrari was overshadowed throughout the season.

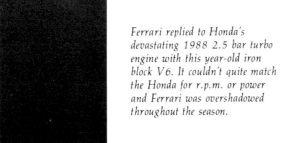

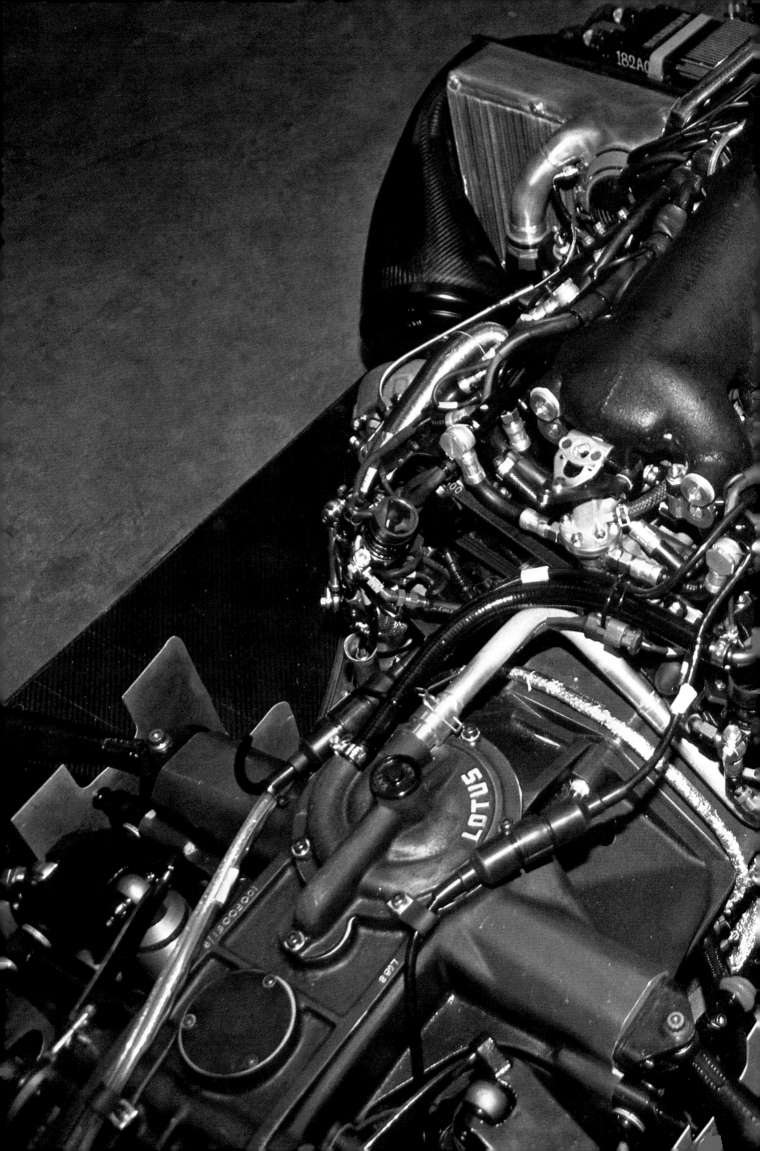

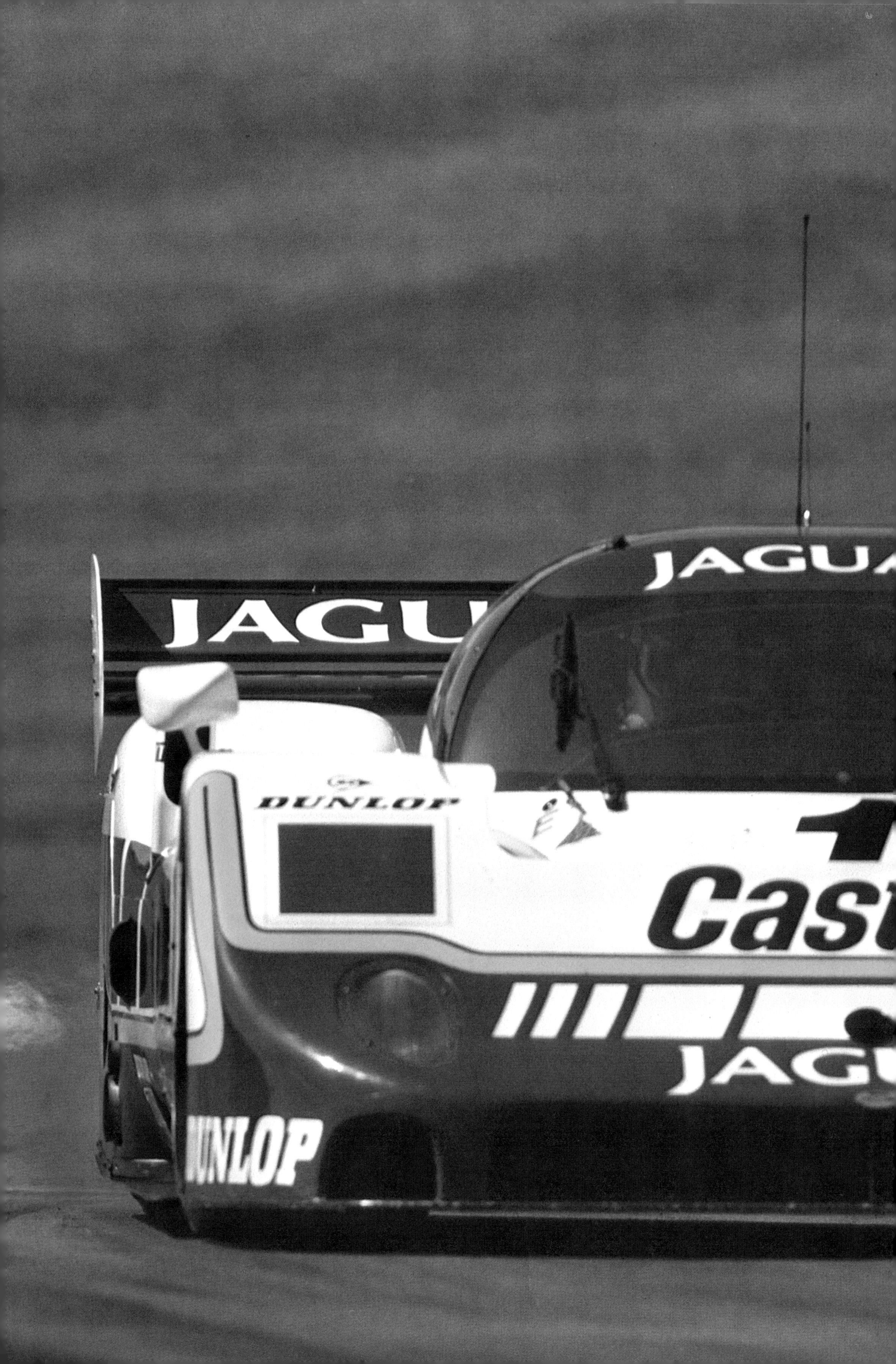
JAGUA
JAGU
DUNLOP
Cast
JAGU
DUNLOP

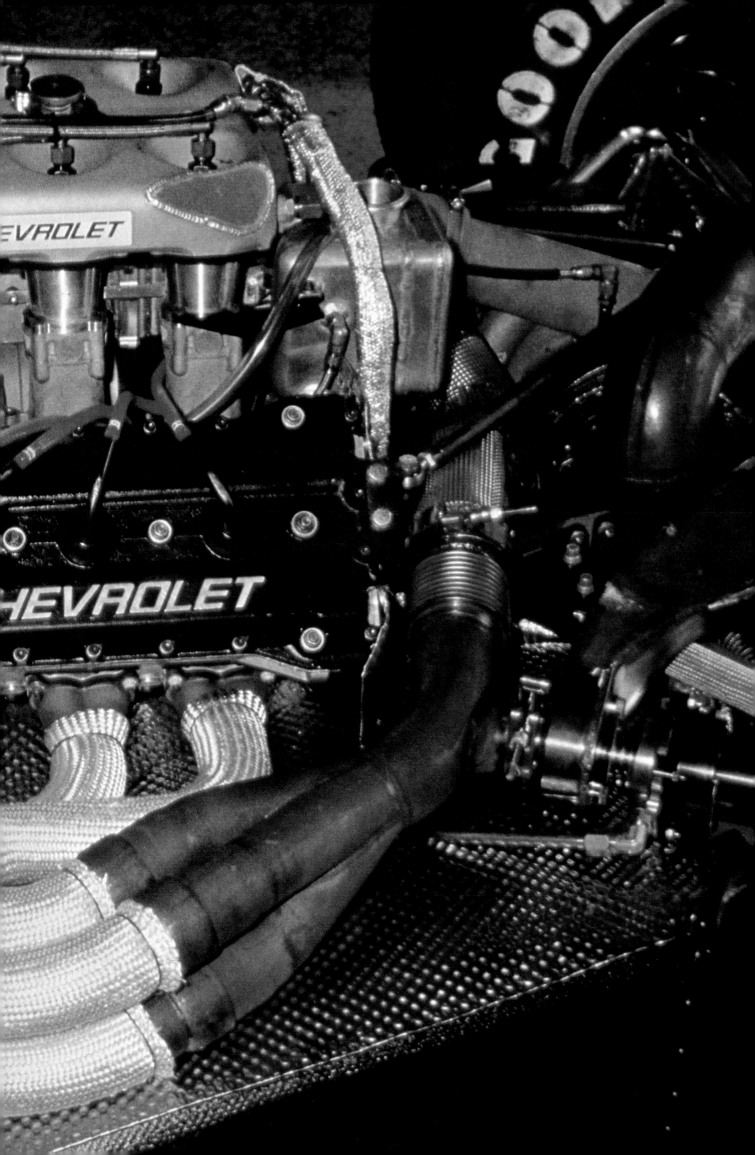

THE EIGHTIES GALLERY
continued

Jaguar fought the Group C and GTP turbocars with its atmospheric V12 engine from 1982 until 1988, then introduced its own forced induction engine. This is the 1989 XJR-11 with turbocharged V6 in Group C guise.

The Chevrolet V8 was by far the most successful engine in 1988 Indy Car competition. Cosworth's title defence had been weakened by loss of many top teams to the Chevrolet camp and of Champions Truesports to Judd.

Sauber introduced its Mercedes-engined C9 chassis here at Silverstone in 1987. The car ran Mader prepared engines but the following year would have full Daimler-Benz factory backing in its World title bid.

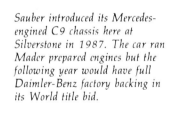

Megatron was the label given to Heini Mader-prepared BMW M12/13 engines run by Arrows in 1987 and '88. The hardware had been bought by computer leasing firm USF&G following the end of the works programme.

Grand Prix Cars 80-81

As Renault Sport strode into the Eighties having inspired Ferrari and Alfa Romeo to follow the turbo route, Dudot took over its technical direction, Castaing quitting over a policy dispute. In 1980 Renault was a serious World Championship force with its RE20 propelled by a revised EF2 that boasted Nikasil rather than steel liners for better heat rejection, and improved water circulation. Running 3.0 bar boost, or thereabouts, Arnoux won at Rio and Kyalami, Jabouille won at the Osterreichring. Elsewhere mechanical failures were rife, and Michelin radials still proved a handicap on occasion. And the same weight and throttle lag penalties had to be faced, and once again valve springs proved troublesome.

The progress made by Renault in the late Seventies hadn't gone unnoticed by other engine manufacturers and by 1980 Ferrari was busy developing its own turbo engine. This was again a V6 but had a 120 degree angle offering excellent balance and keeping the package low and compact. The turbochargers were located within the relatively wide valley. The block and heads were aluminium and the engine had a significantly smaller bore than the Renault V6, displacing 81mm. × 48.4mm. Ferrari favoured chrome plated aluminium rather than Nikasil liners. It employed conventional four valve, single plug pent roof combustion chambers with a 38 degree valve angle and ran a 6.5:1 compression ratio.

The Ferrari 126C's twin overhead camshafts were gear driven off the front end of a four bearing steel crankshaft. The short crankshaft was equipped with a vibration damper and the engine was designed to run to 11,000r.p.m. The crankshaft ran in plain bearings and was turned through titanium con rods by Mahle oil gallery pistons. Ferrari used the same Mahle, Goetze (ring) and Schmitthelm (spring) suppliers as Renault. However, it developed its own electro-mechanical injection system in conjunction with Lucas while Marelli supplied a CD ignition system.

As we have seen, Renault was exploiting mechanical injection responsive to throttle opening and boost pressure. However, while it was responsive to load, it was not also responsive to speed in terms of the quantity of fuel injected. The same fuel quantity was injected for a given load at 10,000r.p.m. as at 5,000r.p.m. and the fuelling had to be a compromise – as it always had to be sufficiently rich to avoid overheating disasters it was often too rich causing unnecessarily high consumption for a given power level. Improved control could make an engine more economical and more driveable.

The electro-mechanical system retains the basic mechanical injection equipment but employs an Electronic Control Unit (ECU) to control the fuel cam according to a set of operational instructions which cover all possible engine operating conditions. Engine operating conditions (speed, load, water temperature, and so forth) are monitored by various sensors, all of which feed information to the ECU. The ECU processes that information, identifies the correct cam setting for the prevailing situation and controls the cam accordingly via a servo motor. The programme under which the ECU runs is known as a map and clearly takes the form of dictates that tell the ECU the cam setting appropriate to any given combination of sensor readings.

The key sensors are throttle opening and boost pressure for load and crankshaft r.p.m. for speed and the map is compiled from endless hours of dyno testing. For example, a reading will be taken every 250r.p.m. and every 0.25 bar boost for a given throttle opening to determine the appropriate injection setting at each step. The ECU will then fine tune the injection according to other sensor readings and the basic laws of physics – example, low water temperature indicates warm up and the fuelling will be richened accordingly.

Enzo Ferrari was particularly pleased with Ferrari's pioneering injection system, saying: 'we have embarked on a new road with turbocharging and we have used our own injection system that has given us lots of advantages in so far as petrol consumption is concerned. Today (he was speaking at the end of the '81 season) with our six cylinder engine that if necessary can produce up to 600b.h.p., we have managed to limit petrol consumption in such a way that it is only 12% worse than that of a normally aspirated engine'.

Ferrari has always put a heavy emphasis upon the exploitation of engine technology so its adventurous approach was to have been expected. Another, less successful manifestation of this approach was an experiment with the Brown Boveri Comprex supercharger, another spin off from the world of commercial vehicles. This device was engine driven (and was geared to run at 30,000 rather than 90,000-plus r.p.m.) and employed the exhaust gas as a means of compressing the incoming air. The rotor assembly consisted of a cylinder divided longitudinally into cells in which pressure waves were induced by the exhaust gas flow, these waves compressing the charge air. The key advantage of the system was improved throttle response (since it was engine driven) and it made its only appearance at Long Beach where it was bugged by rotor shaft failures. The Comprex system was, it transpired, a technical blind alley in Formula One terms.

KKK equipped, the Ferrari 126C had first been seen at Imola in 1980 and was run throughout the 1981 World Championship season, driven by Villeneuve and Pironi. The machine was awesomely quick in a straight line, emphasising its power advantage over the 3.0 litre runners, but was regularly lacking in the handling department as Ferrari learned to come to terms with the complexities of a turbo car package. Nevertheless, Villeneuve took pole at Imola and amazing wins at Monte Carlo and Jarama, driving around obvious chassis deficiencies. Elsewhere the challenge was less impressive, as was to be expected in the Prancing Horse's first turbo season.

On the other hand, in 1981 Renault had an engine with improved response yet apparently lacking the performance of the new electro-mechanically injected 120 degree V6 from Maranello. Renault produced new cars for the start of the European racing season but it wasn't until the weather gods intervened on home soil that the team won a race. Already Ferrari had won two races...

Initially, Renault found an aerodynamic problem with its new chassis but that was soon overcome. More significantly, the Regie was reluctant to bend the new anti-skirt rules and that cost it development time. Renault considered the hydraulic lowering systems introduced by the English Cosworth teams to be a form of cheating. Morally Renault might have been right but FISA had left a loophole it could not quickly plug and since FISA could not outlaw chassis lowering systems in 1981 Renault was forced to follow suit.

However, reliability was improving and a valve seat problem that reared its head in the summer was rapidly overcome. Once up to speed, the Renault RE30 was quick on the European power circuits – the new car took six successive pole positions over the summer – had better all round competitiveness than the Ferrari 126C and took third place in the constructor's championship. Nevertheless, the season's tally for Arnoux and new boy Prost was still a total of only three wins. Renault's tally compared badly in the face of two wins for newcomer Ferrari – largely due to a number of silly faults that cost likely race wins.

There were no fundamental problems bugging the season as a whole. Team Manager Jean Sage commented: 'Nowadays, when we have a problem we concentrate on that problem and our response time is very quick. The Cosworth people are still blowing up engines . . . Everyone looks at us because we are in the lead or in pole position but there are other people who have the same reliability problems. Compared to the other turbocharged cars, we are satisfied with our reliability'.

This season Renault faced two rival turbo engines: at the other end of the scale from the efforts of the major manufacturers was the low budget Hart Grand Prix engine. This came from the small Essex workshop of Brian Hart, a one time Formula Two driver and long time Formula Two engine builder. In the early Seventies Hart had been closely involved in the development of the Cosworth BDA Ford-based in line four and when this was outstripped in Formula Two by a rival BMW four Hart designed his own 2.0 litre race engine, again of in line four configuration. It was raced in Formula Two from 1977 facing BMW and V6 Renault opposition.

While the BMW and Renault Formula Two engines were heavily funded by their respective manufacturers, Hart 420R development was financed by Brian Hart Ltd of Harlow, Essex. Nevertheless, the privateers serviced by the 420R found it useful, particularly after Renault's withdrawal in 1978, and Hart notched up two wins in '77, four in '78. For Hart, the turning point was the winter of 1978/79 when along came the ambitious, well financed Toleman team. Toleman undertook to finance Hart development and, running works assisted Ralt chassis, lost the 1979 European Formula Two Championship by only one point. In 1980, running its own chassis on Pirelli radials, its drivers Henton and Warwick dominated the series, ending a run of BMW-March title successes. At this stage the Lucas mechanically injected 420R was rated 300b.h.p./9,500r.p.m.

The young Toleman team was warming up for the big time while the emergence of the 1.5 litre turbo engine as a competitive proposition had theoretically put Grand Prix racing within Hart's reach. In the light of that Hart had quietly started funding 1.5 litre turbo engine research from his own pocket. Having already developed a turbocharged 420S for rallying, Hart's plan was to develop a blown small bore, short stroke 1.5 litre version of the 420R for testing in 1981 then, given sufficient funds, to develop a purpose designed spin off '415T' for the 1982 World Championship.

Meanwhile, Toleman was reluctant to adopt the Cosworth V8 for its graduation in the light of the obvious long term potential of turbo engines. It had discussions with Lancia, but realistically no major manufacturer was going to entrust its World Championship programme to a team without Formula One experience. Before the end of 1980 Toleman had taken the bold decision to fund Hart's turbo programme. But it was December before Toleman had firmed up team sponsorship arrangements and to keep its momentum going and its sponsors keen it wanted to start racing in 1981.

Hart had casting patterns for the planned 415T, which would have an integral head, but couldn't ready the purpose-designed unit quickly enough to meet Toleman's programme. The Essex engine builder therefore resigned himself to having to produce the interim, reduced

capacity 420R as a stop-gap race engine and to doing fundamental development work in public. A further headache was that of confirming a turbocharger deal, while Toleman's inexperience and its decision to continue to run on Pirelli tyres were obvious handicaps. Pirelli had been absent from the World Championship since 1951.

Although rushed, Hart had the advantage of being able to work closely with Toleman chassis designer Rory Byrne on installation and cooling requirements and found close co-operation from Lucas on injection and ignition systems development. However, he couldn't secure state-of-the-art KKK turbocharger technology, having to rely on off the shelf units from Garrett, the company abandoned by Renault in 1979. Mindful of the response problem inherent in turbocharging he opted for a twin turbo installation, initially trying to feed from each cylinder's siamesed exhaust port to two turbos. A split exhaust manifold proved more practical, the system working well on the bench.

The reduction to 1.5 litres was achieved through a shorter crank, modified piston and alternative liner, with three bore sizes investigated: 93.5mm., 90mm. and 88mm. Hart settled for the 88mm. bore, working with a 6.5:1 compression ratio on pump fuel, injected via the regular (throttle opening governed) Lucas shuttle valve mechanical metering system. The charge air came through an air:air aftercooler which Byrne slotted into the righthand of two 'wheelbarrow' legs which extended back from his modified Toleman Formula Two car's monocoque to carry the 420S unstressed. Four cylinder in line blocks do not lend themselves to running fully stressed.

A very wide car. At Jarama in 1981 Villeneuve had enough turbocharged Ferrari V6 power to stay ahead of his 3.0 litre 'atmo' V8 and V12 engined pursuers on the straights. Around the many tight turns the more agile, instant response atmo cars were faster but Villeneuve won.

The prototype Hart-Toleman turbocar took to a cold Goodwood track on December 9, 1980. The car completed 50 trouble free laps, reaching an estimated 176m.p.h. top speed. By the time a purpose-designed Formula One chassis was ready, in March 1981 Hart had concluded that a single, slower revving turbo offered a more practical installation. The turbo was mounted over the transaxle with the aftercooler still in the righthand 'wheelbarrow leg', Byrne retaining rearward-reaching box members to support the drive package. The box members were a proven alternative to A-frames but limited the scope for aftercooler provision. The planned aftercooler was assisted by an engine driven fan, the idea being to maintain cooling irrespective of speed. Alas, early tests revealed a serious charge cooling problem due to a miscalculation somewhere between Essex and Garrett's California base. Inadequate cooling restricted boost, as high as 2.1 bar on the bench, to a mere 1.4 bar.

Due to the 'wheelbarrow legs' Byrne couldn't get sufficient airflow to the aftercooler. He was later to admit that, from the moment the overweight TG181 first scrubbed its Pirelli radials, it was an obsolete chassis. Had a higher aftercooling requirement been specified he would have opted for A-frames. And Hart couldn't see the way to go on engine development until charge temperature was brought under control.

Although Hart had originally requested a year for development work Toleman needed to set off for Imola at the end of April. Having been allowed to miss the pre-European season races, to keep on the right side of sponsors and the powers that be it now had to join the fray and to contest each subsequent event. Desperately lacking test time, the team failed dismally to qualify for Imola, and the next race, and the next race...

The team was advised that its aftercooler fan was of dubious legality and action might follow should the car manage to qualify for a race. Hart recalls that at this stage it was hard to get charge temperature below 60 degrees even on a cool day. He was looking for something in the region of 40 degrees. For the fourth race at Jarama Hart and Byrne relocated the turbo in the airstream atop the engine and switched to air:water aftercooling. The alloy engine was over water cooled at this stage, but it had proved difficult to produce an adequate heat exchanger. Nevertheless, it was worth the effort: charge temperature dropped by the required amount and shorter primary pipes provided improved response. The drawbacks were weight and complexity: the car was now in the region of 620 – 640kg.

Alas, whereas for Ferrari there was a second turbocharged Grand Prix win to celebrate, for Toleman still the DNQ's mounted... By the team's sixth event at Silverstone Team Manager Alex Hawkridge reckoned the heavily overweight, under-developed package had the potential to qualify, given some luck. At least Pirelli, frustrated by lack of tyre testing opportunity, had by now developed a tyre suited to the cumbersome car. Encouragingly, the following race at Hockenheim saw the it faster than the Cosworth runners in a straightline in spite of its higher drag, but poor acceleration was still evident from the heavy machine.

Hockenheim briefly witnessed the first public outing of the promised 415T. Having an integral head, the 415T was an expensive-to-produce development that offered a lighter, stronger structure. Dispensing with a head gasket eliminated a barrier to the conduction of heat and also removed the thick sections of adjacent faces of two separate castings which can lead to thermal distortion of the structure. The integral head would help check the inevitable tendency for the liners to go oval under the extreme forces involved in extracting over 500b.h.p. from a 1.5 litre engine. It also promised to help keep the valves free from distortion while providing greater freedom in the provision of cooling passages. Since a long, tall structure doesn't lend itself to be a fully stressed chassis member Hart designed the 415T to run semistressed, carried by conventional A-frames.

The heart of the 415T, then, was a stout linerless monobloc that reached down to the level of the crank axis. It was closed by a lower crankcase that formed the two end main bearing caps, allowing a low crankshaft axis and forming a rigid structure. The block was cast by Sterling Metals in the UK, then was sent to Mahle for the cylinder bores to be Nikasil treated. The four valve integral head was of the conventional pent roof layout with a single central plug.

The regular 'mirror image' flat crank was machined from solid by Allen Crankshafts and nitrided. It was driven through conventional H-section con rods by flat topped, valve clearance notched, three ring Mahle pistons cooled by a simple spray to the underside of the crown. Both the crankshaft and the camshafts ran in five plain Vandervell bearings. Camshaft drive was by toothed belt off the nose of the crank. Sloping down to the ports at 45 degrees, each siamesed inlet tract was fed from above by a Lucas injector upstream of the butterfly throttle. Charge air came from a plenum chamber outrigged to the right of the integral head via a short horizontal feed to the inlet manifold. The twin entry turbo was mounted low to the left of the block, at the junction of a steel four branch manifold which was fed by siamesed exhaust tracts. The 415T employed Lucas ignition and injection. The ignition was Lucas CD while the injection was the mechanical shuttle system, now with a cam sensitive to throttle opening and boost pressure.

Byrne wasn't able to produce a new chassis to take advantage of the 415T and, indeed, due to financial considerations it wasn't the intention to replace the interim engine overnight. The 415T was not seen at the following race on the Osterreichring, then again only the prototype was available, for Henton at Zandvoort and Monza where, at long last, a Hart-Toleman qualified for a Grand Prix. Running on three cylinders for much of the duration, Henton finished a distant tenth. Toleman had a turbocharged Grand Prix car but had a long climb to match the heights now scaled by Renault and Ferrari...

The 1981 Ferrari turbo (overleaf) tucked its twin turbos within its 120 degree vee for a compact installation with short charge plumbing for good response. Another unusual engine was the integral head Hart in line four 'monobloc' which powered the Toleman (this page). ⟱

Prototypes 1980-81

Although the era of Porsche versus Renault at Le Mans was over, as we have noted in 1979 Porsche was tempted back to the classic race by the Essex petroleum company, which offered to sponsor a two car 936/78 entry. That year World Championship for Makes races admitted Group 6 cars and Porsche used Silverstone to warm up for Le Mans. The sole 936/78 entered was comfortably faster than the private 935s that now disputed the Makes series between themselves and was well in charge in spite of a time consuming off track excursion, then Mass mysteriously felt the front wheels go light . . .

This chassis and the one Mass had wrecked at Le Mans in '78 were both rebuilt for Le Mans where there was no powerful opposition. Nevertheless, both cars hit problems and a Kremer-entered private 935 won!

The Porsche 935 Group 5 car was now a well established part of the endurance scene with precious little class opposition. It ran a larger displacement version of the two valve boxer turbo engine, though factory cars run in 1978 had employed four valve engines. Mezger's four valve engine was not made available to customers and the two valve boxer engine had been taken out to 3.2 litres for late Seventies silhouette racing.

By this stage, aside from the Essex exercise, Sports-Prototypes had all but faded away and the World Sportscar Championship had been laid to rest. Without factory participation, the World Championship for Makes was ailing and now accepted Group 6 as well as Group 5 cars in an effort to help make up the grids. For '79 Joest had been able to equip his 908/4 with a twin turbo engine and 936/76-style bodywork and he contested selected rounds. Concentrating on 'handling' circuits, he took two wins over the more powerful but cumbersome privately entered big capacity 935s that formed the bulk of the field.

In 1980 the factory was absent from Le Mans but it lent Joest a two valve 936, which Ickx agreed to drive. A broken fuel injection drive belt and a stripped fifth gear handed victory to Jean Rondeau's Cosworth DFV propelled Sports-Prototype team. Elsewhere, the 935 continued to dominate endurance racing. It was much the same in 1981, but this year the factory came back to Le Mans with a re-engined 936 spyder – the chassis taken from the factory museum – which drew on an abandoned Indy Car programme.

The stillborn Indy Car employed engine 935/72 – a 2650.0cc. derivative of Mezger's mid Seventies four valve design with single turbocharger and without aftercooler as per Indy Car regulations. However, since the oval racer ran on alcohol Porsche was able to dispense with the cooling fan. Engine Typ 935/72 had the classic 66mm. stroke crankshaft together with a 92.3mm bore (for 2649.65cc.) and, with a compression ratio of 9.0:1 was rated 630b.h.p. at 9,000r.p.m. on the contemporary regulation maximum 2.03 bar absolute. Alas, Porsche's Indy Car plans had been shelved before the car could even be entered for a race. Six cylinders was an increasing disadvantage as the boost pressure limit was progressively reduced, the engine configuration was a disadvantage in the face of the development of 'wing car' technology and the Indy Car establishment was in turmoil as entrants fought the administrators. Everything was against Porsche participation at the turn of the decade.

Although stillborn, the 2.65 litre Indy engine was perceived as having the ideal capacity for a twin turbocharged unit to meet the requirements of Group C, which was slated to replace Groups 5 and 6 from 1982. Group C had no displacement limit, but set a minimum weight of 800kg. and a specific fuel allocation, according to the length of race. It called for a high level of fuel efficiency and the 2.65 litre displacement was perceived as ideal to meet the Group C ration of 600 litres for a 1000km. race and 2600 litres at Le Mans. Thus, the combination of 66mm. stroke and 92.3mm bore surfaced at Le Mans rather than Indianapolis. The 935/76 engine for Porsche's 1982-launched 956 Sports-Prototype was first race-tested at Le Mans in '81 then, having won easily, its specification was finalised. Porsche was ready for a new era of turbocharged endurance racing.

Derek Bell (pictured) won the 1981 Le Mans 24 hours with Jacky Ickx in this Porsche 936 turbo taken from the factory museum. The chassis was old but the engine was a new generation 2.65 litre version of the boxer six with four valve heads intended for the forthcoming Group C.

Grand Prix Cars 1982

1982 was a sad yet remarkably successful year for Ferrari: due to accidents the team finished the season with two different drivers from those with which it started, yet it won the Constructors Cup with three victories to the credit of its powerful turbocar and finished second in the Drivers series with a driver who had missed five races and still lay in hospital. That driver was Pironi, who won two races before crashing at Hockenheim. Tragically teammate Villeneuve had earlier crashed fatally at Zolder.

On the technical front, the team had switched to advanced composite monocoque construction – Englishman Harvey Postlethwaite overseeing a much more satisfactory chassis – and had found good reliability from Mauro Forghieri's impressive 120 degree V6 turbo, aided by a new so called 'emulsifying' technique which improved cooling and boosted power. As we have seen, Ferrari was prepared to be far more experimental in its approach to turbocharging than Renault.

The crudest method of internal engine cooling is to run rich. The very act of injecting fuel into the charge airflow offers a cooling effect thanks to the latent heat of evaporation of the fuel. However, petrol offers significantly less cooling effect than methanol and Formula One was restricted by FISA regulations to 102 octane petrol. Running rich nevertheless offered a beneficial cooling effect, particularly as it speeded up the combustion process – the effect was to drop both charge and exhaust temperature. Turbo cars ran rich in qualifying on high boost but in the race it was a compromise, the weight of extra fuel a significant handicap.

In qualifying, a large amount of valve overlap could be (and often was) employed causing a blow through of unburned or partially burned fuel which was similarly kind on the turbine. In fact, Ferrari went further, by-passing compressor air over the turbine while the throttle was shut and injecting extra fuel to burn with it, ignited by the red hot turbine blades! In effect, this created a second engine and other engine manufacturers quickly spotted what the crafty Scuderia was up to. The technique was quickly and quietly dropped.

Of greater long term significance was Ferrari's emulsifying technique – AGIP 'Emulsistem' – which was a sophisticated method of water injection. The practice of water injection was an old one, having been used by supercharged aircraft before the war. Injecting water into the charge air (at the plenum) assisted cooling but also, for reasons that had no formal, text book explanation, increased power. Power boosting additives were specifically banned but since there was no theoretical basis on which the rule makers could prove that the injected water added power it could not be deemed illegal!

Renault did not follow suit, once again reluctant to embrace anything it considered outside the spirit of the regulations. As a mass car manufacturer it could not afford to risk its reputation. This year it was, nevertheless, highly competitive with an updated car, living up to its reputation as pre-season favourite. Arnoux and Prost took two wins each but Renault reliability had slipped again and the team did not amass title winning points. Indeed, it could not better third in the constructors league headed so impressively by Ferrari. Renault could count 10 pole positions but no less than 26 retirements from 32 starts. In fact, a Renault led all but three of the season's 16 races at one stage or another yet there were only three wins on the road. A great deal of disillusionment crept into the French camp as the season wore on.

On the technical front, the turning point was Monaco where Renault followed Ferrari's lead with electro-mechanical injection. Subsequently, though, an injection control problem was the most easily pin pointed chink in the RE30B's armour. The more flexible, more frugal EF3 engine which debuted at Monaco, introduced both DPV (as later used by Boudy on the Peugeot Turbo 16) and electro-mechanical injection. DPV – Dispositive Prarotation Variable – was a compressor performance-enhancer which employed variable-incidence blades both to give incoming air a pre-swirl in the direction of rotation and to cut off the air supply when the throttles were closed. Cutting the air supply left the compressor in a partial vacuum, the better to maintain its momentum. However, since the blades had to be arranged in a circumferential ring ahead of the compressor eye the incoming air had to take a somewhat convoluted path to the impeller.

Renault's electro-mechanical injection system saw the cam on its Kugelfischer metering unit controlled by a servo motor which responded to signals from a microprocessor based, in-house produced ECU. However, the system was not, Dudot admits, as sophisticated as that developed for the similarly Kugelfischer injected BMW engine which arrived in 1982. The processor developed by Bosch for BMW could cope with more than the five parameters dealt with by Renault's black box. Nevertheless, the new Renault system brought major improvement.

Alas, there was a long delay in supply of the servo motor ordered from an aeronautical company. Dudot says: 'it was ordered right at the start of '82 but was not available until September. Before that we had to use a Japanese servo that could not adapt to Formula One conditions'. The Japanese motor found it hard to survive in the environment of a hot, high revving race engine. At first it worked fine but later servo failures cost the team two wins and any chance of the accolade of World Champion. A title that would be even harder to come by in 1983 thanks to the participation of BMW.

BMW's in line four cylinder engine was of considerable vintage. It had been designed in the late Fifties by a team working under Alex von Falkenhausen and including Paul Rosche, Technical Director of BMW Motorsport in the Eighties. Contemporary practice had then favoured pushrods and a three bearing crank. Von Falkenhausen had opted for a chain driven s.o.h.c. and a five bearing steel crank running in a deep iron monobloc which extended down from the deck to well below crank axis, forming a rigid beam structure well capable of handling future power increases.

From the initial 1500cc engine producing 80 b.h.p., by 1964 the two valve unit had been developed into a 160 b.h.p. 1800cc. unit capable of winning the European Touring Car Championship. Following successful experiments with an unusual Apfelbeck four valve head that had inlet and exhaust valves diametrically opposed and radially disposed, and operated by double rockers, BMW went Formula Two with a 1600cc Lucas injected version that produced a promising 225 b.h.p. at 10,500 r.p.m.

Alas, the complex Apfelbeck head engine was heavy and lacked the torque and the reliability to win. In 1969 an 'M12' derivative with upright but still diametrically opposed valves and three plugs per cylinder, producing 220b.h.p. at 10,500r.p.m., took Hahne to the runner up slot in the ungraded drivers' championship. In 1970 came the M12/2 with conventional four valve head. The 'compromise' head had allowed bigger inlet valves for extra top end power but additional air friction in the inlet tracts was at the expense of torque. Following a short absence from official competition activity came a 2.0 litre M12 for the increased displacement Formula Two of 1973, again with conventional four valve head, and only a single plug. The M12/6 and its derivative, the M12/7 introduced in 1974 took the BMW-March works team to victory in 67 of 142 races contested over the years 1973-83.

When BMW Motorsport GmbH was founded in 1973 its 2.0 litre Formula Two engine was rated 275b.h.p./8,500r.p.m.: by 1983 Technical Director Rosche's ultimate development of the M12/7 was producing 312 – 315b.h.p./10,000r.p.m., with maximum revs of 10,250 and a dyno 'high' of 321b.h.p.. The classic Formula Two power plant featured a gear driven alloy head with a 40 degree included valve angle. Each camshaft ran in five bearings and was enclosed by its own slim casing, so that the four plugs nestled in a deep vee. The inlet cam was on the right and drove a Kugelfischer metering unit while a Bosch distributor ran directly off the exhaust cam.

Inside the stock five bearing monobloc was a nitrided steel crank turned by Mahle valve clearance notched flat top, three ring pistons via titanium con rods. The stroke was 80mm., while the bore was 89.2mm. and an 11.0:1 compression ratio was run. At its outset, the BMW Motorsport contender had brushed aside Ford's Cosworth BDG and alloy Hart BDA engines, reaching 300b.h.p. by the middle of the decade. Following the admission of pure racing engines, it had shared spoils with Renault's two-season wonder V6 then, in the early Eighties, with the Hart in line four and Honda V6 – all its sparring partners purpose designed alloy units. Its career was ended only by the demands of the Formula One turbo programme.

Of course, the idea of turbocharging was an old one in Munich. As we have seen in 1969 BMW had won four E.T.C.C. races with a lightly turbocharged 2.0 litre saloon racer, while in the mid Seventies it countered the 935 with a twin turbo derivative of its six cylinder CSL saloon racer, a project sub-contracted to Schnitzer. The base CSL racer had an M12/7-style head (though chain driven) on a 3.5 litre straight six block and was good for around 475b.h.p. The 3.2 litre version blown by KKK turbos to 2.3 bar was rated 750b.h.p. Alas, neither was this BMW turbo engine fully developed as the CSL had become an obsolete model. However, in 1977 BMW Motorsport developed a turbocharged four cylinder 320i lookalike in conjunction with McLaren Engines of Detroit, USA, primarily for IMSA silhouette competition.

The IMSA 320i carried a 2.0 litre M12 series engine blown by a single Garrett turbo. Codenamed M12/9, it drew heavily upon the Indy turbo experience of McLaren engineer Gary Knudsen and featured American pistons (TRW) and con rods (Carrillo) as well as an American turbo. Blown to 2.3 bar it was reckoned to produce 550b.h.p. Although at a disadvantage against larger capacity Porsche 935s, it won the July 1977 Road Atlanta IMSA GT race. Late in the year a sister car surfaced in Europe, run by English tuner John Nicholson. However, the Atlantic crossing was not successful, poorer octane (pump rather than American racing) fuel blamed for loss of reliability.

While Nicholson was grappling with the problem of running the fire-breathing 2.0 litre in long distance Group 5 races, German tuner Schnitzer was running his own turbocharged 1.4 litre M12/7 derivative in the 2.0 litre category of national sprint races with a fair amount of success. BMW Motorsport had its own 1.4 litre turbo on the dyno, coded M12/12 and equipped with a single KKK turbo. The idea was to produce a batch of turbo cars for the 1979 German silhouette series. Alas, the series

organisers hastily weighted the dice in favour of atmospheric 2.0 litre cars. All was not lost. From the outset, Rosche admits he had produced a 60mm. stroke crank, as well as the standard 56mm. version. The 1.5 derivative for 1980 was to be coded M12/13...

The 1.4 litre had run well on the bench. Fitted with a 3D metering cam (as used by Renault) to adjust its mechanical injection according to boost pressure as well as throttle opening, and Bosch CD ignition with fixed timing, at around 2.6 bar it gave 550b.h.p./10,500r.p.m. Pushed to 2.8bar and beyond, it had proved capable of handling over 600b.h.p. BMW Motorsport Director Jochen Neerpasch had told Lauda about it. Eager for a new challenge, Lauda had been keen to drive a BMW-McLaren in 1980, and Marlboro had been prepared to back it. Neerpasch had put it to the board, but hadn't played the political game well enough: the answer had been 'nein'. Shortly afterwards Lauda had abruptly quit Formula One and Neerpasch had gone off to head Talbot's new, Grand Prix aspiring competition department.

Neerpasch had arranged for BMW Motorsport know how to be sold to Talbot: Rosche's emerging turbo engine would be given a Talbot badge and raced by Ligier on behalf of the French marque. Supported by two members of the main board, Sales Director Hans-Erdmann Schonbeck and development chief Dr. Karlheinz Radermacher, Neerpasch's successor Dieter Stappert and Rosche protested that the production basis of the engine was reason enough for BMW to invest in its own race programme. The support of the sales and marketing and Press/PR departments was important here: this time the main board said 'yah!'

Although talks continued with Talbot on the basis of the French company entering 'BMW-Talbot' cars, on April 24 1980 it was officially announced that BMW would equip Brabham with the M12/13. Blown by a single KKK turbo, the M12/7 based unit was officially rated at 550b.h.p./9,500r.p.m. at a conservative 2.3 bar. However, it had only just started bench testing.

The iron block designed by von Falkenhausen in 1959 was still in series production powering the 316, 318 and 518 saloons and BMW Motorsport used essentially 'stock' blocks, treated via a heat and chemical process to relieve inherent stresses. During the Formula Two days the company had sometimes instead employed well run in (around 100,000km.) examples. As in those days, the stabilised block had its internal walls machined smooth to assist oil return, while surplus ribs and water channels on the inlet side were machined off, to save around 7kg.

The deep iron monobloc was closed by the aluminium M12/7 type head secured by five pairs of studs, and by a shallow magnesium sump pan. Each of the crankshaft's five bearings was retained by a two-bolt cap. Conveniently, the standard production journal diameter of 48mm. could be employed, the plain bearings supplied by Glyco. The shaft itself, otherwise than for the 60mm. rather than 80mm. stroke, was still the regular Formula Two forged item with deep nitriding, in which the oilways had been modified for greater oil circulation. It was a typical 'mirror image' in line four shaft, with extended balancing webs to reduce bearing and crankcase loads.

The con rod journals retained the same 45mm. diameter as the production 'shaft, and again plain Glyco shells were employed. The H-section rods, 153.6mm. long, were milled and turned from a titanium forging and were shot peened for strength. The big end caps were secured by two titanium bolts with steel nuts. At the other end, a hollow steel gudgeon was fully floating and was retained by Rosan-type nuts rather than conventional circlips. The three ring Mahle pistons were of a 'semi-slipper' form, with short thrust pads integral with the crown. Each weighed little more than one third of a kilogram, complete with gudgeon pin. A vast piston stock was held, allowing a piston to be selected for a precise fit in each bore. The bores, machined directly into the cast iron block, were very precisely honed.

Rosche denies that the M12/13 engine was ever run with Nikasil coated bores or conventional Nikasil liners, as alleged by some of his rivals, saying that coated bores were 'not necessary'. Piston cooling was taken care of by a simple spray to the underside of the crown, the piston not of the oil gallery type.

The conventional steel valves and bronze-based valve seats and guides of the M12/7 head had been changed to cope with the heat, new exhaust valves being nimonic, seats, beryllium bronze. Conventional double springs and sintered steel bucket tappets were retained, with shims inside the buckets for clearance adjustment. The head was sealed to the block by a regular gasket and carried alloy cam carriers, located by studs which projected up through the caps for the five camshaft bearings. Again, plain Glyco bearings were employed. Naturally, the hardened steel camshafts were profiled specifically for the engine.

Timing adjustment was available through movement of the drive gear in relation to the shaft. Those gears were rubber mounted and acted, in effect as vibration dampers for the engine. Driven through a train of three intermediate gears, they rotated in the same direction as the engine. The intermediate gears ran on needle roller bearings, the uppermost one carried by the head, the others by a thick aluminium plate bolted to the front of the block. This wide plate carried oil pumps to the left, acted as an oil gallery and also carried water pumps and metering unit to the right.

The pressure pump fed through a filter screwed into the plate at the front of the block to the distribution gallery within. Early turbo experience had revealed a problem of blow by blocking the return of oil from head to sump. Consequently of four scavenge pumps, one was to service the head while another looked after the turbo.

Fuel was supplied by a Lucas mechanical pump driven directly off the front of the inlet camshaft. This fed the Kugelfischer metering unit via a filter, the plunger-type unit in turn continuously supplying four injectors screwed into the carbon fibre plenum chamber, one directly above each inlet trumpet. From the outset the metering cam had been servo controlled but at this stage the ECU was analogue rather than digital based.

Track testing got underway in late 1980 with a Brabham BT49 wing car converted from fully stressed Cosworth-Ford to unstressed BMW, turbo system and all. Both parties were set for a long hard slog and a proper chassis for the M12/13 engine, the BT50 wasn't produced until mid 1981. The BT50 was a development of the contemporary Cosworth car with bigger fuel cell and slightly longer wheelbase and carried engine telemetry equipment, allowing Rosche's team to sit in a receiver van and monitor the engine while the car was on the move. Telemetry was developed as a spin off from the electro-mechanical injection.

Early on, the BT50 was taken to Donington to adjust its electronics and the test went so well that it appeared soon afterwards in qualifying at Silverstone, where it proved high on top speed and cut a lap quick enough for the second row in Piquet's hands. However, it wasn't quicker than Piquet's regular Cosworth car and the Brazilian was able to win the 1981 World Championship without once resorting to turbo power. The original plan had been to start racing the turbo at Monza, but that had been shelved so as not to jeopardise Piquet's strong position by using unproven equipment. Nevertheless, the writing was on the wall for atmospheric engines and Piquet was determined to help develop the BT50 to a high state.

Alas, problems were rife – the new electronics largely to blame, Rosche recalls. Kyalami in January approached faster than the development programme could cope and, under pressure from the BMW board for concrete results from its big, two year investment, 'M Power' made its entrance in South Africa on purely mechanical injection. The high altitude of the Kyalami circuit favoured turbos

and Piquet and teammate Patrese were second and fourth in qualifying, up with the Renault and Ferrari V6 turbos (and with Piquet over two seconds clear of the fastest Cosworth car). Alas, Piquet made a poor start and then spun out while Patrese retired due to a failed turbo.

With the analogue-based injection control troublesome, Brabham reverted to Cosworth power, joining in with the controversial use of a large water tank ostensively for brake cooling. Piquet won the Brazilian Grand Prix on the road after a late stop for water, only to be disqualified as his car, allegedly, hadn't conformed with the minimum weight ruling throughout the race. The upshot was that the majority of FOCA stalwarts (among whom only Brabham had a turbo deal) had boycotted Imola, round four of the 1982 World Championship.

Having abandoned the BMW engine since Kyalami, and having become embroiled in a fight with FISA, Ecclestone hadn't endeared himself to the BMW board. A week prior to the next Grand Prix at Zolder he faced a public ultimatum from Munich: 'field two BT50s at Zolder or we shall terminate our association'.

Piquet and Patrese qualified the BMW cars just inside the top ten and although Patrese spun out this time, Piquet finished fifth. Thereafter, Piquet persevered with the turbo car while Patrese reverted to Cosworth power – and won straight away, at Monte Carlo. Piquet's gearbox failed in Monaco then in first qualifying at Detroit the engine blew in the race car while the T car refused to run cleanly – Piquet was off the grid. With second qualifying washed out, there was no race for him.

Rosche recalls that '50% of the electronic boxes at Detroit were no good!' In the few days prior to Montreal qualifying: 'we worked to make four good boxes from eight'. Murray wanted to give the World Champion one BMW and one Cosworth car for Montreal but Stappert insisted he stick to the two BMW machines. The race car misfired in first qualifying but this time the T car ran sweetly. One decent ECU made all the difference, transforming the engine from 'undriveable' to smooth and progressive. Piquet qualified fourth up with the Renault and Ferrari turbo cars. Come the race and he quickly dispatched them, going on to win round seven of the World Championship.

Over the remainder of the season both Brabhams were BMW powered and Murray devised the pit stop tactic whereby the cars could run hard on soft tyres and a light fuel load, hopefully building up a sufficient lead to allow for replenishment. However, it wasn't until the fourth attempt that either car lasted long enough to make the planned stop. The engine was still bugged by problems with its electronics and Montreal remained the high of 1982.

Meanwhile, at the other end of the scale, Hart had made progress in '82 with detail improvements including a slightly higher compression ratio. The tyres improved and mid season Byrne was able to heavily revise the chassis – the upshot was fastest lap in the Dutch Grand Prix! Toleman had an advantage over the Cosworth runners who comprised the bulk of the field on the few occasions when the whole package clicked and Warwick ran second in the British Grand Prix before retiring. Engineering expertise and sheer hard work could still shine through even on a very, very tight budget.

By 1982 both Ferrari (upper photograph) and Renault were serious World Championship challengers with turbocharged cars. The 'atmo' was on its way out and even Toleman's low budget Hart turbo car went well on occasion – Warwick is seen challenging Pironi's Ferrari at Brands Hatch.

Indy Cars 1980-85

As we have noted, after Sneva's Penske run McLaren-Cosworth won the '77 National title it was Cosworth all the way into the Eighties in spite of progressive boost cuts down to 48ins (a whisker over 1.6 bar absolute) following another brief taste of 1000b.h.p. Indy Cars. The final cut to 48in. for the early Eighties was the most dramatic and slashed power to around 600b.h.p. However, Cosworth struck back with a high compression ratio – 11.0:1 – and higher revs and a package of improvements. The basic philosophy was now to consider the 'DFX' as a DFV running in a more favourable atmosphere.

For the 48in. engine Cosworth introduced contemporary DFV-sized valves and ports, DFV-type cams and DFV-style intake and exhaust system tuning, with a 4 into 1 exhaust manifold. It also developed its own constant flow mechanical fuel injection system which, in essence, offered a more sophisticated metering valve system. The valve was operated by a 3D cam which responded to pressure in the plenum as well as throttle opening to provide more accurate fuelling over the entire operating range. This was primarily in the interest of improved fuel consumption since these days there was a fuel allocation of approximately a quarter of a litre per mile.

Slotted into the centre of the vee and driven at engine speed in the manner of the DFV's Lucas shuttle metering unit, the new metering unit was used in conjunction with a single butterfly just ahead of the plenum rather than individual cylinder throttles. There was less of a pressure drop with the single butterfly, which was quite adequate for oval racing. The turbocharger (only one was permitted) was carried in the bellhousing in the manner of an Eighties Formula One oil tank, keeping its weight as low as possible and allowing a short run from compressor to plenum (no aftercooler was permitted).

Engine weight was addressed wherever possible. The use of Nikasil rather than traditional iron liners would save the best part of 5kg. from the top end of the engine but unlike the DFV the DFX had not been, and could not be converted. The higher cylinder pressure called for a thicker Nikasil liner: this could not be accommodated together with adequate water passages given the constraints of the DFV based block casting. The DFX continued on iron liners.

By the early Eighties the DFX was equipped with CD ignition – usually Lucas. Running a DFV compression ratio and to DFV-type revs power went to a quoted 720b.h.p./11,000r.p.m. with torque quoted as 350lb.ft./9,500r.p.m. It wasn't until 1986 that the engine faced serious competition, other than at Indianapolis where USAC allowed stock block turbo engines to displace 3425cc. and to run 10in. additional boost.

USAC had first given stock block turbo engines a shot in the arm in 1979, by offering an 8in. Hg. mercury (approximately 0.27bar) boost advantage over the Cosworth DFX. Already turbocharged stock blocks had a capacity advantage – 209cu. in. versus 161cu. in. Chevrolet had responded by offering Indy Car racers a special version of its V6 production engine.

The Chevrolet V6 was a 90 degree engine that had been produced essentially by lopping two cylinders off a V8. The V8 in question was, of course, the classic Chevrolet pushrod V8 engine, introduced way back in 1955. Its farsighted designers had produced an engine with tremendous tuning and long term development

potential and the five/six litre (300 – 360cu.in.) small block Chevrolet had become an American motorsport tradition. In particular it formed the basis of the most popular competition on the North American continent, NASCAR Grand National Stock Car Racing which had downsized in the Seventies, forcing a switch from seven litre big blocks to small blocks of up to 358 cu.in. (5867.62cc.). In Grand National competition fuel of high (107 octane) was permitted in the interests of 500 mile reliability and on a 14:1 compression ratio the late Seventies/early Eighties dominant 358cu.in Chevrolet V8 produced approximately 620b.h.p. at 7,750r.p.m.

Since the Chevrolet V6 was based on V8 tooling it employed reciprocating parts from the small block. A 90 degree V6 with a straightforward three pin shaft (the pins naturally disposed at 120 degree intervals) is burdened with an uneven firing order and will have an unbalanced secondary rocking couple – inherently smooth V6 engines are those with 60 or 120 degree vee angles. The Chevrolet V6 was fitted with a split pin crank (in other words, there were two staggered con rod journals between each pair of webs) but since the pins were phased at only 18 degrees it was still an 'odd fire' engine which was not to the benefit of racing ignition systems. For racing, Chevrolet offered a high strength nickel-iron V6 block and special lightweight aluminium heads. The block featured main bearing caps that spanned the width of the crankcase and had outer bolts into the 'case walls.

Chevrolet tuner Ryan Falconer built a V6 turbo for the 1980 500, this 209 cu. in. (3425.51cc.) unit running Falconer's own even fire split pin crankshaft produced from a solid billet of steel. On its regulation 58in. (approximately 2.0 bar absolute) it was powerful but it was lacking development time. Falconer subsequently switched to IMSA GTP racing. Development of the turbocharged Chevrolet V6 Indy engine continued through the Eighties but only as a low priority venture by the Cosworth-equipped Foyt team.

More serious was the factory backed Buick V6 turbo effort. By the early Eighties Buick had resolved to shake off its staid 'doctor's car' image. Two major strategies were developed: in NASCAR, the most popular form of national racing, the company would use GM's corporate V8 while elsewhere it would explore every outlet through which it could promote its bread-and-butter V6 engine. As with the Chevrolet V6 , the Buick V6, produced in various displacements from 2.5 to 4.5 litres, was a V8 with two cylinders chopped off. And the V8 in question was essentially still General Motor's 1955-launched Chevrolet engine.

The different displacement Buick V6 versions versions were all produced on common tooling having fully interchangeable parts. In 1977 Buick had introduced an even fire split pin crankshaft. The base engine was a conventional pushrod V6 with two valves side by side servicing a classic wedge shape combustion chamber. It had a linerless cast iron block, cast iron heads, cast iron crank, cast iron con rods and cast aluminium pistons.

Buick's decision to exploit the V6 on the race track led it straight to Indianapolis, where Falconer's similar V6 had already shown promise. Buick rolled in for the 1984 race. For the mid Eighties stock blocks had 57in. Hg. mercury (approximately 1.9 bar absolute), four valve race engines only 47in. (approximately 1.6 bar). CART was not so lenient and so Buick had commissioned McLaren Engines to develop the V6 specifically for the high profile '500'.

Before that engine was ready, a superficially similar spin-off GTP power plant had been debuted in the March of IMSA Camel GT team Pegasus Racing. The GTP car was ready in time for the 1983 Daytona finale and astonished with its speed around the banking. It ran a full programme in 1984 and even took in Le Mans where speed on the Mulsanne was prodigious. Alas, reliable it was not.

Meantime, Buick arrived at the Brickyard powering a pair of March 84C chassis run by the Brayton team. The turbocharged V6 engine developed by McLaren Engines were based on special 'heavy duty' parts produced by Buick's Special Products Engineering division. The linerless block was a high strength 'Stage II' casting. Unlike the production item it was skirted, the crankcase walls extending roughly 60mm. below crank axis, and had solid bulkheads at the centre main bearings to accommodate full width four bolt caps. Further strength was added by an integral lifter valley and by additional ribbing throughout. The casting was produced in chrome-moly-alloyed cast iron claimed to offer 20% more strength than production iron.

The Stage II block featured modified oil galleries and was used in conjunction with a cast aluminium dry sump pan. The crank was retained by steel main bearing caps. Clevite supplied the bearings which ran on 63.47mm. journals. The split-pin big end journals had a diameter of 57mm. The shaft was a steel forging by Buick with rolled fillets on the journals for added strength. It had six extended balancing webs and carried a steel flywheel (retained by six bolts) ahead of a harmonic damper.

Typical H section billet steel rods were supplied by Carrillo Industries and had a two bolt secured big end

which ran on a Vandervell bearing. Diamond Racing supplied both the three ring piston and the circlip retained gudgeon pin. The top ring was Moly coated and the piston was forged. It was slightly dished to provide the desired compression ratio. The basic design of Buick 'Stage II' head provided for a small combustion chamber with extensive squish area both sides of the valves to be run in conjunction with a (clearance notched) flat top piston in the case of normal aspiration.

Buick had both iron and aluminium 'Stage II' heads available to the same basic pattern, which was a clean sheet of paper design for maximum performance. The valve sizes (2.02 and 1.60in.) were not the ultimate that could be crammed in but were optimum from the point of view of gas flow, offering the highest velocity. Only the aluminium head was fitted with valve seats. Both heads were attached by six bolts per cylinder. Head to block sealing was via a composite gasket having stainless steel flanging and in-built steel O-rings, one per cylinder.

The valves were titanium on the intake side and, in the case of the turbo engines, Inconel for the exhaust. They were fitted with triple chrome silicon wire springs and titanium retainers. Operation was through roller-equipped machined rockers, shaft-mounted on needle bearings. Similarly the pushrods, 205mm. long, were equipped with roller lifters. Rockers and lifters were from various aftermarket sources while the camshaft was from Special Products Engineering. It was hardened 8620 billet steel and was ground by McLaren Engines to its requirements. It ran in four bearings and was gear driven off the front end through an idler.

Milodon supplied the gear drive, more precise than the stock chain drive. The drive ran in its own housing ahead of which was a front cover produced by McLaren Engines

which isolated the ancillary drive, taken off the camshaft drive gear, and acted as a water manifold and pump mount. McLaren Engine's aluminium housing set the pumps either side of the engine, the ancillary drive taking the form of a belt which wrapped around a pulley each side of the crankcase. Cosworth supplied the pumps (mounted in classic 'Cosworth fashion'): on the left an oil pressure pump (plus filter) and water pump, on the right two scavenge pumps, one for the crankcase, one for the turbocharger.

The dry sump contained a crank scraper which supplied oil to a central scavenge pick up. In excess of 100p.s.i. oil pressure was run given the demands of turbocharging. The turbocharger was a single unit as demanded by USAC. The exhaust primaries were stainless steel and the turbocharger was mounted just behind the engine. Pressure in the plenum was sensed by Buick's advanced microprocessor controlled distributorless ignition system which adjusted timing accordingly.

The Buick 'Power Source Computer Controlled Stand Alone' ignition system provided three CD coils, each serving a pair of cylinders (thus each plug sparked twice per cycle). The drive signals were delivered by an electronic module which contained the microprocessor and five rotary switches to programme timing advance. This module received information from a crankshaft position sensor and a manifold absolute pressure sensor. Its programming switches set r.p.m. breakpoints and the maximum advance available to those breakpoints, plus correction according to manifold pressure. One pair of switches controlled low r.p.m. ignition while after a given breakpoint another pair took over, its breakpoint a pre-set r.p.m. limit. After that limit the system started cutting ignition to pairs of cylinders (a different pair each revolution to avoid any pair fouling). The fifth switch added a maximum advance available as correction to the basic r.p.m. curve set by the other four in the light of to manifold pressure.

The Buick ignition system fired 14mm. plugs (12mm. in the case of the aluminium head) in the order 1-6-5-4-3-2. Fuel injection was not electronically controlled, being taken care of by the Kugelfischer high pressure mechanical system which offered superb atomisation. The familiar plunger-type injection pump supplied one injector per inlet stack.

Perhaps the greatest challenge in the development of the turbo V6 had been the production of an adequately rigid crank, the split pin arrangement calling for some very clever metallurgy. Iron heads were preferred for the Indy turbo engine while the composite gasket proved adequate. Two combinations of bore and stroke had been tested, 4.00 × 2.75in. (101.6 × 69.8mm) and 3.80 × 3.06in. (96.52 × 77.7mm.) and as power and torque were virtually identical the latter combination (with an 8,600r.p.m. potential) had been adopted for a smaller piston crown. Similarly both 6.5in. (165mm.) and 5.9in. (150mm.) rods had been evaluated, again with no measurable effect on performance so the longer rod was used for less cylinder wall loading. The Indy Car engine was reckoned to produce around 800b.h.p. at 8,200r.p.m. on the regulation 57in. compared to around 720b.h.p. for the smaller displacement DFX on 47in., while the torque advantage was in the region of 150 lb.ft. Limited by the inertia of its valve train, the pushrod engine ran to a safe maximum of 8,600r.p.m. whereas the DFX screamed to over 11,000r.p.m.

At the Brickyard in '84 car owner Scott Brayton put his example on the outside of the ninth row with a 203.637m.p.h. clocking that represented a new stock block record and was the fastest time of the second qualifying weekend, if well off the 210m.p.h. pole speed. Teammate Bedard started from the seventh row only to crash while Brayton suffered engine failure. Could a pushrod engine survive 500 miles? Many doubted it.

In 1985 Buicks were entered by Brayton and Galles racing, each running a single March 85C. And they shocked the establishment by heading qualifying, Galles driver Carter taking pole at 212.538m.p.h. in blustery conditions which cut speed slightly and might have favoured the torquey engine. Alas, both Galles and Brayton were early retirements. Both the Buick and Chevrolet push rod V6 Indy engines, although powerful still lacked stamina. Through the early and mid Eighties Indy Car racing was essentially a single engine formula, even under USAC regulations.

In view of that Cosworth had an agreement with CART whereby there was to be no development of the DFX purely for the sake of it. The idea, of course, was to minimise cost for competitors. The DFX was rebuilt by half a dozen or so American based tuners (headed by VDS' Franz Weis and the Penske team's Karl Kainhofer) and with year after year running the same engine reliability was excellent. Usually an IHI turbocharger was employed rather than the earlier Garrett but Penske came to an exclusive deal with Holset. However, there was no turbocharger trickery and with the pop off valve set at 48ins. power was reckoned to have a ceiling of 730b.h.p.

Prototypes 1982-85

Lancia won the 1981 World Endurance Championship, and came close to success in 1982 – the first year of Group C – racing a small capacity in line four cylinder engine in normally aspirated and turbocharged guises. The policy in '82 was to run in the Group 6 class taking advantage of a lightweight spyder-bodied chassis with very effective skirted ground effect tunnels. Group C cars had to weigh at least 800kg., had to conform to a minimum windscreen height ruling (which virtually dictated a a coupe body) and had to run unskirted with a flat area of at least 800mm. × 1000mm. within the wheelbase. Clearly, a Group 6 runner should enjoy a chassis advantage. However, whereas a Group 6 car was limited to a maximum of 1.4 litres turbocharged for this interim year, a Group C car could run any given capacity. Fuel consumption, however, was limited. There was a maximum tank size of 100 litres and there were restrictions on the number of times the tank could be refuelled during a given race.

As we have seen, Porsche considered its stillborn 2.65 litre 'Indy' engine to have the ideal capacity for a turbocharged unit to meet the requirements of Group C, the 66mm. stroke, 92.3mm. bore blown boxer surfacing at Le Mans rather than Indianapolis. The 935/76 Group C engine remained essentially to the specification of the earlier four valve sports-prototype engines with twin KKK turbochargers (one per bank) and Bosch mechanical injection (one injector per cylinder) and CD ignition and air:air aftercoolers, one for each bank (each having its own plenum chamber).

To briefly recap, the aluminium engine, with its water cooled twin cam four valve heads ran Nikasil cylinders. The gear driven cams drove 35mm. inlet, 30.5mm. exhaust valves, the valves set at narrow included angle of 30 degrees which allowed the heads to be welded to the cylinders. The flat top pistons were Mahle oil gallery type with three Goetze rings driving titanium con rods which turned an eight bearing steel crankshaft. A crankshaft that would have been familiar to a Carrera 6 mechanic almost two decades earlier. Of course, the familiar vertical fan – now cooling just the crankcase – seemed somewhat incongruous in a state of the art Eighties Sports-Prototype! The compression ratio was set at 7.2:1 and (given Group C fuel consumption regulations) on a typical 2.2 bar race boost power was quoted as 620b.h.p./8,200r.p.m. with maximum revs of 8,400r.p.m.

The Typ 935/76 engine propelled Porsche's first ever monocoque racing car, the 956 which made its debut at Silverstone in 1982. It comfortably took pole but Lancia won the race. Although it had a 1000km. race fuel ration, Silverstone was run as a six hour race and the fleet little 450b.h.p. Lancia spyder clocked up over 1100km. in the time available. Soft pedalling drastically to save fuel, Porsche had to watch it run away. Revenge came at Le Mans (after Lancia had won the Nurburgring 1000km. in Porsche's absence): three factory 956 models finished first, second and third while Lancia had hit trouble right at the start and failed to last the night. Thereafter, Porsche fought Lancia in 1000km. distance races and retained the upper hand.

The first season of Group C showed that even an enlarged capacity Cosworth DFV engine could not use up the fuel ration. Cosworth started a turbocharging programme at Ford's behest but political changes left Group C as Porsche versus Lancia in 1983. Porsche built a batch of 956 customer cars while Lancia replaced its spyder Group 6 car with a Dallara produced monocoque chassis propelled by an Abarth-developed turbocharged Ferrari V8 engine displacing 2.65 litres. Abarth had done the same sums as Porsche and had come up with the same ideal capacity for a twin turbo race engine, given the Group C fuel allocation.

A Ferrari engine was available to Lancia since the two marques shared membership of the Fiat Group. The base unit was the 1973-introduced 90 degree 'F105' V8 that propelled the 'Dino' road car. This two valve production engine had belt driven twin cam heads and since '83 four valve heads. It was a light alloy unit specifically designed to accept vast future power increases.

That was tested in 1981 when Carlo Facetti/ Martino Finotto's Milan-based 'Carma FF' concern developed a twin turbocharged version of the Ferrari 308 for Group 5 racing. Over 800b.h.p. was coaxed from the unit with KKK turbochargers but the project lacked factory backing and it proved too expensive for a sustained private effort. The later factory Group C engine programme was initiated by Ing. Gianni Tonti working within Fiat's Abarth competition department which was run by Claudio Lambardi. Abarth started with a dozen engines supplied by the Ferrari factory, which had its own foundry at Maranello.

The F105 engine offered a compact and deep mono-bloc, having siamesed Nikasil liners and skirts that extended below crank depth. It was an all alloy unit with four valve, single plug heads attached by 10 bolts and offering a 33.5 degree included valve angle. The combustion chamber was of the regular pent roof pattern and naturally had been designed to run in conjunction with a flat top piston. Mahle oil gallery pistons were fitted with Goetze rings for the Group C version.

The five bearing crankshaft was of the flat plane configuration and the twin overhead camshafts per bank were driven off its nose. A crankshaft power take off gear drove a pulley either side, each bank then having its own belt drive. In production form the unit had a wet sump and on K-Jetronic injection and with four valve heads it still offered 250b.h.p.

The dry-sumped race engine was initially run with Bosch mechanical race injection and featured no expense spared refinements such as titanium con rods. Each KKK turbocharger blew into a individual plenum chamber for the respective bank. The engine was pressurised to around 2.5 bar absolute and could match Porsche's claimed 1982 1000km. race power of 600b.h.p. It made its entrance at Monza in 1983 in the 'Lancia LC2' chassis after precious little testing. The Lancia Group C project had commenced too late for comfort.

For its part, Porsche introduced fully electronic injection with the Bosch Motronic MP1.2 engine management system. Fully electronic injection sees the microprocessor-based ECU activating triggers that control solenoid-operated injectors, determining the timing and duration of each injection pulse. There is no need for a mechanical metering unit: the fuel merely has to be kept at a constant pressure ready for delivery by the injectors. Mechanically, therefore, the system is far less complex. However, the solenoid injectors worked at a far lower pressure than a mechanical metering unit.

Whereas the Kugelfischer metering unit supplied fuel at a pressure in excess of 20 bar, the Bosch solenoid injectors worked at a maximum of 5.0 bar. Higher pressure electro-mechanical injection promised superior atomisation while fully computer timed electronic injection offered superior control. And it was possible to integrate ignition timing control to produce a full engine management system. Motronic MP1.2 controlled injection timing and duration and ignition timing, the conventional ignition system incorporating a Bosch CD coil, distributor and plugs. The Motronic control unit took readings of r.p.m., throttle position, charge air pressure and temperature, oil and water temperature and ambient temperature and there was a manual mixture control facility in the cockpit, weakening or richening the mixture up to 7%. Available only to the factory 956 team, the Motronic engine – coded Typ 935/82 – allowed the four valve boxer engine's compression ratio to rise, first to 8.0:1, then 8.5:1 over the '83 season, power rising to 650b.h.p. without an increase in race boost. First time out at Monza, the factory was beaten by Joest Racing's mechanically injected Typ 935/76 engined-customer 956 but thereafter the works team was in charge.

Lancia's car was too fresh to press home its challenge. In general the LC2 could match or better Porsche qualifying pace and on race day it had sufficient speed to outrun the private 956s. But it lacked reliability. Early on a problem arose of insufficient head rigidity and new castings could not be phased in until after Le Mans '83. By the end of the season the LC2 was running well and in the absence of factory Porsches Lancia won the Imola 'European Championship' race.

For 1984 Lancia was ready to challenge the works Porsches with a full engine management system claimed to improve fuel consumption by 15%. The system was that developed by Marelli Weber for the Ferrari Formula One engine and controlled low pressure solenoid injectors and the timing of the conventional CD ignition system (which incorporated a distributor for each bank). With the engine management system the compression ratio was 8.0:1 and at 3.0 bar absolute over 800b.h.p. was produced. Maximum revs were 8,800r.p.m. and race boost was in the region of 2.5 bar absolute. A further development in '84 was the introduction at Silverstone of an enlarged capacity engine displacing 3.01 litres. and this put the model on pole position. Later Esso supplied a special fuel brew. However, the LC2 still lacked the reliability to match its speed and the factory Porsche team dominated 1000km. races once again. Lancia had a winless '84 season.

The factory 956s underwent little development but in 1984 the customer cars benefited from supply of the Typ 935/82 engine. Nevertheless, in the absence of the factory Joest Racing won Le Mans running a mechanical injection Typ 935/76. Both versions were produced in 2.65, 2.8, 3.0 and 3.2 litre displacements, the bigger displacement versions at first run in German national sprint races, though some customers tried them in World Championship races.

Converting a 2.65 litre to a 2.8 litre engine was simplicity itself: it was simply a case of buying the appropriate stroke crankshaft and con rods to suit. The 2.8 litre version ran a 70.4mm stroke and to produce a 3.0 litre version it was then simply a case of taking the bore out to 95.0mm. with a set of new pistons and rings. It was possible for teams to run larger capacity engines without disclosing the fact. And there was much mystery surrounding the performance of the Joest 956 at Le Mans in 1985. In spite of the return of the factory team Joest's car won for a second time in a row . . .

Elsewhere, the Rothmans backed works team was the class of '85. Lancia had managed to improve the performance of its LC2 with engine and chassis refinements and ran very high boost in qualifying, exploiting around 1000b.h.p. as it collected a string of pole positions. On race day it could run a more competitive pace than ever before to the fuel but good reliability still tended to be elusive. However, the team did win the Spa Francorchamps race.

One other marque won a World Championship race in 1985: Nissan. This was the Japanese event, from which the European based teams withdrew in the face of a washed-out track. The Nissan engine was a development from the marque's 3.0 litre V6, as used in the ZX300 production car. This was an iron block engine with a 60 degree vee angle and two valve aluminium 'hemi' heads of which the inclined valves were operated through rockers by a belt driven single overhead camshaft.

The so called VG30 engine was equipped as standard with a sophisticated engine management system and that at first had caused problems for racers trying to modify it for competition. However, American tuning concern Electramotive had managed to properly re-programme the V6 for Trans Am competition and its efforts had come to the attention of Nismo, the Nissan competition wing. Subsequently Nissan developed Group C and GTP versions of the VG30 in association with Electramotive. The units retained the stock block and aluminium heads and the production 3.0 litre displacement. However, a new electronic injection system was developed, employing Bosch injectors and Electramotive's own control package.

The single turbo GTP engine was first out of the box, at Laguna Seca in May 1985, while the Group C engine started its career in the Japanese national endurance series. On the World Championship trail, it was only seen at Fuji. Toyota, on the other hand, contested both Fuji and, earlier, Le Mans in 1985. Toyota had first entered the international Group C stage at Fuji back in 1983.

Toyota made a quiet entrance. Its 1983 representatives were locally produced Dome prototypes running factory supplied, production based in line four cylinder engines of only 2.1 litres and blown by a single turbo. These 4T-GT engines were based on a five-bearing iron block and had an aluminium two valve, twin plug head. Blown to 2.5 bar absolute, the 7.0:1 compression ratio engine was rated '480b.h.p.' That was very low by Group C standards yet in 1984 some encouraging performances were registered against locally based 956s on the national scene.

In 1985 Dome and Toms – a large Toyota tuning company – entered a car apiece for Le Mans, fully backed by the factory. The engine now had a Nippon Denso engine management system and was officially rated '503b.h.p.' at 7,600r.p.m. Although still underpowered, the engine had enough stamina to see the Toms car home 12th overall.

That was better than the Group C record of the only all-French Le Mans prototype seen in the early to mid Eighties, the WM-Peugeot. Run by Peugeot stylist Gerard Welter and engineer Michel Meunier, the WM team had been active at Le Mans since the mid Seventies, originally running a Peugeot-propelled prototype in the Le Mans GTP category. The engine was based on the ZNS4 90 degree V6 unit that had been developed as a joint venture between Peugeot, Renault and Volvo. This was the so called 'PRV' engine that in Renault guise had inspired the pioneering V6 turbo Le Mans and F1 engines. WM had not looked to turbocharging until 1977 and, essentially an amateur venture, had been interested only in GTP class Le Mans success in the Seventies.

The first WM car ran in 1976, with an unblown 2.7 litre version of the alloy, two valve Peugeot engine breathing through three Weber carburettors. Bosch K-Jetronic (road car) fuel injection was introduced for the '77 car, which was blown by a single KKK turbocharger. Then, in '79, came the more appropriate Bosch Kugelfischer racing injection system and WM's own four valve heads. Unlike the production engine, WM's engine was dry sumped and the team was gradually phasing in its own parts – crank, con rods, pistons and so forth. It cooled each piston via a single spray to the underside of the crown. The new d.o.h.c. four valve alloy heads were produced outside of Peugeot and retained the production based chain drive.

In 1979 WM won the GTP category for the first time, posting a 14th place finish. By 1980 its 2.7 litre engine was rated 500b.h.p. and in 1980 it managed a fourth place overall. Peugeot was delighted and helped with engine modifications as the Group C era arrived. There was a revised sump, a new front cover and new cam covers, allowing the engine to run fully stressed. The bore was taken out from the traditional 88mm. to 91mm., while retaining the production 73mm. stroke for a 2850cc. Group C displacement.

In 1982 WM ventured away from Le Mans for the first and only time, without success. Its car was fast but fragile. And there was no luck at Le Mans in 1982 or '83. And then the team was forced into liquidation by a change in the French tax laws affecting charitable organisations. However, regular driver Roger Dorchy was able to purchase its assets and keep it alive. Engine preparation was put in the hands of DMC – Denis Mathiot Competition – based near Paris and a digital electronic injection control system was introduced for '84, this making the Kugelfischer cam responsive to revs, boost and throttle position. Race power for the mid Eighties was officially 600b.h.p./7000r.p.m.

In '84 Dorchy's narrow track, low drag WM 'P83' ran 227m.p.h. down the Mulsanne and he used that speed to lead the race before spinning at Mulsanne corner. The car later retired. For '85 oil gallery Mahle pistons and a higher compression ratio pushed power higher but again there was no result. And WM was still an amateur effort, with little realistic hope of challenging the might of Porsche.

While the Porsche Typ 935 engine dominated Group C in the early to mid Eighties, IMSA GTP had seen the arrival of the Typ 962. GTP regulations charged four valve turbos with a maximum capacity of 2.1 litres so Porsche produced an alternative 3164.0cc. two valve engine (having a 95mm. bore plus a 74.4mm. crankshaft) to run at the heaviest, 900kg. weight break. Unlike Group C, GTP regulations equated engine type and displacement to car weight. Although restricted to single plug heads and a single turbocharger this engine produced over 700b.h.p. on 2.4 bar absolute and, in a March chassis, helped Al Holbert win the 1983 Camel GT title over Chevrolet V8 and Jaguar V12 propelled prototypes. In 1982 a trailblazing Lola-Chevrolet GTP car had overthrown the Camel GT rule of the customer Group 5/GTX Porsche 935 and for 1984 Porsche offered customers its own GTP chassis.

Porsche introduced the 962 with a 2869.0cc. (93.0mm. bore/ standard 70.4mm. stroke) version of the two valve engine, taking advantage of the fact that its light chassis could then be run at 850kg. However, track experience suggested that the 3164.0cc. alternative engine, although having to pull 900kg., was a more competitive proposition.

Consequently, 962 customer cars were offered with the smaller Typ 962/70 engine or (ballasted to 900kg.) with the Typ 962/71 which retained the '83 bore and stroke dimensions. The two versions were otherwise identical (right down to valve sizes) aside from the longer throw crankshaft 962/71 needing a 125.8mm. rather than a 127.8mm. con rod to maintain the same deck height. They ran a horizontal fan and were fitted with the Bosch Motronic MP1.2 engine management system, as developed through the Group C programme, this driving one solenoid injector per cylinder and timing the (still mandatory single plug) CD system.

The smaller engine was rated 680b.h.p./8200r.p.m. at 2.4 bar absolute and revved to 8,450r.p.m. while the larger engine was red-lined at 8,000r.p.m. and on maximum boost officially produced 720b.h.p./7,300r.p.m. This was on IMSA legal high octane fuel. That fuel was as high as 114 octane and its use was permitted primarily to help keep the Chevrolet V8 stock block alive. The time it took the 962 to get up to speed allowed a fast-starting March-Chevrolet team to claim the 1984 Camel GT title. The unblown 6.0 litre Chevrolet offered a solid 600b.h.p.

with, of course, instant response.

That wasn't enough to make a mark in 1985. In 1985 the Porsche Typ 962/71 engine dominated GTP racing and Al Holbert won his fourth IMSA title. During the course of the season IMSA admitted 'the 3.2 litre Porsche engine is stronger than we expected' and announced measures to handicap its performance in 1986. Meanwhile, Chevrolet was in the process of switching to turbo power.

The Chevrolet turbo GTP engine had been around since 1981 but the project had taken a long time to get up and running after a false start in the early Eighties. After his 1980 Indianapolis adventure, Ryan Falconer had concentrated on GTP racing with the turbocharged V6 unit. The GTP programme commenced in 1982 with a twin turbo Lola for the Interscope team. 1983 regulations cost one turbo then early in the season the team collapsed. Undaunted, Falconer helped set up a deal whereby GM sanctioned a racing car for the first time in 20 years. This was the 'Corvette GTP', an evolution from the Interscope car with a body styled by Chevrolet engineers and a chassis built by Lola. The car didn't start racing until 1985 when the Hendrick NASCAR team was charged with running it. Falconer claimed 650b.h.p. race power, pressurising the 3.4 litre V6 to 2.0 bar absolute via a single Warner ISHI turbo. For qualifying 750b.h.p. was available and the Hendrick-run car was quick. However, it did not arrive until mid season – properly sorted, in 1986 it would show its true colours.

At this stage Buick also had a V6 turbo GTP engine, again a spin-off from its Indy Car V6. Like the Buick Indy engine, this was developed by McLaren Engines in Detroit. Essentially it was the same engine running high octane racing gasoline rather than methanol. The pioneering, privately run March-Buick had been debuted in 1983 and in 1984 it ran a full IMSA season and also ventured to Le Mans where its speed on the Mulsanne was impressive. However, it made little other impression in France and at home it was far from a worry for the Porsche runners. Nevertheless, it was powerful, offering in excess of 900b.h.p. at 2.2 bar absolute qualifying boost from its 3.4 litre displacement which was pressurised by one Warner ISHI turbo.

The power was attractive, as was Buick's support and the '84 IMSA Daytona finale found two new March-Buick teams, Miami Motorsport and Conte Racing, both equipped with new 85G chassis. The Conte car led but both teams suffered new car bugs. Conte ran a full '85 season but while its car was fast it suffered transmission unreliability and a rear suspension weakness. Mid season it was revamped as the Hawk-Buick and the team entered two cars. Yet concrete results remained elusive.

Similarly, Ford was finding it hard to make an impression on the Camel GT trail. It ran a wild front-engined GTP car in 1983 and replaced that with the more conventional 'Probe' in 1985, this equipped with a Zakspeed developed turbo four. This four valve alloy 2.1 litre racing engine, replacing a production based iron block had advanced Motorola electronics and at 2.3 bar absolute race boost it was rated 650b.h.p./ 8,800r.p.m. on a compression ratio of 6.5:1. The Probe started its career at Laguna Seca in 1985 but there was no instant success and, like Chevrolet, Ford was looking for a longer term pay-off. Nissan was in the same boat, with the GTP version of its V6 turbo. 1986 promised more intense competition on the GTP trail...

In the World Endurance Championship the four valve, twin turbo Porsche boxer six (upper photograph) swept all before it from 1982 through to the mid Eighties. A bigger displacement two valve version ran strongly in IMSA, here powering the March which won the '84 Daytona 24 hours.

Grand Prix Cars 1983

For a number of years the specialist British racing teams running off-the-shelf Cosworth DFV engines had staved off turbo power through clever chassis technology. Without the burden of a turbocharging system there was scope to build a lightweight car – right on the 540kg. minimum – with sophisticated ground effect aerodynamics. However, for 1983 all cars had to have flat bottoms within the wheelbase. Big wings came back, and it needed turbo power to drag them through the air. A 500b.h.p. normally aspirated engine was no longer a competitive proposition: the pacemakers were the 650b.h.p. turbos from Renault, Ferrari and BMW. And Brabham had showed that it could be worthwhile starting a thirsty turbo car with less than a full tank of fuel, on soft tyres, and making a mid race pit stop. The pit stop tactic was spectacular and put the turbo cars yet further ahead of the 'atmos', at least on fast circuits. On slow circuits the driveability of a lighter, more agile atmo could sometimes even the odds and Williams, McLaren and Tyrrell all won races this year. However, during the course of the season both Williams and McLaren went with the tide and introduced new generation turbocars.

With its powerful water injected V6 engine and an effective flat bottom version of its composite chassis Ferrari was well placed and in spite of tyre difficulties and bouts of unreliability the team won four races and amassed sufficient points to retain the Constructors Cup. However, in Arnoux and Tambay it didn't have a driver of the calibre of Prost (Renault) or Piquet (BMW). For much of the season Prost looked likely to win the World Championship, in spite of the late entrance of Renault's first advanced composite chassis.

With its '82 chassis down close to the weight limit, lighter and more aerodynamically efficient air:air aftercoolers and reliable electro-mechanical injection Renault had entered the season full of confidence. Prost (now partnered by Cheever) had matured into an outstanding driver and Renault followed Ferrari in the use of water injection to give him enough power to do the job. The new RE40 chassis arrived after the opening races, accompanied by a new alloy block cast by sub contractor Messier that replaced the familiar spheroidal graphite casting from Renault's own foundry, saving a further 12kg. The switch to alloy was primarily to save weight, Dudot confirms, and the alloy EF3 brought the RE40 right down to the new 540kg. minimum. An initial problem of block rigidity soon overcome, the EF3 was rated a healthy 650b.h.p./10,500r.p.m. on 3.2 bar race boost.

In qualifying Renault used 3.4 bar boost and water-sprayed its aftercoolers but didn't match Ferrari turbo power. And just as Prost looked to be sailing to the title, BMW made a surge in race power, to which Renault failed to respond...

In the light of BMW's '82 problems Bosch had commenced work on a digital-based control system, and this had been readied for 1983. To meet the flat bottom ruling Murray had rush-produced the Brabham BT52, a dart-shaped car without conventional sidepods, the coolers fanning out either side of the engine. With that layout, a long wheelbase, the driver sitting well back and a heavy engine, the rearward weight bias was pronounced. Faced with a loss of aerodynamic grip and increasing power Murray had put the emphasis on traction. The static weight distribution was in the region of 35 – 65, compared to 42 – 58 for a typical '82 Cosworth wing car.

The digital-controlled M12/13 started racing at around 2.9 bar, producing in the region of 640b.h.p. on a 6.7:1 compression ratio and was pushed to over 700b.h.p. in qualifying. The four cylinder engine's single turbo was hard worked and a pits cooling blower was introduced to help its bearings. Qualifying also saw the use of a water spray onto the aftercooler. Rosche tried water injection on the dyno but found it more beneficial to concentrate upon fuel chemistry. Zandvoort, round 12, was the turning point. BMW had commissioned fuel from BASF subsidiary Wintershall to replace its regular doctored Avgas, and Rosche confirms that improved fuel and a bigger turbo released more race and qualifying power. Consequently, Piquet could come out of the shadows and grapple with Renault and Ferrari in qualifying.

Although overshadowed in qualifying for much of the season, Piquet had usually been a factor on race day. He had won the Rio opener with ease, then had suffered a rare off day at Long Beach. Thereafter, as a rule the Brabham-BMW had either been the class of the field, or second only to Prost's Renault. However, small, infuriating problems had left Piquet's pickings as three seconds, a third and two fourths prior to Zandvoort. He languished 14 points behind Prost. Piquet and Prost tangled at Zandvoort but thereafter, with the improved BMW engine raced as high as 3.4 bar, producing almost 750b.h.p., there was no stopping Piquet. Prost could not respond as Piquet strode ahead of him to claim the world title.

The controversial Wintershall fuel revolutionised Formula One. Formula One regulations restricted fuel to 'petrol having the following characteristics – maximum 102 octane; maximum 2% oxygen and 1% hydrogen by weight, the remaining 97% consisting exclusively of hydrocarbons and not containing any alcohols, nitro-compounds or other power boosting additives'. Surprisingly, in spite of the apparent exactness, that definition of 102 octane petrol opened the door to the fuel chemist.

Strictly speaking, 'petrol' is but the European name given to refined petroleum (or a synthetic substitute produced by chemical process) as used in motor cars. The act of refining petroleum produces many different liquid hydrocarbons and there are over 200 chemicals present in pump petrol, which varies from manufacturer to manufacturer and from country to country. The Formula One fuel chemist was able to ensure the presence of the precise hydrocarbons which, while not recognised 'power boosting additives' work particularly well in a high boost turbo engine.

Examples of hydrocarbons derived from petroleum are octane, toluene and aniline. Octane is commonly found in pump petrol, unlike the other two which are more useful in the turbo engine. High boost slows flame spread. The chemist was able to brew an arguably legal fuel that under conditions of high boost burned more rapidly, generating more heat energy and had a higher resistance to detonation – in effect, a higher octane fuel. Nevertheless, it registered 102 octane on the mandatory slow speed, low load laboratory test designed to rate fuel for atmospheric production car engines.

Renault's Bernard Dudot reflects, 'we were running a high grade of fuel but this was very close to pump fuel – not completely chemical like BMW's fuel'. For 1983

Renault had come to an agreement to supply engines to Lotus, a team which was in the doldrums until the recruitment of Gerard Ducarouge in mid '83. When Ducarouge, whose talents had been squandered by Euroracing, unpacked his bags at Ketteringham Hall in rural Norfolk in June '83, Lotus was struggling with the 93T. That car had taken it from the Chapman/Cosworth era into the Renault age. Within five weeks Ducarouge had prepared a lighter, more agile chassis based on the previous year's carbon fibre/Kevlar monocoque. It retained unfashionable rocker arm suspension, yet was as competitive as its Pirelli radials allowed – competitive enough to outqualify the Renault works team at the Osterreichring, Zandvoort and Brands Hatch, where de Angelis took pole.

While major manufacturers fought for pole, Hart made further progress in mid field. The new Toleman 'TG183' was a flat bottom derivative of the '82 car featuring a novel aerodynamic package that included front mounted water radiators and side mounted air:air aftercoolers. Feeding the charge air through two matrixes, one either side of the car, the new aftercooling system was designed to save weight over the previous air: water cooler. It helped Toleman reach 575kg. and Warwick was a splendid sixth fastest in qualifying at Rio, fifth fastest at Long Beach. Alas, that early season pace flattered to deceive: thereafter Warwick and new partner Giacomelli were midfield runners, in spite of the development of a twin plug version of the 415T.

Hart was still running pump fuel, which limited the boost that the engine could sustain as flame spread was slow and uneven. The second plug reached into the chamber from a horizontal position, where the head/block interface would have been on a conventional engine, on the inlet side and utilising the space left between valve seat arcs. This upset the form of the chamber a little but allowed the plug, firing at the same time as the central plug, to light an area prone to detonation. It worked very well, and was worth something like a second a lap.

Alas, in '83 ten races passed before Toleman posted a finish, uncharacteristic Hart unreliability partly to blame. Hart explains this as part of the normal 'learning process'. He was, of course, still working to an extremely limited budget. One particular drawback was lack of turbocharger development, Garrett still supplying off-the-shelf diesel engine units. In the light of that, Hart struck an agreement with Holset. The single Holset turbocharger was introduced at the tenth race, on the Osterreichring. Round 11 at Zandvoort brought Toleman its first points, for fourth place, and the team subsequently claimed two sixth, a fifth and another fourth place from the final three races of the season. By that stage, on 2.8/2.9 bar race boost and a 6.7:1 compression ratio the twin plug 415T, still running on Lucas mechanical injection, was producing 630b.h.p. at 10,500r.p.m. Although still low on boost Hart again had a reliable race engine. There wasn't the budget for special qualifying engines – 'there was hardly a budget for ordinary engines', Hart notes. 'The budget didn't increase with increased performance. We were running engines longer and needed more money to do that'.

At least Hart had valuable experience under his belt. Alfa Romeo had likewise conceived a turbo engine in 1980 but it had taken three years for it to achieve a state of race-readiness. Alfa Romeo was represented in Formula One by the Milan-based Autodelta concern, headed by Carlo Chiti, the former Ferrari Technical Director and creator of Alfa Romeo V8 and V12 Formula One engines in the Seventies. Chiti was given the go ahead for a turbo engine at the end of '79 and plumped for a V8 configuration.

Chiti says he opted for eight cylinders as the best compromise between power potential and considerations of complexity and dependability. His was only the second clean-sheet-of-paper design for a 1.5 litre Formula One turbo engine (following Ferrari). It was designed by Chiti

and three assistants over the first half of 1980 and the prototype was unveiled at the mid September Italian Grand Prix in which the turbo-Ferrari made its public track debut. Whereas the six cylinder Ferrari was a 120 degree unit with exhausts and either Comprex supercharger or twin turbos within its wide vee, Chiti's offering was a traditional 90 degree Italian race engine with a KKK turbocharger set either side of the crankcase, Renault fashion.

It was an all alloy engine with Nikasil cylinders and four valve, twin cam heads driven by belts. Alfa Romeo dictated that it should employ in-house Avio turbos and Spica mechanical injection and this extended the delay. For 1983 Alfa Romeo entered into an agreement with Euroracing to run its Formula One team, leaving Autodelta as engine supplier. Euroracing designer Gerard Ducarouge produced an evolution of the prototype turbo car adapted to flat bottom specification, for the V8 the 183T. Winter testing was promising but the season kicked off with two unimpressive races followed by the infamous empty fire extinguisher bottle incident during qualifying at Paul Ricard for which Ducarouge was forced to carry the can.

The departure of Ducarouge left the team an all-Italian affair with engineering headed by Luigi Marmiroli. He saw the 183T regularly qualify in the top 10, in spite of high boost often cracking the Avio turbos, and Cesaris convincingly led the Francorchamps race before a wheel change was fumbled. Chiti says there was nothing inherently wrong with the V8 engine in '83, but emphasises that the Avio turbos, forced onto him by 'in-house politics' were 'a big problem'.

Given the scheduled '84 fuel ration six cylinders looked more practical and both Honda and Porsche launched six cylinder turbo engines in '83. Both engines were unveiled at the 1983 Geneva Motor Show, the Honda offering an hour or so before the Porsche arrival. And whereas the Porsche engine was a clean sheet of paper design, the Japanese newcomer was clearly derived from the existing Honda Formula Two engine.

The Ralt-Honda works Formula Two team had made its debut at Silverstone in June 1980. The engine was an 80 degree V6 with an iron block and gear driven aluminium four valve, single plug heads. The piston was a flat top design, running in conjunction with a conventional pent roof chamber in a Nikasil cylinder and driving a four bearing, three pin steel crank through I-section steel rods. The engine had been designed by a team of young engineers guided by Yoshio Nakamura and Nobuhiko Kawamoto. Nakamura had designed the Honda Sixties Formula Two and Grand Prix engines and was now a consultant to Honda while Kawamoto had worked on those engines as a young engineer and was now President of Honda R&D.

Information about the RA-263 engine's internals was slim. A likely bore of 90mm. was never confirmed but it later transpired that the valves were worked by finger-type cam followers rather than through conventional bucket tappets. Finger followers had long been favoured by Honda. Tended by Nakamura and his team of young engineers, the Formula Two engine unveiled in 1980 started running at 10,500r.p.m. (just a little above the BMW's red line) and was subsequently coaxed to give 12,000r.p.m., going on to win the 1981 European Championship with Ralt, and advice from John Judd of Engine Developments. Honda used Judd's base for engine development work. Early in 1981 it had to overcome problems with the Bosch electronic injection it had adopted for the new season, switching to a Lucas mechanical racing system. Later, with advice from Judd, it designed a head with revised porting (which was manufactured back in Japan).

In 1981 the Honda RA-263 had plenty of mid range punch but had a very narrow power band and while it revved freely to 12,000r.p.m. it tended to run out of breath well before that. However, it was reliable and faced only four cylinder opposition. Once the Honda-

Ralt package was fully sorted on Bridgestone tyres it set the 1981 standard.

By the summer of 1982 work was well advanced back at Wako on the spin off 1500cc. turbocharged V6 and discussion took place with Ralt and Spirit, a new Formula Two team, as to a deal to race it. Spirit was keen to get into Formula One and by the end of '82 the prototype turbocharged engine was track testing in a converted Spirit Formula Two car. The wraps then officially came off the RA-163-E at the Geneva Show.

It was a low-key unveiling on the Honda stand: an engine looking very much like the contemporary Formula Two V6 with a turbo system added and precious little technical information. The external similarity to the Formula Two engine suggested Honda had retained its 90mm. bore in search of high revs and that left 39.35mm. as the stroke that would give the quoted displacement of '1.5 liters' (sic). Almost certainly, the internals were only modified in response to the heat generated by turbocharging (oil cooled pistons, heat resistant valves and seats) and certainly the unusual finger followers remained. The most interesting aspect of the unveiling was Honda's early deployment of an engine management system with computer timed low pressure injection. Precise control of injection and ignition timing was to play a key role in Formula One turbo engine development.

Spirit tested extensively prior to a debut at the Brands Hatch Race of Champions, then joined the 1983 World Championship trail at Silverstone, still employing a converted Formula Two chassis. It contested six Grands Prix, finishing in three albeit well down the field. However, Honda had already announced that it would be switching to a bigger, established team. For the next three seasons Williams Grand Prix Engineering would get free engines and maintenance.

Williams decided to get race experience as soon as possible, preparing the first Honda-Williams for a 1983 debut in the season-closing Kyalami race. With some furious design and build work it made it just despite the engines arriving virtually bare. Technical Director Head was later to reflect: 'we had to improvise a lot. Honda hadn't the least idea of heat generated or air consumed once the engine was in a car. We had to do the whole installation ourselves.'

Williams successfully got the latest, 'D-spec' RA-163-E not only onto the grid, but into the points with fifth place for Rosberg. Probably as much due to Rosberg's incomparable talent with a virtually untried new car equipped with an engine that went off like a bomb when the power came in. It was a considerable feat which provided a wealth of information for winter development.

In contrast, Porsche had produced a more civilised engine. It had been produced at the request of the McLaren International team, run by Ron Dennis with John Barnard its Technical Director. Barnard had produced one of the most effective of all Cosworth powered wing cars but the team clearly needed a turbo engine to take it into the mid Eighties. For a time, the BMW unit was seriously considered but Barnard was not convinced of the long term potential of any in line four. The same went for the iron block Renault V6, a development of an old sports car and Formula Two engine. Heidegger's straight six project, which was being hawked around, was quickly rejected on the grounds that its configuration was unsuitable to be central to a competitive package. So it was that Porsche's R&D operation at Weissach was contracted to produce a brand new engine. On October 12 a contract was signed. The prototype engine was ready in December 1982, by which time Dennis had formed a relationship with TAG (*Techniques d'Avant-Garde*) a company investing Saudi oil revenues. A new company TAG Turbo Engines would fund the rest of the programme.

Barnard's ground effect package demanded a compact engine, either a V6 or a V8, with a maximum angle between the banks of cylinders of no more than 90

degrees. Mezger chose an 80 degree V6 and the base engine would fit into a two foot cube. The mechanicals broke no new ground, though were as advanced as any. The block was cast by regular Porsche race engine sub contractor Honsel, extended to the depth of the crank axis and carried Nikasil wet aluminium liners. The liners were secured by a flange at the top and were sealed to the head via metal sealing rings. The heads were aluminium with integral cam carriers and were closed by magnesium cam carriers. The lower crankcase-cum-sump was a structural magnesium casting forming each of the four main bearing caps. A conventional three pin steel crank was produced by Maschinenfabrik Alfing Kessler, another long standing Porsche ally. The crank ran in four plain Glyco bearings (lead bronze in a steel shell) and was driven through titanium con rods by Mahle oil gallery pistons, fitted with Goetze rings. Each three ring piston's crown was slightly concave with valve clearance notches.

Twin overhead camshafts were driven by straight cut spur gears from the front of the crank. As usual, there were four valves per cylinder the two 30.5mm. diameter inlet valves were inclined at 14 degrees, the two 27.5mm. diameter exhaust valves at 15 degrees. Made by Glyco, the valves were of Nimonic steel and were sodium cooled, as was long Porsche practice. In order to protect the exhaust valves Porsche first experimented with ceramic inserts, then settled for drilling minute waterways between the valves.

There were two Bosch solenoid-operated injectors per cylinder angled downwards at 30 degrees in the intake tract, positioned between the throttle butterfly and the valves. These were operated by a Bosch Motronic MP1.2 engine management system, as seen in Group C on the Porsche 956. However, the requirements of Group C racing were not as subtle as those of Formula One and in a Group C car it was easier to protect the sophisticated circuitry from 'spikes'.

The electronic TAG engine was pressurised by twin KKK turbos. Bore and stroke dimensions of 82.0 × 47.3mm. gave a capacity of 1499cc. while the compression ratio was 7.0:1. McLaren had undertaken to have a turbo car running in 1983, as part of its commitment to its sponsors. Barnard consequently designed an interim car, the MP4/1E, based on his Cosworth design. The 'interim' turbo McLaren made its competition debut in late August 1983 at Zandvoort in the hands of Niki Lauda. By Barnard's standards the car was a poor compromise which had not been properly wind tunnel tested and refined. In a straight line the turbo McLaren was as quick as anything but it still had essentially a Cosworth chassis designed for about 535b.h.p.: the car's aerodynamics could not use the power and the brakes proved inadequate. The Motronic system was also troublesome.

Lauda retired, from 14th place, on lap 26 with the brake fluid boiling. By the time of the 1983 finale at Kyalami the car featured improved aftercooling and running at 3.0 bar the engine was now producing 700b.h.p. at 12,000r.p.m., whereas at Zandvoort it had run at 2.5 bar, developing around 630b.h.p. at 11,500r.p.m. As usual there were Motronic headaches and there was no significant race result. However, a glance at lap times made interesting reading. Piquet's BMW-Brabham had set the fastest lap by a clear margin, and early in the race at that, but second quickest lap went to Lauda's Porsche/TAG-McLaren. That provided plenty of food for thought for anyone considering the 1984 season.

The first turbocharged engine to power a Formula One World Champion driver was this BMW in line four, a rugged old iron block engine pressurised by a single KKK turbo. Special fuel introduced mid season was the key to Nelson Piquet's defeat of Renault favourite Alain Prost.

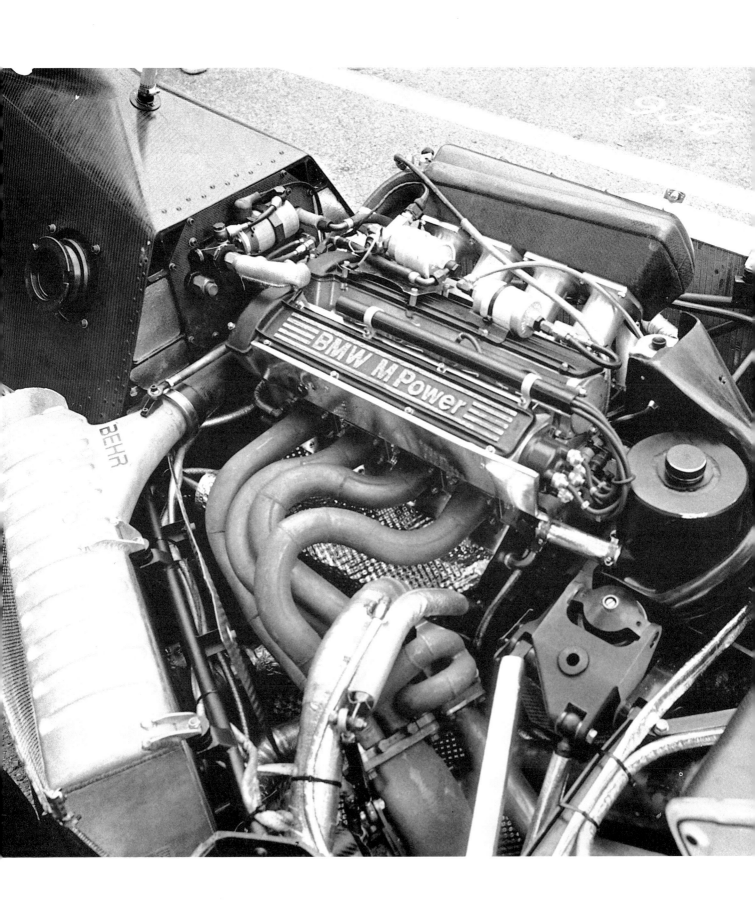

Grand Prix Cars 1984

The 220 litre fuel ration hit engine builders hard. Previously, running rich had helped keep temperatures down. Now every last drop of fuel counted and it was necessary to run lean to avoid running dry. It took a lot of electronic and mechanical development work and generous engine cooling and aftercooling provision merely to make the engine and turbocharger survive. To win, it was necessary to run as efficiently as possible. That implied running right on the verge of detonation without actually suffering piston crown or turbine wheel melt down. Digital control was essential: the engine management system came into its own. Porsche was clearly well placed with the Motronic MP1.2 system and proved able to run a 7.5:1 compression ratio – higher than any other '84 turbo engine. However, at first Porsche ran doctored Avgas whereas BMW continued to exploit more advanced fuel. With its digitally-controlled electro-mechanical injection system ensuring better atomisation and toluene based fuel, BMW had the more powerful race engine in '84. It also had the most powerful qualifying engine of all. Nevertheless, where it counted – at the chequered flag – the McLaren-Porsche/TAG was the car of '84.

Running 3.2 bar absolute, the race power of the Porsche engine had increased to a quoted 750b.h.p. at 12,000r.p.m. with maximum torque of 466Nm. In 1983 Renault and Ferrari had been surprised when the Porsche engine arrived with bespoke turbochargers. KKK hadn't done such development work for them, but then Porsche had a much longer relationship with KKK. For Monaco KKK delivered specially commissioned turbocharger casings which tightened internal tolerances. They were standard fitting from then on and later lightweight, thin wall turbine housings were introduced. Three different sizes of turbines and two sizes of compressor were used and these were used in different combinations depending on weather conditions, the individual circuit, or weather the cars were running in qualifying or the race itself. Larger turbos naturally gave more power at a cost of response.

Ironically, pre season testing at Rio with the MP4/E suggested that 1984 was going to be a difficult year for McLaren – spikes played havoc with the Motronic system once again, and on occasion basic components vibrated apart. Nevertheless, by the time the MP4/2, the proper turbo car, appeared for testing at Paul Ricard many of the bugs had been ironed out. Back in Rio for the Grand Prix, Prost qualified fourth, Lauda sixth. McLaren policy was not to employ sacrificial engines in search of pole. The team's philosophy was that the right fuel efficient package would win, regardless of who led into the first corner. And that efficiency was a function of both engine and chassis performance. It was important to find a good race set up during the practice session, more important than searching for pole.

At Rio, Lauda led before retiring and Prost came through to win. A key to McLaren's success was revealed at Kyalami, the next race, when Prost's car developed a misfire and he had to start the race from the pit lane in the team spare. On that occasion he finished second to Lauda but later would come times when Prost would win in a spare car fired up at the last minute. It was this rare ability not only to give equal treatment to two top-line drivers but also to have a spare car prepared to race standard which marked out the team. And McLaren more quickly adapted to running fuel-restricted turbo cars than any other outfit.

Even before it was over, McLaren's 1984 season had passed into motor racing legend. By the end of the 13th round, it had passed Lotus' record of wins in a season, and then it went on to win the remaining three with a cliffhanger of a final race in Portugal when, by coming second to Prost, Lauda won the Championship by half a point, the smallest margin ever. Not only did McLaren International win the Constructors' Cup with the highest score (143.5 points) ever known but its winning margin (96 points over Ferrari) was easily the largest in the thirty year history of the Cup.

The main opposition to the McLaren International domination had come in form of Piquet's Brabham-BMW which was often the quickest car in the field. However, more often than not Piquet retired, typically through engine or turbo failure. Further, whereas McLaren was running two Great drivers, Piquet was teamed with one or other of the Fabi brothers, neither of whom looked like a race winner. Piquet's Brabham BT53 was a 220 litre tank evolution of the BT52 with bigger, sidepod housed coolers and more sophisticated aerodynamics. The '52 had been produced in a rush and the '53 benefited in particular from a certain amount of wind tunnel work.

Significantly, though, the six cylinder rival enjoyed more efficient aerodynamics – this was particularly noticeable at the sweeping Osterreichring, where the MP4 chassis required less road, enjoying greater grip. Consequently, Piquet had to drive harder, to the detriment of tyres, fuel consumption and chassis reliability. And neither chassis, nor engine, nor turbo reliability was good. At first BMW suffered since it had under estimated the amount of power that would be required to be competitive under the new conditions. Race boost, 3.3 bar from the outset, had to be significantly increased, reaching 3.8/3.9 bar: power was then far in excess of 720b.h.p. (the official power figure at 10,500r.p.m. on 3.1 bar).

Early on there was a problem of sub-standard components, the first six races witnessing a succession of engine failures as a consequence. Motorsport had found itself overstretched as a host of problems came at once and its quality control department was too small to cope. Most failures were blamed on parts from outside suppliers, BMW confessing only to incorrectly machined big end bolts which failed at Zolder in spectacular fashion. However, the most common problem was failure of the highly stressed single turbo. Rosche admits that as power climbed over the period '83 – '84, the turbo supplied by KKK was pushed to its limits in terms of turbine operating temperature and revs. Montreal, round seven, saw the BT53 boast a nose mounted oil radiator which Rosche confesses was 'very important – everything was too hot . . .'

Piquet won Montreal, then repeated the feat at Detroit. Rosche had, of course, prepared specific street race engines. The second half of the season saw retention of the nose radiator but there were no more wins. However, Piquet could turn the boost high enough to challenge the dominating Porsche-TAG McLarens every where, if he hadn't the stamina to beat them. On balance, BMW's electro-mechanical injection system was highly effective. Chilling fuel was a common tactic in '84 but for BMW was a low priority, and was undertaken only spasmodically, and only in Europe. Murray considered

1984: 'the most competitive year I'd ever had in Grand Prix racing – the car was quick everywhere. Overall, it was the most competitive car, but we didn't get the results we deserved. Engine and turbo reliability had disappeared...'

Rosche reflects: 'we had no problem on 220 litres, and had more power than the Porsche engine, but lost half a dozen races through turbo failure. The turbo was the biggest problem'. While he was running, Piquet was a real menace to the McLaren drivers and he led 243 laps of '84, in comparison with 347 for Prost and 165 for Lauda. However, he added only a second, a third and a sixth to his two wins, collecting 29 points whereas both McLaren drivers, for whom he was the most serious rival, amassed over 70. Piquet was, however, the King of Qualifying. Nine poles came his way. Rosche denies that he ever produced specific qualifying engines. However, the rugged old iron block took high boost well and a larger turbo was available for qualifying. Qualifying power was quoted officially as '850b.h.p.', but by the end of '84 boost was nudging 5.0 bar and Rosche admits that power was then in excess of 1000b.h.p. Almost certainly, M qualifying Power was the first to reach four figures. The water spray onto the aftercooler was essential as boost soared.

Increasing boost had seen the old Ferrari V6 engine 80% redesigned for 1984. The 120 degree vee aluminium block was modified for greater strength with less weight and a lower cross-section. However, the bore and stroke were retained, as were chrome plated rather than Nikasil liners. The heads were modified, having revised porting and combustion chambers designed to match the advances in fuel pioneered by BMW, though the 38 degree included valve angle was retained. And the turbochargers still nestled in the wide vee. Most important of all was the introduction of fully electronic injection as part of a new engine management system developed in conjunction with Weber-Marelli.

Ferrari had a lighter, more compact car in the 126C4 which was campaigned by Alboreto and Arnoux, who started the season full of confidence. Alboreto looked extremely competitive at Rio but retired early and neither driver was in strong contention at Kyalami. The biggest problem was the new injection system and this came off the cars for Zolder. Here the team's Goodyear tyres worked better than the Michelins run by McLaren, Brabham and Renault. Alboreto won. Arnoux finished third, then second at Imola. However, Arnoux had been no threat to Imola winner Prost and though electronic injection came back at Detroit Ferrari would not find winning form again in 1984. The 126C4 was not as fuel efficient as the McLaren-Porsche/TAG, and reliability slipped. Indeed, only in Dallas, Austria, Italy and Germany did either driver stand on the podium.

Generally, Ferrari was most competitive on slow circuits. With the predominance of fast circuits over the second half of the season the team extensively reworked its aerodynamics. Nevertheless, it was clearly in trouble and mid season Technical Director Mauro Forghieri was ousted from his post within the racing department. Engine development saw the 120 degree V6 reach a maximum of 730b.h.p. in race trim, 820b.h.p. in qualifying, running 3.6 and 4.2 bar respectively. It wasn't enough to make a mark on fast circuits and in general the Michelin runners had a tyre advantage as Goodyear started its to switch to radials. Overall, 1984 was a poor year for Ferrari.

It was also a poor year for Renault. In 1984 Renault switched back to Garrett turbochargers. Dudot: 'in '83 we had a lot of turbo development to do but KKK didn't want to assist. It believed its turbos were OK. Ferrari and Renault had the same turbo - it was correct for the Ferrari engine, but not for our engine as we had a higher airflow'. In crude terms, the turbos were too small to deliver the necessary flow at full power. Renault signed a three year technical agreement with Garrett. 'We needed special constructions - it was very difficult to get specialist turbos from KKK. We knew the possibility of development working with Garrett. Garrett was completely implicated in the project and developed turbine wheels from special steels and a high speed compressor wheel machined from solid in a special aluminium'.

With turbochargers employing exotic materials and advanced processes, Renault had insured itself against the hammering that would be dealt by lean running 220 litre race conditions. With aftercoolers designed to be positioned upright either side of the rear bulkhead (Porsche/TAG-McLaren style) rather than angled alongside the tank, the '84 turbo system was more compact and its plumbing was shorter, providing improved response and better full throttle running. Renault admitted that the most fundamental improvement of the EF4 engine was its turbo system. In addition, it planned to introduce fully electronic injection. Dudot wanted the superior control offered by low pressure solenoid injectors and work started on a full engine management system at the start of '84. However, it would take some time to complete...

Warwick and Tambay replaced Prost and Cheever at Renault driving the RE50 – an evolutionary design offering better rigidity and weight distribution as well as improved aerodynamics. The season got off to an encouraging start with Warwick seemingly destined for victory at Rio when his suspension broke 10 laps from the finish, legacy of an earlier bump with Lauda. Only at Dallas would things look so rosy again. The rival German engines surged to the fore at Kyalami, then Ferrari similarly overshadowed Renault at Zolder. Thereafter, it was German horsepower all the way, with the exception of Dallas – and that freak race went the way of Honda...

Tambay managed to lead at Dijon and Monza – but on both occasions found himself overhauled by Lauda. A higher compression engine introduced at Monza followed a heavily revised unit introduced at Dallas which had featured new camshafts and pistons and revised electro-mechanical injection. It wasn't until after Monza that Renault was able to test fully electronic injection, the technology exploited so well by Porsche/TAG. It was clear that lack of the late arriving 'Renix' system had put it at a disadvantage. Generally it had been strongest on slow circuits where consumption is less of a problem. The early races had been a struggle with fuel waxing: it was chilled to 30 degrees below zero and fuel line heaters had to be introduced to overcome misfire in the early laps.

At Dijon larger aftercoolers reduced charge temperatures, while revised Elf fuel was said to offer a much needed 4 – 5% consumption improvement. Just before the home race Larrousse had declared that the works team would withdraw temporarily for further development if consumption hadn't been improved by mid season. He was clearly trying to galvanise the effort to produce an engine management system to match Bosch Motronic. Poor fuel consumption was deeply embarrassing to a company selling mass market road cars. Nevertheless, it was Estoril before the long awaited Renix equipment was ready to race. The system was based around a more powerful processor than that used to control the superseded electro-mechanical injection and incorporated more sensors. Dudot considers: 'the Motronic system was a little more sophisticated than the Renix system, but it was very close'. With Renix Renault reckoned it had finally achieved competitive race power.

Not surprisingly, a four turbo engine that had tested at Kyalami before the season got underway hadn't resurfaced. 'It was a two stage system', Dudot admits, 'but we had no time in which to develop it. There was much work to do to develop completely this installation'.

1984 was the first year since 1978 in which Renault failed to win a race. However, if Renault was on the way down, Lotus was on the way up, enjoying a promising ongoing relationship with Renault. It switched from inconsistent Pirelli radials to Goodyear's new radials and produced an elegant development from the compromise 94T, the 95T. Lotus introduced a fuel warming heater before Renault, at Zolder, but had to wait until Imola before both cars could run Garrett qualifying turbos and until Montreal for the larger aftercoolers seen on the works cars at Dijon. Nevertheless, the 95T emerged as the most competitive Goodyear runner of a Michelin dominated year. If, in the final analysis, Ferrari came out with a higher Constructors Cup total, that was thanks to a slightly superior finishing record.

In the drivers table de Angelis took the honour of highest placed non-Porsche/TAG driver thanks to a string of solid finishes. Qualifying highlight for de Angelis was right at the start: pole at Rio, while Mansell took pole at Dallas. Both drivers generally qualified solidly in the top ten. The 95T handled well and its aerodynamics were clearly sounder than those of the RE50. It was a superb chassis handicapped by a lack of race power and often by inferior race tyres. The 95T did not frequently outrun the RE50 on race day, probably due to Goodyear's lack of radial experience. Zolder was a rare Goodyear weekend but saw Ferrari rather than Lotus profit. The the next spurt of Akron competitiveness came at Monte Carlo where there was a new construction front and Lotus went to the top of its client list. From the front row, Mansell would probably have won the wet race but for driver error. Hockenheim brought a competitive dry race tyre and this time de Angelis led – only for his engine to fail.

In terms of qualifying speed and points gathering, Lotus was the top Renault team of '84 and its chassis was arguably the equal of the McLaren MP4. Certainly it was the best chassis of all on Goodyear tyres, and the best chassis with Renault power. Ligier, by way of contrast, had the poorest of the three Renault chassis. For '84, Ligier had acquired Renault engines on the same basis as Lotus, and Michelin continued supplying the team, which ran de Cesaris and Hesnault in its first composite chassis. The JS23 was a brand new model, with a rearward weight bias and getting to grips with turbo power proved a struggle. Ligier was a midfield team.

Another struggling team was Euroracing Alfa Romeo. In the light of the fuel ration the thirst of an eight cylinder engine looked inappropriate and at the start of 1984 Autodelta did not even have electronic injection control. Without micro processor control the detonation threshold was low, and in '84 the 890T couldn't safely be boosted high enough for competitive qualifying or race pace. Avio's qualifying turbo was inadequate and a long drawn out attempt to engineer a high compression qualifying engine was only moderately productive. The 890T chassis had questionable aerodynamics and the sad fact is that throughout '84 the Alfa Romeo V8 tended to detonate on qualifying boost then run dry on race day as meeting after meeting passed without any sign of the fruits of a Bosch Motronic programme. Euroracing was not a force in '84, and nor was the small Osella team which also used the V8 engine.

Much more was achieved by Hart. Hart had not the clout to get digital control from Bosch or Marelli Weber and introduced a system devised by ERA (later known as Zytek), a small company based on Lucas' doorstep in Birmingham and run by two ex-Lucas employees Brian Mason and Bill Gibson. Monte Carlo saw the introduction of the system on Senna's Toleman TG184. It utilised Bosch solenoid operated injectors. Using solenoid injectors allowed four per cylinder, Hart doubling up on the usual down feed and adding another row of eight to feed up into the tracts. Early tests had employed two, sometimes three injectors per cylinder. Clearly, using more injectors allowed the injection of a greater quantity of fuel in a given space of time.

At Monaco Senna reported an encouraging improvement in throttle response from the prototype engine, which he used in qualifying. It offered more progressive power in a wider band, but was new and unproven. The team chose not to race it: Senna was happy with the regular engine, fuel consumption was not a problem at Monaco, and the electronic engine was still undergoing

development. However, from Brands Hatch the combination of the electronic engine and a revised Holset turbo: 'unlocked a new area of development in terms of b.h.p., response and fuel consumption', according to Hart. He adds that the additional power also put him in a new area in terms of reliability.

Since Montreal a solid top 10 qualifier, Senna rewarded Hart with a third place finish in Britain. From Dallas until the Estoril finale his was the only Hart car equipped with the electronic engine, and it kept him well up the grid even on the continental power circuits. With it he could never be discounted on race day, though various problems stopped him backing up strong showings with further rostrum finishes until Estoril. By Estoril, Hart had really got to grips with the potential of the electronic 415T and with a supply of Michelin's best rubber the Hart-Toleman flew. The TG184 chassis had won acknowledgment as one of the best handling in Formula One and Senna managed a resounding third on the grid, just 0.4 second shy of pole. He finished third in the race.

The end of season electronic Hart was reckoned to be worth over 800b.h.p. in qualifying, while it could survive a 220 litre race on 3.3 bar boost, producing around 720b.h.p. In contrast, the mechanical engine as used throughout by Spirit and RAM was restricted a little on boost and both teams lacked systems experience. Both Pirelli shod outfits were impoverished; neither rose above also ran status. A similar status was held by ATS and Arrows – teams supplied BMW in line fours looked after by Swiss tuner Heini Mader. In contrast, Williams and Honda were making real progress. This year the team's performance was patchy but the underlying trend was upwards.

Honda had taken the attitude that its engine could only be as good as its turbocharger and engine management system and consequently was taking the difficult route of producing electronics in house, while popping round the corner for turbochargers rather than continuing to rely on general supplier KKK. The IHI company was willing to do special development work for the programme, but had plenty to learn. Although Honda achieved much over the winter of '83/'84 this did not prevent a series of spectacular piston failures. And, worst of all, the block was showing clear signs of unhappiness at having its already excellent race output doubled. Any flexing would obviously lower reliability, as well as producing handling problems in any car in which it was a stressed member. The FW09 chassis – one of the 'last of the metal honeycombs' – gained a probably undeserved reputation at the time for flexibility and gross understeer.

The Goodyear shod FW09 started as a short stubby car based on the earlier 08, carrying a heavy, untidily packaged and only partly developed Honda V6. At this point the engine was some 20kg. heavier than the Renault V6. During the season the car underwent a radical 125mm. wheelbase extension while later Williams produced the improved but still troubled FW09B. 1984 season had opened on a high note: second place 'out of the box' at Rio for Rosberg. Although there was the even better first place at Dallas in mid season, combined with a handful of lowlier placings, the rest of the year was total disaster. This despite thousands upon thousands of hours of work and experiment by Honda and Williams technicians. Would it eventually pay off?

The most powerful Formula One car of 1984 – the first year of fuel rationing – was the Brabham-BMW, in which Piquet (upper photograph) is pictured ahead of Lauda's McLaren. Yet the McLaren-TAG Porsche dominated the season while Brabham and likewise Ferrari (below) floundered.

Grand Prix Cars 1985

Overall, 1985 was another McLaren year. However, right at the end of the season the tide turned – at Brands Hatch, Kyalami and Adelaide Honda triumphed convincingly. After its '84 problems Honda is reputed to have built 25 different engine specifications for its winter test programme, each a significant variation on the theme, as part of a ferocious attack on its shortcomings. It then produced a massively modified (yet still officially 'D-spec') engine with lowered and re-sited turbos, modified exhaust system, flattened plenum chamber, inlet tract alterations, not counting those invisible refinements to combustion chambers, piston tops, turbo wheels, scrolls and materials, valve timing and electronics. Simultaneously, Williams was making the leap to its first advanced composite chassis, moulded in-house and tailored to new and stiffer engine mountings.

The awful season of 1984, far from crushing the Williams Honda effort had galvanised it and while the opening season results of 1985 were not dramatic, perceptive watchers soon spotted the major difference. The cars were crossing the finishing as well as the start line, and both Rosberg and Mansell were moving the better handling FW10 up the grid in practice. The power band, however, was still all-too-sudden in its arrival; it even caught out the lightening reflexes of Rosberg, putting him off the road in Portugal, which left him with a broken thumb. Still down the pipeline at that stage was a fundamentally new engine incorporating not only all the lessons learnt to date, but a seriously stiffer block, skilfully employing cast-in ducts and piping to add to its structural strength. Much rumoured, and highly likely but never confirmed was a move to a much smaller bore: it is believed to have gone from 90mm. to 82mm. Certainly the rest of the world's Formula One V6 engine builders were moving to the region of 80 – 82mm.

What was not denied was the arrival of the new 'E-spec' RA-163-E at Francorchamps. With that race called off, it debut was Montreal (fourth and sixth place) followed by Detroit, where Rosberg won convincingly.

This new strength coincided with the opening of a purpose-built engine 'shop within the Williams factory at mid-season. It could not have come at a better moment, playing a vital role in curing a series of bottom-end failures. Honda's involvement not only in the engine, but also in the electrics and electronics had produced an ultra-sophisticated computerised fuel read-out telling the driver precisely how many litres were left in the tank. For the late-season races the overall engine height was reduced via a flattening of the plenum chamber by a remarkable 100mm., helping Williams improve airflow to the rear wing. With those three consecutive end of season wins the writing was on the wall.

Indeed, in '85 both Renault and Honda made long strides while M.I., Porsche and Bosch concentrated upon detail refinements. Bosch had redesigned its management system using the mass of data gathered from the original system and this was now housed neatly in one box. As part of the package, the on-board computer read-out included the number of laps at current boost which the car could complete. From the German Grand Prix onwards the cars had the 'mirror image' KKK turbos which gave the design team more space to play with as well as cleaning up the gas flow to the right-hand turbo. Until mid-way through 1985, McLaren ran a 40/60 mixture of Avgas and pump fuel but after that Shell came

up with a more sophisticated, denser toluene based fuel.

In race trim, the '85 engine is quoted as having run 3.3 bar, producing 800b.h.p. with torque increased to 497Nm., while for qualifying 890b.h.p. was available. Part of this increase came from the improved management system, part from the mid season introduction of 'rocket fuel'. The McLaren-Porsche/TAG remained the most competent all-round package but while Prost finally clinched a World Championship title with five wins (a sixth win at Imola was discounted when it was discovered his car was 0.7kg. underweight – less than the weight of the fuel it had used on its slowing down lap), Lauda managed only three finishes from 14 starts. Luck was not on the Austrian's side but in a memorable Dutch Grand Prix he used all his race craft to keep Prost at bay to win his 25th (and last) Grand Prix victory.

On behalf of Renault, Larrousse had started talks with Lauda at Detroit the previous year and into the autumn of '84 it had looked increasingly likely that the Austrian would accept the challenge of the slumped works team. Chairman Hanon had given the nod but a story in the French press alleged that employing the star would cost a king's ransom and in the face of poor productivity and hostile unions Lauda's Renault deal had fallen through.

Larrousse felt uncomfortable running Renault Sport in the wake of the rejection of the deal and spoke of increasingly trying conditions. The Ligier team offered fresh motivation, and before the year was out chassis designer Tetu had moved with him down the road to Vichy.

On the technical front, it had been recognised that the V6 needed a major update for '85. The EF4's architecture was inherited from its 2.0 litre ancestor and in conjunction with Renault's Rueil R&D Department Dudot's team set about evolving a smaller bore version to challenge younger generation rivals. That entailed heavy revision of the V6, the modified, (80.1mm. rather than 86.0mm. bore) block incorporating improved waterways. With a revamped combustion chamber and smaller piston crown Renault was looking for improved combustion and a shorter heat flow to the cylinder wall to assist heat dissipation. Of course, a longer throw crank promised more torque, and the unit would keep maximum revs as 12,000r.p.m. The compression ratio was 7.5:1 and race boost went up to 3.5 bar at the outset. Renix engine management was now standard, this year operating two injectors per cylinder. The ECU was programmed to keep the wastegate setting within certain limits, though ultimate boost control lay within reach of the driver in the form of a five position switch.

Mindful of qualifying engine requirements, an updated EF4 was developed alongside the EF15. This so called EF4*bis* was equipped with the revised turbo installation and with certain EF15 internals, and was reckoned to contain around one third new parts. It was produced in both low (7.0:1) compression, high boost qualifying trim and higher compression, more economical race configuration since the EF15 would initially be in short supply. In qualifying trim it was found to fly without wastegates, Garrett's '85 qualifying turbo pushing out a solid 4.5 bar boost: around 1000b.h.p.

This year there would, in effect, be two works teams, for Hanon had promised Lotus 'works' status – it would get Renault Sport developments as soon as the works team. Ducarouge produced a refined 95T in the 97T which retained Goodyear tyres. De Angelis stayed on to drive it and Senna was lured from the Toleman team. Senna requested joint number one status, as Tambay and Warwick shared at Renault. Tambay and Warwick were equipped with the RE60, a straightforward development of the '84 Renault with strengthened transaxle, suspension to suit Goodyear tyres and aerodynamics that took advantage of the repackaged turbo system.

Of the four Renault leading lights, Senna shone most brightly. Poor Tambay and Warwick didn't have a chance, burdened with an uncompetitive chassis that left them floundering in midfield. In contrast, Senna took over from Piquet as King of Pole Position and broke Lotus' long winless streak. Before the season was very old he had established himself as a more equal number one than de Angelis, the team gelling around him. Senna was a revelation, early on dominating the streaming wet Portuguese Grand Prix: in that performance driving skill was everything, power was insignificant.

The Renault cars were always short of race power, even with the EF15 which offered more torque and greater fuel efficiency but was in very limited supply at the start of the season. Only one car could be equipped at Rio; Lotus had to wait until Imola. Senna's Estoril performance highlighted the smoothness and driveability of the superseded engine. However, the stronger EF15 was reckoned to be 4-5% more fuel efficient. And that still wasn't good enough by '85 standards. Renault introduced 'periscope' compressor air collectors in mid season and race boost went as high as 3.8 bar but the EF15 never looked as efficient a race engine as the title winning Porsche/TAG and towards the end of the season Honda overshadowed both Renault and Porsche/TAG.

Clearly the equal of its predecessor, its 97T was a superb chassis, and it enjoyed consistently good qualifying tyres and plenty of qualifying power from the low compression EF4bis with wastegates removed. While the KKK blown BMW four offered more qualifying power, it was less drivable and Brabham was often let down by its Pirelli tyres. Overall the most successful qualifying combination was that of Senna, the Lotus 97T, Goodyear tyres and the Garrett equipped EF4bis. Renault-Lotus took a total of eight pole positions and was unrepresented on the front row on only half a dozen occasions.

The 97T chassis worked well almost everywhere, the exception to the rule the Osterreichring where Lotus had not attempted to test. Ducarouge recalls that, 'some fuel efficiency was lacking but in general Ayrton considered it a good car'. If the 97T was a first class chassis, clearly the EF15 race engine was another matter. It served both 'works' teams and Ligier from the aborted Francorchamps meeting and, equipped with it from Monaco, Senna led more laps than anyone else but, frustratingly, winning was often just out of reach. After Estoril, he won only one more race, in the damp at Francorchamps, while de Angelis, who adopted a tortoise rather than a hare policy, inherited victory at Imola. Using an EF4bis, Senna had run out of fuel while leading, and on no less than eight other occasions he was let down by engine or ancillaries. It did look as though Renault was trying to service too many cars.

While Renault's own team slumped without Larrousse and Tetu, Ligier started to pick itself up. Laffite replaced Hesnault and throughout the season the JS25 model rush-produced by Tetu was a good midfield runner, well capable of collecting useful points (unlike its predecessor). Tyrrell also made progress, though from a lower level, having absolutely no experience of turbocharged Formula One. The first Renault engine arrived in May '85 and the 014 made its race debut at Paul Ricard, after a limited amount of testing, equipped with an iron block based EF4 engine. For the first four races there were only sufficient engines for one entry. Tyrrell was the last team to switch to a turbo engine and Austria marked the end of an era, Brundle understandably failing to qualify a 500b.h.p. atmospheric car (without even appropriate tyres) on the high speed circuit. Zandvoort

became the first Grand Prix since 1967 without a Cosworth/Ford car in the paddock. Sadly, though the 014 wasn't competitive – it was a difficult transitional season for the under financed team with so much to catch up on.

Ferrari produced more than the Renault runners in the final analysis, running a further modified version of its 120 degree V6 engine. For aerodynamic reasons the turbos were relocated outside of the vee in more conventional fashion and the unit was dubbed the 156. The ECU took the space vacated by the exhaust primaries and the turbos and there was still a separate plenum for each bank, now above rather than below the heads. To switch the exhausts outside of the block it was necessary to redesign the heads but the fundamentals of the engine went unchanged. However, the control system was improved, the compression ratio was increased to 7.0:1 and race power rose close to 800b.h.p. at around 3.6bar, the engine running to 11,000r.p.m.

The revised engine propelled a new chassis, clearly influenced by the McLaren MP4 and at Estoril Johansson joined Alboreto in the driving chores. The car went very well on power circuits and was good enough as an all round weapon for Alboreto to collect second at Rio, Estoril and Monte Carlo and to win in Canada. That put him in the lead of the World Championship. With the return to fast circuits qualifying power went over 1000b.h.p. for the first time and with engine modification following failures at Ricard, race power went as high as 840b.h.p. This went up further to 880b.h.p. and Alboreto won the German Grand Prix. However, the 156 package had reached the limit of its potential and over the rest of the season the Ferrari challenge crumbled amid broken engines, turbos and transmissions. Runner up position to Prost in the Championship was a worthy result for Alboreto but more had been expected.

Brabham also had a difficult de-briefing session at the end of '85. The team had switched to Pirelli rather than Goodyear tyres following Michelin's withdrawal and Murray had produced a revised car, the BT54, with improved aerodynamics and even longer wheelbase through a longer transaxle. As more downforce was found from the underbody, the centre of pressure moved forward and traction was less of a problem, so the centre of gravity could be shifted forward. Cooling improvements, the product of over 10,000 miles running by an interim machine at Kyalami, then a further developed example in the February Rio test, were, according to Rosche, the key to improved engine performance.

This season Motorsport again provided a 25-strong M12/13 pool and, officially, power was quoted as '800b.h.p.' in race trim, with '950b.h.p.' available for qualifying. Throughout qualifying power was in four figures and Rosche says 5.3/5.4 bar was seen on occasion, representing short bursts of 1150 – 1200b.h.p. But brute power wasn't enough.

Over the first half of the season the BMW Brabham pole quest was disadvantaged by poor Pirelli qualifying tyres. That was understandable, given that winter work had concentrated on development of a good race tyre. Yet Pirelli race rubber also posed headaches. Between Rio and Ricard, race power had to be compromised to tyre life. The nadir of Pirelli performance came at Estoril, where all its cars were undriveable on its wet weather offering. However, the same tread pattern in a softer compound subsequently proved acceptable. On dry roads, lack of grip left Piquet struggling to get into the grid top 10 and out of the picture on race day – until Ricard, which, Murray reflects, 'was night and day': Piquet qualified fifth and went on to win.

Immediately after its Ricard boost, Pirelli produced a qualifier that let Piquet in on the battle for pole at Silverstone. However, it was the low powered Hart-Toleman that gave Pirelli its first ever pole position, in freak circumstances at the Nurburgring. From the latter half of the season Piquet claimed but one pole position, though the BMW-Brabham could be counted on to be in the top six slots. On race days there was no repeat of

Ricard. Second at Monza following the introduction of another new tyre was the only other podium position: this year, even with the improved Pirelli race tyres, Piquet wasn't a major factor.

Murray admits the BT52/53/54 chassis series was nearing the end of its development potential. 'We tried for the whole year, and couldn't find more downforce. We needed a 10% bigger wing but the greater depth of such a wing would have "hidden" it behind the rear deck'. It was a fundamental problem of the height of the engine package. In view of that Murray concentrated hard on the genesis of a radical replacement with a lay down engine. Inferior aerodynamics naturally compromised race day performances. Overall, the BMW engine package was more reliable this year, but wasn't wholly dependable, and nor was Brabham's transmission. The most positive aspect of the season, other than Pirelli's eventual improvement, was Motorsport's switch to Garrett, another step taken at Ricard. Following the problems experienced with KKK's offering, BMW had eventually managed to conclude a contract whereby it paid the American company to develop special turbos for its use.

The Mader engines supplied to Arrows continued throughout with KKK, this year Arrows benefiting from more appropriate turbine and compressor sizes for its needs. In May Arrows tried an IHI turbo in a private test. The team however, remained a midfield one. With BMW no longer dealing with ATS, Mader had a frustrating season.

Hart's season started out that way. He had received Toleman's contribution towards his 1985 programme in good time and had refined his engine while starting work on a small (86mm.) bore engine, having found it impractical to secure funding for an all new six cylinder design, which existed in outline form. The problem was the size of the piston crown. An 86mm. bore was a practical response, but with Toleman finding early problems it went into the pending file.

Toleman had a very effective new car but could not get tyres for it and missed the opening rounds of the World Championship. Hart found himself 'shot in the leg'. He lost all important continuity of development and was left represented by RAM and Spirit. They could afford only 'customer' electronic 415Ts, which were rated 'in excess of 740b.h.p.' at 10,500r.p.m. in qualifying with '700b.h.p.' on 3.2 bar race boost. RAM produced a radically small chassis without generous cooling provision and the team ran into endless engine problems. It failed to score any points. Spirit had a worse time, ended its programme early and sold its Pirelli tyre contract to Toleman.

Toleman was able to rejoin the circus at Monaco with a Benetton backed entry for Teo Fabi. The first four races were unmemorable, Fabi no better than midfield runner. However, the TG185 chassis worked well and the team was getting to grips with it, making up for lost time, as was Hart who had seen the best part of three months development slip away. Importantly, he had been able to procure 'advanced fuel' for Toleman from an undisclosed source. Everything clicked at Silverstone where Fabi was sixth in first qualifying – the Hart-Toleman was up to speed. At the Nurburgring Fabi took a splendid pole position on the Friday, which was protected by rain the following day.

Thereafter, the Toleman was often competitive but rarely finished. For Hart, as the engine was run leaner the main problem was a persistent burning out of valve seats. That took a lot of development to overcome. With an integral head the seats are difficult to access, as are the adjacent water passages. Eventually detail work paid off, but Hart admits that it was not until the end of the year that he got the best out of the toluene based fuel supply. At that stage qualifying at 4.0 bar, the 415T was producing over 800b.h.p.

Sadly, for '86 Toleman arranged to switch to BMW power. In fact, Hart had lost four teams by the end of '85: RAM, Spirit, Toleman and newcomer FORCE, a team created by Carl Haas. FORCE debuted a Hart car at Monza and achieved nothing of note over the balance of the season, lacking testing time. In 1986 it would run a new Cosworth turbo engine. Although he had lost all his customers, Hart didn't end his development work, though, and for '86 promised more power and improved cooling, having modified the block to improve combustion chambers and waterways. There was always hope . . .

Euroracing had little hope left. Sources close to Autodelta say that it was fundamental problems rather than any shortage of cash that postponed the debut of a planned in line four from the start of the 1985 season. In fact, Autodelta didn't even have Bosch injection ready for Rio '85. The early season races might have been no more inspiring than '84 had been but Imola brought long awaited Bosch injection control equipment. The system supplied was based on BMW's electro-mechanical Motronic equipment (doubled up), but was apparently a generation or so behind. However, it provided better calibration than the Jofa system, further improving fuel consumption and throttle response, if doing nothing for top end power. With Bosch electro-mechanical injection the V8, still AGIP fuelled, still qualified at 3.8 bar and raced at 3.0 bar and was officially rated over 800b.h.p. Properly sorted, it was a revelation at Monaco, Patrese setting second fastest time in first qualifying before slipping to 12th, while Cheever moved up to fourth place. Alas, an early alternator problem cost him the advantage of that grid position. And that early promise flattered to deceive.

In 1985 Euroracing failed to score any points. With its chassis designer elsewhere and its engine, even with electronic injection, something of a dinosaur, it had excuses for lack of pace but endless race retirements were less easy to explain, although to be fair a good number were down to engine or turbo failure. Osella had continued to run the V8 but was still an also ran team.

Meanwhile, having quit Autodelta Carlo Chiti had debuted his new engine. This was a V6 produced with the support of Minardi team backer Piero Mancini and some help from Ferrari, including loan of the old Lucas-Ferrari injection system. Hence the 'Motori Moderni' engine's V6 configuration, though it was a 90 degree rather than a 120 degree V6. Chiti plumped for a relatively small 80mm. bore for his conventional four valve, single plug alloy 6VTC engine, this choice echoing the new reduced-bore (80.1mm.) Renault EF15 engine. However, with an inexperienced driver, the Minardi-Motori Moderni was an also ran in 1985. Zakspeed was also now fielding its own engine, an in line four which powered its own chassis. Again, however, it lacked electronic injection and was hopelessly outclassed.

Spaghetti-like plumbing of the BMW engine that powered Brabham's 1200b.h.p. '85 Formula One challenge. The turbocharger was a twin entry device specially developed for BMW by Garrett. It could pump over 5.0 bar – five times atmospheric pressure as felt in the plenum.

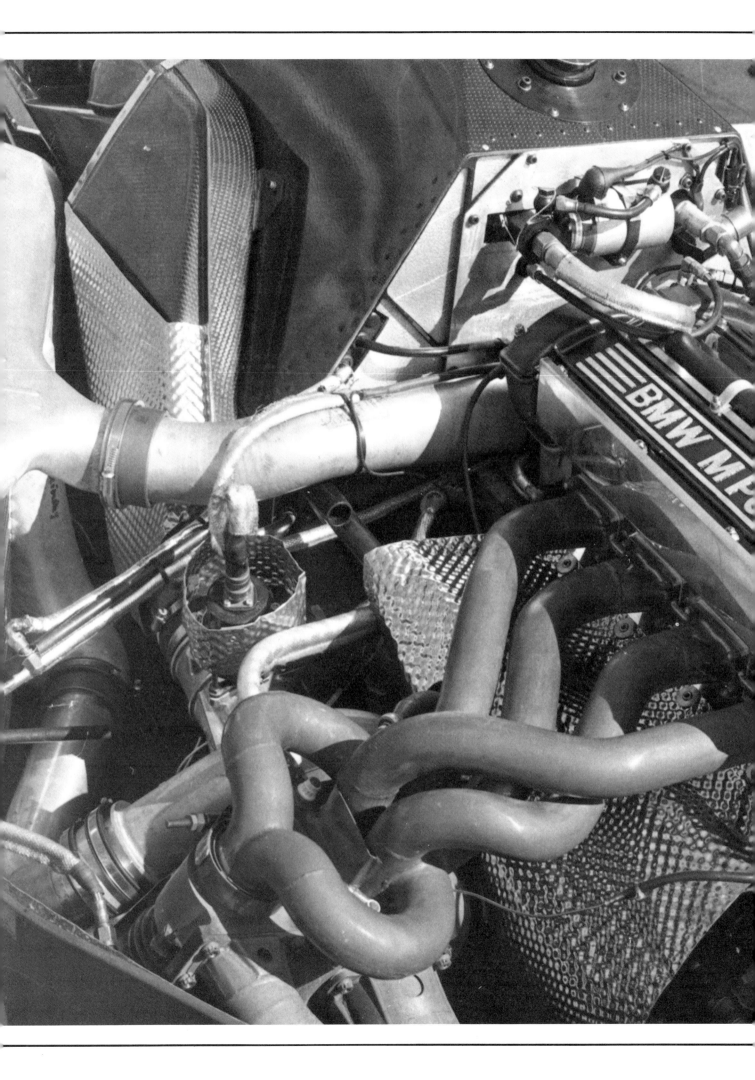

Indy Cars 1986 - 87

As we have seen, during the early to mid Eighties Indy Car racing was essentially a single engine formula, and Cosworth had a 'no development' agreement with CART. While it was committed to that policy, in '85 VDS had gone ahead and experimented with its own short stroke DFX, using the 90mm. DFV block and having a suitable crankshaft forged in the UK at Laystall Engineering. Apparently, the short stroke engine did not show any dyno gain but drivers reported it more responsive and since those drivers were the ones doing the winning a short stroke DFX became the thing to have. Cosworth responded with a kit of parts for '86 whereby a long stroke DFX could be converted to an 89.0mm bore short stroker. Of course, with competition now coming in from Ilmor Engineering and Engine Developments the no development deal was out of the window.

In 1985 CART had sanctioned the use of commercially available engine management systems for the first time. A system employing low pressure solenoid injectors had been developed by Zakspeed and had first raced at Mid Ohio in September '85. However, it did not offer additional top end horsepower and did not set a trend since it posed the usual installation problems and there was a lack of funding for development. Nevertheless, it set Cosworth thinking. 'We didn't think the Ilmor engine would beat us on power', recalls Cosworth's Chief Racing Engine Designer Geoff Goddard of a policy meeting over the winter of '85/'86, 'but we felt driveability and response were possible areas of improvement from engine management'.

In 1986 the fully electronic, Zytek managed Brabham-Honda arrived, as well as the more heavily funded electro-mechanical Chevrolet Indy V8. The Brabham-Honda arrived at Laguna Seca in December 1985 for its first test in Geoff Brabham's Galles Racing run Lola. It came from the Rugby workshops of John Judd, an engine builder who had cut his teeth working on Coventry Climax then Repco Grand Prix engines in the Sixties. Subsequently he had continued to work with Repco's World Championship winning team leader Jack Brabham in the (still UK based) Jack Brabham Conversions tuning firm. Engine Developments Ltd was born out of that: a company run by Judd with Brabham a sleeping partner.

In 1980 Honda re-entered European motor racing via Formula Two turning for help to associates from the days of the Brabham-Honda Formula Two cars. Brabham's designer Ron Tauranac supplied his Ralt chassis and later Engine Developments was used as a base for engine development work. A significantly improved Honda Formula Two engine came out of the Somers Road, Rugby factory.

Subsequently Engine Developments co-operated with Honda in the production of an Indy Car engine. The 90 degree V8 was designed at Rugby and the block was cast in Japan. Valve operation through Honda's favoured finger cam followers reflected the oriental influence while a gear drive at the back end where the inherent shake of a flat plane crankshaft is less severe was a Judd innovation. Bore and stroke were not revealed but rival designers believe that it had a generous 92 or 93mm. bore. Clearly, the so called 'AV' was far from a DFX clone and, apart from the finger followers, the rear drive and the bigger bore for larger valves, better breathing, key

differences were a lighter non-structural sump, allegedly lighter reciprocating parts and less overall weight.

A major headache of the DFV in its early years had been breakage of its timing gears thanks to the aforementioned crankshaft shake. A 90 degree V8 needs an in line four-type flat plane crank to achieve an in-line four type exhaust system on each bank for the most effective exhaust pressure wave tuning. Such a crank causes pronounced unbalanced secondary forces: the DFV had required a special vibration-cushioning gear hub in its timing drive to make it dependable.

Engine Developments had not only positioned its drive at what it says is a 'calmer' point in the shaft, between the rearmost main bearing and the flywheel, but also claims it achieved less reciprocating weight through careful parts design hence suffered less severe shake. Lighter overall weight was further assisted by the non-structural sump and much emphasis had been given to keeping the weight both as low and as low down as possible.

Like the DFX, the AV had an aluminium block carrying cast iron liners. From the decks, the block extended down to just below the crankshaft axis, with further depth accounted for by lugs either side of each main bearing to allow side bolting into each full width main bearing cap. Thus was a very rigid bottom end created without resort to a Cosworth-type structural sump, with its attendant weight penalty.

The sump was a light magnesium casting while the aluminium heads carried detachable magnesium tappet blocks in which were the finger cam followers, as also employed in the Honda Formula One engine. Head attachment included five pairs of primary studs and sealing was attended to by conventional bronze sealing rings.

Plain bearings were run throughout, generally supplied by GKN though some cam bearings were from Japan. The five bearing steel crank (with elegant extended balance weights) was forged locally, in Coventry, by Farndon Engineering, and was machine finished. Farndon also forged the I section con rods, designed to be as light as possible given the use of steel rather than titanium. Two bolt big end caps were employed, while the pistons were retained via conventional steel gudgeon pins and circlips. Judd shunned the usual Mahle pistons and Goetze rings for UK forged pistons and uncoated rings – only two on each piston – produced by the small Omega company.

The engine ran a regular pent roof style combustion chamber (with valve angle undisclosed). The rear-located drive pinion was sandwiched between the rear bearing and the flywheel. Either side of the small crank drive pinion was a large gear with a small idler attached, this pairing running on a needle roller bearing supported by the block. The idler turned a large gear on a needle roller bearing supported by the head which in turn drove the camshaft pinions.

The rear gear train drove only the camshafts: there was another drive at the front for the ancillaries, which are less prone to vibration-related problems. A small pinion on the nose of the crank, outside the block, transmitted drive (via three gears running on plain bearings) to pumps either side of the block and to an intermediate shaft above, which ran down the valley of the engine. Engine Developments positioned the alternator and distributor on a common shaft between the heads towards the rear of the engine and this shaft was driven from the intermediate shaft via a short belt.

At first, the interesting new Brabham-Honda engine provided motivation only for Jack Brabham's eldest son. An IHI turbocharger was employed – IHI was in the process of becoming the major supplier of Indy Car turbos in the mid Eighties – and maximum r.p.m. was in the region of 11,700r.p.m. The AV ran its Zytek engine management system from the outset, Engine Developments pioneering the Birmingham firm's re-programmable on board memory (rather than plug-in EPROM) development. After early problems forced withdrawal from the '86 Indy 500, the AV engine proved reliable and reasonably competitive. As we have seen, its rear drive and allegedly lighter than usual reciprocating parts were credited with prevention of drive train problems. Such problems bugged the early days of the Ilmor Chevrolet...

The Ilmor engine emerged on paper shortly before the Brabham-Honda. Aside from the illfated Drake V8, it was thus the first clean sheet of paper Indy car engine since the pre war offerings of Leo Goossen. Designer Mario Illien had only one constraint: that his design should slot into a chassis developed around an existing 90 degree V8. Illien was ex-Cosworth, as was partner Paul Morgan. It had taken Illien and Morgan only a week in late November 1983 to decide to join forces and to outline plans for Ilmor Engineering Ltd, a company created specifically to produce a new generation Indy Car engine. 'Indy Car racing was a single engine formula', Morgan explains, 'and we felt it was possible to design a new engine to produce more power than the DFX'.

The vital backing for the project came from Roger Penske, the influential and highly successful team owner that the aspiring company had quickly approached. By the end of November Penske had accepted the invitation to become involved and had approved a budget and a time scale. Illien first put pen to paper on January 3 1984 and after three months intensive work two detail designers became Ilmor's first employees. Throughout the remainder of 1984 the design and Ilmor's own, purpose built factory on the edge of Brixworth, Northampton came together. By this stage Ilmor with the help of Penske had signed a contract with General Motors whereby the design had become the 'Chevrolet Indy V8'.

The Ilmor engine had eight cylinders since that was the maximum permissible under the regulations: with manifold pressure limited to 1.62 bar absolute, power had to be found from revs. A traditional 90 degree vee configuration produced a light, compact structure while ensuring the unit would fit Penske's existing chassis. Of course, there was no question of an uncompromised race engine being anything other than a fully stressed member of the chassis and Ilmor logically adopted the simple but effective method of mounting pioneered by the DFV, time honoured and widely followed.

The Ilmor engine was not intended to be a radical departure from conventional wisdom. Rather, it was a very carefully thought out design intended to offer a better overall car package with improved ground effect aerodynamics and lower centre of gravity, and also, through detail improvements, to offer an higher output. And it was very tidily finished with, for example, the major pumps combined in one module attached by two bolts. Reflecting the thoughtful design, that helped maximise serviceability.

Illien went for the 'smallest, lightest, most powerful' engine, carefully packaged to the benefit of the chassis designer. Thus, the pumps were mounted at the front of the engine where it could afford to be wider in plan since chassis regulations demanded a width of at least 16" for the rear of the monocoque. From that point the form of the engine package tapered back to the transaxle where it was a narrow as possible in the interest of maximum width diffuser upsweeps. The exhaust manifolds were kept high and the sump was angled upwards 2 degrees to further benefit the underwing.

Illien admits he was 'obsessed with saving weight', in the interest of lowering a car's centre of gravity. Weight was reduced, not by resort to exotic materials but through 'the optimisation of design in traditional materials'. To minimise weight Illien went for an integral head and cam carrier.

Illien designed a pent roof head with the notably narrow valve angle of 24 degrees to run in conjunction with a flat top piston following existing four valve practice. However, he was unwilling to reveal valve sizes and the detailing of his combustion chamber. In this area lay one of the secrets of the innovative new engine. The bore size was set at 88mm. with consideration to overall engine length and crankshaft rigidity as well as to compression ratio and piston area.

The crankshaft reflected further fresh thinking. It was based on an original balancing principle and featured only four main extended webs. As we have seen, a flat plane crank is necessary but presents the inherent problem of secondary imbalance. Illien preferred the precision of a gear drive and located this at the rear of the engine. He says that close to the flywheel the amplitude of crankshaft vibration was only a third of that to be found at the front end. Similar logic to that which saw the Judd engine gear driven from the back. The rear drive made for a more compact engine but presented packaging difficulties, the area near the flywheel becoming very congested. There was also a danger of weakening the block near the transaxle pick up.

.Another feature of the Ilmor V8 was a structural sump incorporating all five main bearing caps for maximum rigidity with each sump chamber scavenged by its own small pump. The main bearings were of the smallest possible width to minimise frictional loss.

The use of methanol presented special problems, in particular due to the sheer quantity of fuel involved: around 20% of the charge was fuel. Consequently, Ilmor took the unusual option of producing its own bespoke electro-mechanical fuel injection system. This worked on the same principle as Lucas' familiar shuttle metering system but was specifically designed as a high flow electro-mechanical system with a servo motor adjusting the fuel cam according to boost.

By the time of the first dyno test Ilmor had parts for an initial batch of 10 engines. Intensive dyno testing was carried out through the summer of '85 with mapping controlling development. Maps followed airflow and were drawn up to 400r.p.m. intervals and around 20 throttle positions. Illien says, 'we concentrated on the fuel system and the engine came along fairly swiftly on the dyno'.

From the outset the compression ratio was 11.0:1 while early on maximum r.p.m. was 11,400. At that level the engine was rated at 'approximately 700b.h.p.' on the mandatory boost level while torque was quoted as 480Nm. at 8,500 - 9,000r.p.m. The quoted power level was that claimed by Cosworth at 11,600r.p.m. Impressively, 90% of the peak torque figure was available through the working rev range, which went from 7,000 r.p.m. all the way to 11,400 r.p.m.

By August the Chevrolet Indy V8 was ready to take its place in a Penske test chassis and on the 10th on the month the car barked into life on the disused Bruntingthorpe airfield, Rick Mears at the controls. 'Nothing broke. It was fairly encouraging', Morgan recalls. A week or so later another exploratory run was made and the car was pushed harder. Gears broke in the drive train. 'We had tried strongly to avoid this', Illien admits; 'we discovered some fairly heavy loadings in the gear train and that gave us some major work'.

Once again the secondary imbalance inherent in a flat plane crank V8 had shown a designer no mercy. An interim solution was found by mounting the compound intermediates on a torsion bar with a friction damper between the two gears. In this form the Chevrolet-Penske started serious track testing at Michigan International Speedway in September. The engine performed 'reasonably well' and encouraging track testing over the winter months was matched by intensive development work on the gear train. By the time the '86 season arrived 'the vibration problem had been reduced', says Illien, 'we could go race distances without hitting major trouble'.

Around 25 engines were produced for the first season during which the unit would be serviced by members of the Penske crew trained at Brixworth. The engine was reckoned to take 120 hours to assemble and 70 hours to rebuild. At this stage Ilmor Engineering had grown to the extent that it had 26 employees working at its Quarry Road base.

The first race for the Chevrolet Indy V8 was at Phoenix in April 1986. Al Unser Snr. qualified seventh only to suffer a flat battery at the start. 'Once he got going he was the quickest on the track', Morgan recounts. Alas, it came to nought due to a shunt. Then came two disastrous bottom end failures at Long Beach due to oil starvation. Was this an inherent engine problem or a chassis installation fault?

Two culprits were eventually identified: an inadequate oil tank on the chassis and an inadequate filter in the engine. Instrumentation revealed that the high flow and high vibration could cause filter collapse, starving the engine of oil pressure, but that the filter would then hide its guilt by recovering. A new type of filter had to be developed. Another headache was still the gear train which was given a harder hammering as drivers explored the region above 11,400r.p.m. A characteristic of the engine was a power band that continued beyond the red line, tempting the driver to gamble. Over the season the Chevrolet-Penske made 11 starts, two from pole position and achieved two third place finishes. Ilmor was, says Morgan 'encouraged with the engine's potential'. It had demonstrated that it had the promised performance edge and if it could summon enough stamina it would win in 1987.

In '87, having done typically thorough development of its own engine management system, Cosworth phased in a fully electronic DFX and Andretti Junior opened its account winning at Nazareth. However, the electronic system was on and off Andretti's and others' engines since testing was necessary to fully sort it on the track and reversion to the proven mechanical injection – as run by the standard setting Truesports team – was an easy option.

'It was a conservative attitude by the competitors', says Cosworth DFX Project Manager Malcolm Tyrrell: 'the electronic engine ran well on the dyno but in car development was protracted since people weren't prepared to test with it'. Proof of improved driveability came right at the end of the season in the form of a one-two in the wet at Miami.

The DFX engine management system was similar to that seen on the DFZ 3.5 litre Formula One engine but employed Weber injectors (larger than Bosch could supply), two per cylinder and pointing upwards rather than feeding downstream for improved atomisation. Conventional Lucas CD ignition was retained, with the alternator taken out of the vee via a cable drive since the valley had become cluttered, there now being low mounted fuel rails inside as well as outside each bank.

Another '87 development that only slowly gained acceptance due to conservative attitudes was a smaller, lighter turbocharger for better packaging – it enabled a smaller 'lump' to be set lower, lowering a car's centre of gravity. This in house turbocharger was designed along the lines of the Holset item run by Penske (these days, on a Chevrolet Indy V8, of course). Like the Holset, it was intended to offer only a packaging gain, the existing IHI offering optimum 48in. performance. Says Tyrrell: 'Indy Car folklore had it that a large turbine was necessary to reduce exhaust back pressure – our dyno tests with the new smaller turbine housing shot that one down!'.

Replacing the clumsy production-based IHI turbocharger, Cosworth's replacement had its more compact turbine again of stainless steel but a thinwall casting that offered a lighter method of pipe attachment, dispensing with the usual heavy flange. It was run with a more compact bearing housing (again cast stainless) and a lightweight aluminium rather than stainless backplate for the traditionally aluminium compressor. Saving just over 8kg, the new turbocharger matched the weight of the Penske Holset.

In '86 most DFX teams had played with short stroke engines and revs were edging towards 12,000 with a shorter trumpet and revised cams. For '87 customer engines, both long and short stroke, were tested right to 12,000r.p.m. For some mysterious reason the DFX could safely run to 12,000r.p.m. whereas the normally aspirated members of the DFV family needed to be restricted to 11,000r.p.m. Officially red lined at 11,900r.p.m., the short stroker was kinder to its bottom end and rods than the identically red lined long stroker. Running iron liners, the DFX block was reckoned to be good for around 3000 miles. It was still a popular, dependable customer engine but many customers were starting to look enviously at the heavily funded Chevrolet engine...

In 1987 the Newman Haas and Patrick teams joined Penske in the use of the 'Chevrolet Indy V8', the new customers serviced by Franz Weis' VDS concern. As it started the season, the oil filter was still undergoing development work while the gear train was still not 100%. The engine was capable of running to 11,800r.p.m. and a rev limiter cut the ignition progressively from that level. However, the gear train suffered if a driver leaned on the limiter. Nevertheless, the engine was race distance dependable and the first victory came at Long Beach right at the start of the season.

Andretti won Long Beach in the Newman Haas car then Fittipaldi's Patrick March won at Cleveland and Toronto, then Mears took the first 500 mile win, for Penske at Pocono. Andretti took a further win at Elkhart Lake and over the season amassed eight poles. He was the fastest man of the year, led twice as many laps as anyone else and dominated the Indy 500 only to retire due to valve spring failure...

During the course of the '87 campaign 'general refinements' improved ease of manufacture and servicing. Development saw the filter problem overcome and in September 'a major breakthrough' made the gear train 100% dependable. Ilmor was unwilling to reveal the discovery.

Clearly, 1988 was shaping up to be a very interesting year for Indy Car racing. The Chevrolet looked ready to dominate but Cosworth was not going to let its Indy Car grip go without a fight. Then there was the quietly progressing Judd engine with which Brabham had come close to winning the '87 Pocono 500. To its credit were second places at Pocono and Elkhart Lake and though Galles planned to switch to Chevrolet power for 1988, the Truesports team signed a deal to exploit the AV. And Buick was still keen to promote its V6 at Indianapolis where its impressive torque had continued to be evident, though reliability was still a problem. Nevertheless, some very influential engineers – including March boss Robin Herd – felt it was a problem that could be overcome. Not only that, but Porsche had now pitched in with another V8 engine. The Indy Car engine war was hot...

In 1986 the Cosworth DFX faced serious V8 opposition for the first time. This challenger was produced in the UK by John Judd's Engine Developments concern with the support of Honda. It featured Honda-favoured finger cam followers and the alloy block was cast in Japan.

Prototypes 1986 - 87

In 1986 Porsche met its match in the form of a normally aspirated engine, the Jaguar V12. The Jaguar V12 had become a familiar GTP runner thanks to the efforts of the Group 44 team. The American operation started its Camel GT campaign in 1982 with a 5.3 litre carburettor engine developing 570b.h.p. and by the mid Eighties had a full 6.0 litre version equipped with a Lucas Micos engine management system. This produced around 650b.h.p., enough to make the American prototype a strong GTP runner, if not a consistent winner.

Jaguar backed Group 44 Le Mans bids in 1984 and '85 but, developed on a diet of high octane fuel, the GTP engine did not take to the mandatory fuel supply. Group 44's lack of Group C experience lent weight to Jaguar Group A team TWR's bid to move up to Group C. TWR argued that its in-house Engine Division could develop a competitive Group C engine and that a clean sheet of paper chassis design could give it a clear advantage over Porsche. Porsche lacked rolling road wind tunnel developed underbody aerodynamics and an advanced composite chassis. Jaguar gave TWR the chance to exploit both factors.

Soon after Le Mans '85 TWR introduced the XJR-6 Group C car with a carbon fibre/Kevlar tub, advanced aerodynamics and a two valve V12 engine running a 12.0:1 compression ratio on pump petrol and producing around 650b.h.p. at 7,000r.p.m. from a 6.2 litre capacity. It was equipped with a Zytek engine management system. However, the car was overweight and with an eye to the fuel allowance raced at around 6,500r.p.m.

For 1986 TWR rolled out a lighter, more efficient chassis with a 6.5 litre engine: power was then in the region of 700b.h.p. at 7,000r.p.m., which was the regular race rev limit. It was too soon to hope to win Le Mans – TWR lacked vital experience of the event – but the XJR-6 won the Silverstone 1000km. race and looked capable of winning elsewhere. Silly problems cost further victories. However, TWR learned how to fine tune its sophisticated car from circuit to circuit for the best fuel efficiency and for '87 went up to 7.0 litres, primarily for extra torque. With more torque there was less gear changing, the car pulling a higher gear and thus saving fuel. The chassis was further refined and the so called XJR-8 was the car of 1987, taking the World Endurance Championship away from Porsche for the first time since the advent of Group C.

The increased competition provided by TWR in '87 (which toppled Porsche from its World Championship superiority but not its Le Mans rule) saw the development of a fully water cooled 3.0 litre engine, the Typ 935/83. Other than for the replacement of the fan by additional water jacketing to envelop the cylinder barrels, this was still essentially to the regular Motronic engine specification. However, Porsche introduced a new Bosch injector in '87 that offered a revised spray pattern for better atomisation. This was run with an internally revised black box and new camshafts.

For the Typ 935/83, maximum r.p.m. was up from 8,400 to 8,800r.p.m. In spite of mandatory pump fuel, the compression ratio remained 9.0:1. Porsche had always developed the 935/82 engine to run pump petrol (and apparently it had not responded well to attempts made by some customers to feed it a 'special brew'). At 2.4 bar race boost power went over 700b.h.p. (rivalling that of the 3.2 litre two valve IMSA engine which had run on high octane fuel).

While the '86 and '87 seasons saw the Porsche 962C steadily overhauled by the performance of the Jaguar V12 propelled TWR contender, a newer turbo car was gradually gaining speed. This was the Sauber-Mercedes. Swiss race car constructor Peter Sauber had built his first Group C car, the C6, in '82 in conjunction with composite material specialists Seger and Hoffmann. At the end of the season they parted company and while Seger and Hoffmann developed the 'Sehcar' from the Cosworth powered C6, Sauber produced a BMW engined car which was the only non-Porsche in the top 10 at Le Mans in '83.

The Sauber C6 and C7 cars were designed with the assistance of a number of Daimler-Benz Research and Development engineers working in their spare time. The contact between Sauber and the Daimler-Benz R&D department led to the availability of a Mercedes V8 turbocharged Group C engine. Sauber's efforts with the C6 had impressed the R&D hierarchy while Sauber had seen the potential of the all alloy, chain driven s.o.h.c., 16 valve M117 engine as the base for a powerful and reliable turbocharged Group C power plant. The M117 was the latest in a succession of Mercedes V8 engines stretching back to 1963.

The original 6.3 (later 6.9) litre V8 had been followed in 1969 by a new generation 3.5 litre M116 V8 which sired the M117. The M116 had iron block and alloy heads with chain driven s.o.h.c. Its two valves per cylinder were offset 20 degrees from the vertical in a wedge-shaped combustion chamber surrounded by generous squish area, run in conjunction with a flat topped piston. Although the offset valves were set in parallel they were operated through finger cam followers which pivoted on spherical-headed adjuster studs. The M116 engine was taken out to 4.5 litres then, 10 years after its introduction, was replaced by the alloy block M117.

While the M117 generally followed the pattern of the iron block engine (retaining the wedge heads) the most important difference was a massive weight saving in the order of 125kg. This was made possible through a new production technique offering a linerless block, as introduced by General Motors with the famous Vega 2300 engine. In fact the Reynolds Aluminium developed process and material had been pioneered through racing having first been employed as a means of producing blocks for the works Chevrolet-McLaren Can Am car. Reynolds' replacement for the traditional cast iron Chevrolet big block was able to offer increased capacity (8.1 litres) since it was linerless and was, of course, a lot lighter.

The new generation linerless block was subsequently adopted by both Daimler Benz and Porsche as a means of producing new lightweight V8 engines. The process saw the block diecast by the new 'Accurad' method in a new aluminium alloy, Reynolds A390, which combined good fluidity in the molten condition with a fine dispersion of silicon after heat treatment giving good bearing properties and ease of machining. After machining an electrochemical etching process was used to expose the glasshard silicon particles on the walls providing a wear resistant and oil retaining surface. This was run in conjunction with an iron-plated piston skirt to prevent any possibility of aluminium to aluminium contact since that would cause galling (reversing the usual combination of alloy piston on iron bore).

Though Daimler Benz' M117 production engine was not turbocharged, the research engineers at Stuttgart were already familiar with the challenge of forced induction, having worked with turbocharged engines for 15 years. However, Daimler-Benz AG was not yet ready for a direct involvement in motor racing so the parts and technical information were supplied to Mader who built the first Mercedes Group C engine.

The project echoed that of Aston Martin, on behalf of which offshoot Tickford Engineering had toyed with a Group C V8 turbo engine early in '84. The longer-lived Mercedes challenger was a superficially similar, large capacity, lightly blown 90 degree V8. Likewise, it was essentially stock and consequently had a two plane crankshaft for smooth running. Of course, the two-plane configuration made for a very smooth engine at the expense of exhaust tuning potential. However, that was not a serious concern given forced induction and the smooth, well balanced nature of the unit was ideal for an endurance car.

The M117 race engine had dimensions of 96.5 × 85mm. for a displacement of 4970.0cc. and ran two valve, single plug heads, the valves offset at 22 degrees from the vertical in a wedge-shaped head chamber. The stock engine had a flat top piston but a slightly dished crown was employed to lower the compression ratio of the turbo version. The prototype engine first ran on the dyno around Christmas '84 and started track testing in March '85. Initially the head gasket gave problems but once the Stuttgart engineers had solved this it ran well. The solution was in a modified gasket and a stiffer head, the latter involving a modification to the casting which was carried through to the production car line.

The Mader engine benefited from a dry sump, porting and camshaft work, increased water circulation, special heat resistant valves and oil sprayed pistons. Type 27 turbochargers were supplied by KKK and these were governed by mechanical wastegates which were modified Porsche road car items. The appropriately revised induction system included air:air aftercoolers while injection and ignition were incorporated in the Porsche Group C-type Motronic M1.2 package which was supplied by Bosch. Daimler-Benz had worked closely with Bosch for many years. Together they had pioneered fuel injection for road car engines and engine management systems.

The Mader-assembled 5.0 litre Mercedes engine was pressurised to a maximum of 2.0 bar absolute in qualifying, at which power was in excess of 700b.h.p. Race boost was 1.8 bar absolute while for maximum power the drivers had to look no further than 6,600r.p.m. Sauber went in at the deep end, the Mercedes-Sauber C8 debuting at Le Mans. Qualifying was encouraging until, warming up for a serious attempt to post a grid time, it took off over the brow after the Mulsanne kink. It somersaulted a couple of times and was wrecked, thankfully without injury to driver Nielsen. Daimler-Benz kept faith with Sauber and a short, five-race programme was undertaken in '86, highlighted by victory in the wet at the Nurburgring, aided by the tremendous torque of the low revving, big displacement engine.

In the dry the Mercedes-Sauber was less impressive but with continuing engine development work and an improved chassis, the C9, in 1987 the package was a real contender. The key engine developments were the introduction of a Nikasil bore coating, a new lighter crankshaft, improved, higher efficiency turbochargers and a switch to the Motronic M1.7 engine management system offering more precise control of ignition and injection, plus electronic control of a new wastegate. In addition, a total of 20kg. was saved through lighter internals (including titanium con rods), a lighter flywheel, lighter ancillaries and lighter turbochargers. Even the camshafts were lightened, through a new form of construction.

With the more precise ignition control of the M1.7

system the compression ratio could be increased from an initial 8.0:1 to 8.5:1 while power was then officially 700b.h.p./7000r.p.m. on the 1.9 bar absolute race setting. In qualifying almost 800b.h.p. was extracted. Nevertheless, the base engine remained essentially a production item. In 1987 Sauber's season was again only five races long and this time the highlight was pole at Francorchamps. For 1988 Daimler-Benz announced that it would give the effort full factory support – it clearly had the potential to win consistently.

In contrast, Lancia had given up Group C, in 1986 the Fiat Group dictating that its Lancia division should concentrate upon rallying. Nevertheless, it allowed its Abarth company to service a privately entered LC2. That season Gianni Mussato ran his ex-works car in a couple of events (only for Giacomelli to write it off at Zeltweg) while in '87 he brought out another chassis (based on a new Dallara tub) for a couple more outings. Without any sort of success.

Nor was there any success for a privately entered Cosworth turbo. As we have seen, Ford ended Cosworth's DFL turbo project when it overhauled its competition programme early in 1983. Without turbocharging the DFL simply didn't have enough power to rival Porsche. Of course, already there was a member of the DFV family with light turbocharging: the DFX. Light turbocharging was all a DFL would require to produce competitive Group C power and Graham Dale-Jones felt it was a route that should be explored with or without a factory Group C commitment.

In 1985 Dale-Jones sold the idea to Group C entrant Tim Lee-Davey who was already running a 3.9 litre DFL propelled Tiga GC84. With Tiga's support Lee-Davey set up Team Tiga to run a new turbocharged GC86 (a development from his existing chassis which had originally run a Chevrolet V8 engine). The aim was to contest the 1986 World Endurance Championship but funds were short and the car could not be readied before Le Mans. While Cosworth was prepared to assist and Ford blessed the project, this was strictly a private effort. That was its downfall. The engine concept was right but there was no budget for extensive mapping or engine development and the impoverished Team Tiga entry always lacked development mileage.

It was the same situation for the similarly underfunded WM team, which still concentrated upon Le Mans. At Le Mans in '86 it ran two cars and while one retired (engine), the other, running in C2 with an engine reduced to 2650cc. and only two valves per cylinder, finished 12th overall, third in class. Running in C2 was indicative of hopelessness of outright victory in the mid/late Eighties. However, WM had already planned a realistic target: Project 400. It aimed to field the first car to exceed 400k.p.h. (approximately 250m.p.h.) on the Linge Droit des Hunaudieres. Intensive spare time wind tunnel research, sponsored by Peugeot, produced a car with a drag co-efficient of only 0.27, remarkable for a ground effect race car.

The new P87, its chassis an evolution of the existing equipment to fit a striking new body shape, ran KKK rather than Garrett twin turbochargers for better matching and more boost (each feeding through an air:air aftercooler) and benefited from a Bosch Motronic engine management system. Maximum boost was 2.5 bar absolute with maximum revs of 8,200r.p.m. and a power output of 850b.h.p. It ran 416k.p.h. when tested on an unopened autoroute and, according only to the team, 407k.p.h. at Le Mans. The official radar did not acknowledge that.

Le Mans continued to be the key event for Toyota and Nissan in the mid Eighties, still without success. Both Dome and Toms Toyota teams were back in '86, to no avail. For the '87 campaign (still home-based) Toyota established the Toms operation as a full works team: Toyota Team Toms. Engine development and preparation was still based at Toyota's Higashifuji Technical Centre. And there was a new four cylinder engine, the 16 valve 3S-GT, introduced at the '86 Fuji 1000km. race where it looked very strong. This was similarly based on a linerless iron stock block (the 3S-GT motivated Toyota's Celica and Supra models). At first the unit was envisaged as a potent rally engine but it was switched to the Group C programme before it was ever rallied. Early on it had been recognised that the original Group C unit lacked sufficient power to tackle the likes of Porsche, a major drawback its production-based eight valve head. The replacement 16 valver reached the prototype build stage as a Group C engine early in '86 and was first track tested immediately after Le Mans. The 4T-GT engine was phased out in late '86.

The overall design of the engine followed that of the production unit retaining the standard bore and stroke for a capacity of 2140cc. and with even an unchanged combustion chamber shape, though the water circulation was modified: heat was of course the major adversary. Designer Yamaguchi says he concentrated on the cooling of the combustion chamber and put a lot of work into detailing. The piston was oil sprayed and, unusually, the turbocharger rotor shaft was water cooled.

The twin-entry in-house turbocharger was of the CT44RT variety as developed for the 4T-GT engine by Yamaguchi's department. Of conventional (KKK-style) design, it revved to 110,000r.p.m. and offered up to 3.5 bar absolute. It was equipped with a mechanically-controlled wastegate system also developed by Toyota. A twin turbocharger installation had been perceived as too heavy but the single twin entry unit was run in conjunction with dual water cooled wastegates and this provided excellent response. The turbocharger was of a conventional design (for reliability) with aluminium compressor wheel and inconel turbine wheel in a high-nickel iron casting.

The compressor blew through an air:air aftercooler to the plenum chamber outrigged to the right of the block (the induction side). Each cylinder had its own throttle butterfly and a single injector was placed upstream of that. The solenoid injectors were supplied by Nippon Denso and were larger than the Bosch contemporary, and one per cylinder was quite adequate. Nippon Denso also supplied its CD-type ignition system (together with a 10mm. plug for each cylinder) plus an integrated control system developed jointly with Toyota that governed ignition timing as well as running the injectors. There were two ignition pick ups on each camshaft, a system developed by Toyota for greater accuracy.

The Nippon Denso engine management system took r.p.m. (from the crank), throttle position, manifold pressure and charge air and block water temperature as its key inputs. The mapping process commenced early in '86 with the prototype engine, the aim to produce a relatively 'coarse' map (a reading every 400r.p.m., for example). From the outset the unit was run with a 7.0:1 compression ratio and by the time it was ready to race it was attributed a conservative 550b.h.p. race power on 2.4 bar absolute with as much as 750b.h.p. available for qualifying as manifold pressure was pumped up towards 3.5 bar absolute. Maximum r.p.m. was 9000 with 8,500r.p.m. the regular limit.

From '87 Toyota introduced a smaller CT44ST turbocharger offering 2.8 bar absolute maximum race boost, leaving the higher airflow RT unit for qualifying. The ST model was designed for greater reliability and at 2.8 bar the engine (with well developed software) produced in the region of 600b.h.p. Maximum output was officially quoted as 680b.h.p./8,500r.p.m. with torque 65m./kg. at 5,500r.p.m. though as much as 900b.h.p. had been extracted on the bench.

An important development for the '87 season was an oil gallery piston, the hardware supplied by Mahle. An early valve seat headache was cured through the use of a special, undisclosed, material developed by Toyota. A spate of cylinder bore cracking arose early in '87 and prior to Le Mans a new block casting was introduced with a 2mm. greater wall thickness to cure the problem.

For 1987, Dome supplied a further development of its original chassis design and though a two-car entry for Le Mans was again fruitless, the upgraded Tom's team won national events at Suzuka and Fuji and showed strongly in qualifying for the home World Championship event. Nissan took pole for that event, running a new 3.0 litre V8 turbo engine, designed as a no-compromise replacement for the production based V6. The V6 had raced at Le Mans and Fuji in '86 without success and the V8 did not improve the situation. It was an all alloy, twin turbo engine that unusually employed rockers and hydraulic lifters derived from production car technology. It was clear that the V8 would have to be redesigned extensively for 1988, the so called VEJ30 suffering poor low and mid range torque, poor power at high revs, poor fuel consumption and lack of dependability...

In contrast the Electramotive GTP V6 engine was coming on strongly, taking a first victory at Miami in '87. Nevertheless, and in spite of the efforts of the American motor industry in the form of Buick, Chevrolet and Ford, Porsche continued its GTP domination through '86 and '87. In response to the 3.0 litre displacement limit Porsche developed a revised engine taking advantage of the fact that it could now run twin ignition. The 962/72 engine ran the 127.8mm. con rod and 70.4mm. crankshaft of the Typ 962/70 engine together with a 95.0mm. bore for 2994.0cc. While twin ignition had been run on the two valve 935 engine, timing was now controlled by the Motronic system. Running a 7.5:1 compression ratio the 962/72 engine was strong enough to shrug off the Buick and Chevrolet V6 turbos.

Sadly, the Hawk-Buicks had continued to find little more than high horsepower and early in '87 the Conte team had been disbanded. The Corvette GTP programme was longer lasting, and by the end of '86 had seven poles plus wins at Road Atlanta and West Palm Beach to its credit. Towards the end of '86 Falconer started phasing in electronic injection to replace the original Bosch mechanical system and in '87 he switched the now 3.0 litre engine to an alloy block. Running a production based Chevrolet engine management system this engine took a best of one second place in 1987, the management system a major headache. However, there were another four pole positions.

In contrast, Ford – like Buick – had withdrawn after a disappointing 1986 season. The Probe found winning pace and stamina at Laguna Seca in '86 but otherwise it was a barren season for the four cylinder car. Development work included modifications to the block and head castings. Faced with a host of problems, Ford ordered a 2.1 litre derivative of the DFX from Dale-Jones, who was busy developing the Lee-Davey Group C Cosworth turbo engine. Similarly produced by Dale-Jones at Terry Hoyle Engines, this was dubbed the DFP and was very much a sister for the 3.3 litre engine. It was very promising but had arrived to late to save the Ford GTP programme, which was axed at the end of the year. Porsche had only Nissan and Chevrolet to worry about in '88 – unless a new TWR GTP car lived up to the performance of the XJR-8.

The mid Eighties found the Porsche 962 firmly in charge of the IMSA Camel GT Championship (lower photograph), shrugging off the likes of Jaguar, Chevrolet and Buick. In Group C, however, Jaguar rose to topple the 962C, and Sauber-Mercedes (above) found improving form in 1987...

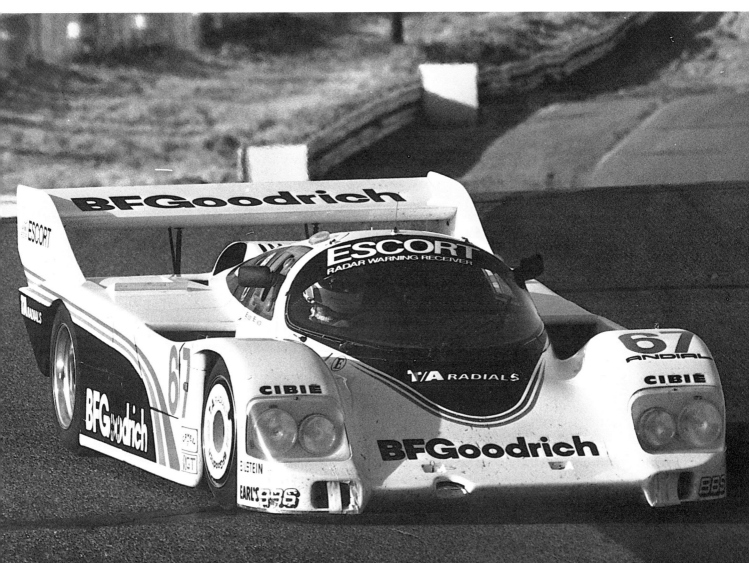

Grand Prix Cars 1986

Having climbed to the top in 1985, Honda stayed there in 1986 with a heavily revised engine running to the new 195 litre fuel allocation. The 25 litre fuel cut was partly offset by the continuing development of 'heavy' toluene based fuel, which Mobil was supplying. The new engine was RA-166-E/'F' spec, and outwardly it was characterised by new lower plenum chambers with double inlets to a single body, new low body air intakes for the compressors, relocated injectors. Internal details were kept secret, though it is known that the bore was now smaller, in the region of 80mm.

The engine was fitted to a new chassis, the FW11, and there was a new driver in the Williams line up, Piquet replacing Rosberg. Williams called the FW11 'a logical development' of its FW10 design, yet it was totally new – lower and more compact with revised aerodynamics. With the '166' engine it was crushingly successful: it started from pole position on four occasions and, more impressively, took no less than eight wins to sweep the Constructors Cup.

The 1986 season was very much the season of the Honda-Williams, with no other engine capable of the same level of race power. The McLaren team was well and truly beaten for the first time since 1983. It replaced Lauda with Rosberg and, as usual, Barnard chose to refine his existing design rather than break new ground. KKK produced new turbines which enabled more boost to be delivered without suffering a penalty in back pressure, which had previously been the case. Indeed, in one early test session M.I. had turned the boost right up to see what would happen and the car went no faster.

From Hockenheim onwards, Bosch came up with an improved engine management system, the MP1.7, and KKK came up with a new turbocharger, the HHB. These improvements allowed both cars to run 3.9 bar at Hockenheim and Rosberg and Prost were able to take over the front row of the grid though in the race the fuel read-out failed and both cars ran out of fuel when lying second and third. Normal race boost was officially 3.3 bar in spite of having 25 litres of fuel less, and at this level the engine developed 850 b.h.p. at 12,800 r.p.m. with an increase of torque to 519Nm. There were again different specifications for qualifying and race engine and that resulted in a difference in power of about 200 b.h.p., but McLaren did not push the engine to its ultimate possible performance.

Although 1986 was the year of the Williams-Honda Prost again had a very consistent season. He retired only twice and won four races. Consistency is the hallmark of a World Champion and Prost won the title for a second successive year, albeit with one less win than Mansell, his closest rival. It was the first time since 1959/60 that a driver had won consecutive titles and the first time ever that a team had provided the cars for a hat trick of drivers' titles.

In contrast, the Renault Sport team had withered away altogether. Nevertheless, Renault continued to equip six cars – two from Lotus, two from Ligier and two from Tyrrell. Of course, Lotus was the number one team, receiving its engines direct from Viry Chatillon. Senna was now its undisputed number one, with rookie Johnny Dumfries in the second car. French sources reckon Renault had spent around $27 million on engine development in '85, and out of Viry Chatillon had come the radical *distribution pneumatique* valve closing system. Its origins could be traced back to the early Eighties, when Renault ran into valve spring problems. Valve springs are subject to fatigue and surge. Surge is tackled by running coaxial springs but the interference that damps surge increases the likelihood of fatigue. And maximum revs are limited by the weight of the valve plus part of the weight of the spring. Renault looked at desmodromic timing but was put off by the extra weight and complication involved. However, in '84 emerged the clever concept of using compressed gas to close the valves.

A flange on the valve stem formed a piston which ran in a nitrogen filled chamber. Each chamber was part of a central network, pressurised to 1.2 – 1.8 bar. Compressed by the flange as the valve lifted, subsequent expansion of the nitrogen closed the valve in a very positive fashion. Overcoming the mechanical limitations of conventional springs, the system offered improved reliability and more scope with cam profiles, helping the quest for fuel efficiency. A self damping effect reduced a potential source of vibration.

Clearly the threat to the system was loss of gas pressure. Consequently, the nitrogen network was monitored by an automatic valve which could let in more gas from a 1/2 litre reserve bottle stored in the central valley of the engine. Intriguingly, increasing gas pressure was equivalent to fitting stiffer springs and, in effect, allowed the use of very stiff springs at no weight penalty. 'It was possible to go to 13,000 r.p.m.', Dudot explains, pointing out that there was also an added measure of security as a driver could over-rev without dire consequence: 'It was possible to get very high r.p.m'. How high? 'Sometimes in excess of 13,500 r.p.m. without problem . . .'

From the start the system allowed the EF15 to go to 12,500 r.p.m. and come '86, the regular limit was 13,000 r.p.m. The so called EF15*bis* also benefited from a distributor-less ignition system. The revamped ignition provided a high tension coil for each plug, which was built into its cap. Each spark could then be individually controlled by the ECU via a low voltage signal. There were no moving parts or H.T. leads to leak away current and there was more programming flexibility promising more efficient combustion. In particular, there was the potential to run just that little bit closer to the detonation threshold. 'We could adjust the timing according to more parameters', Dudot explains, 'making it more accurate. That was very important for fuel consumption. For fuel consumption you must run as close as possible to the limit of detonation'.

With its 13,000 r.p.m. potential the EF15*bis* could be adapted as a fine qualifying engine, allowing the EF4*bis* to be laid to rest. In qualifying the EF15*bis* was similarly used without wastegate. Come Estoril, and a new turbo was offering an honest 5.0 bar boost. Right at the end of the season Adelaide saw a high of 5.2 bar – and well over 1100 b.h.p. For race day Elf had denser fuels, which added 10kg. to a tankful. Race boost was in the region of 3.7 – 4.0 bar. No doubt about it, the 13,000 r.p.m. qualifying unit on which Lotus spent 40% of its engine budget was hugely successful and Senna comfortably retained his crown as King of Qualifying with no less than eight poles.

While the Renault-Lotus was a superbly effective qualifying car, the weakness of the package was the original EF15bis race engine. Renault simply didn't have the fuel efficiency of Honda and it is significant that Senna won at Jerez and Detroit, slow circuits on which fuel consumption is less of a problem. Renault had a real problem on faster circuits and mindful of that a 'C' version of the EF15 was developed featuring revised heads. 'It was a problem of the temperature in the combustion chamber', Dudot admits, 'we changed the cylinder head for improved water circulation. The C specification was much better'. Of course, compression ratio increases were behind the problem, the geometric ratio moving towards 8.0:1, probably beyond.

Dudot reckons the EF15C got 'very close' to the Honda engine and could have been the basis of a highly competitive offering for '87. Alas, it had arrived too late. In '86 Senna's efforts netted Lotus a distant third position in the Constructors Cup chase. Ligier managed fifth in the points league (behind Ferrari), one position higher than '85 indicative of its steady climb with Renault power behind it while Tyrrell failed to break out of mid field. In accommodating Tyrrell Renault had breached the terms of its contract with Lotus and Lotus was thus able to end the contract one year early, switching to Honda power for '87. Left without a top team, Renault ended its Formula One turbo adventure.

At the same time Ferrari ended the adventure of its 120 degree V6, if not its turbo programme. For its final season the 156 engine had its compression ratio increased to 7.5:1 and race power was officially 850b.h.p. at 11,500r.p.m. on 3.8 bar, with 4.6 bar and over 1000b.h.p. for qualifying. However, those were the levels achieved by the '85 engine: there was more to come in '86. To meet the 195 litre ration the engine management system was refined and during the course of the year Ferrari switched from KKK to Garrett turbos.

Early in the season power was disappointing and modifications were made to the heads. By Francorchamps, race power was up to 890b.h.p. and towards the end of the season the management system was improved to incorporate wastegate control. However, this was a frustrating season for Ferrari and the best result was second for Alboreto in Australia. Ferrari needed a new generation engine.

Brabham had a new BMW engine in 1986, but it was essentially unchanged internally. The big difference was that this version of the old in line four was canted over to 72 degrees from the vertical – it was a lay-down engine with an offset crank. This significantly lowered the centre of gravity and opened up a route to major aerodynamic improvement. Rosche says the only significant modification required to allow the block to be tilted was to the left corner of the flywheel area. The M12/13/1 engine had modified scavenge channels in its sump and was fitted with oil gallery pistons. Otherwise, it was to standard 'upright' specification.

Race power was officially quoted at 850b.h.p., with qualifying potential admitted as in excess of 1000b.h.p. However, the engine still had the narrow power band of 8,500 – 11,000r.p.m., with its output virtually tripling from 6,500r.p.m.! On the dyno there was no difference in performance between the regular upright engine and the prototype lay-down engine. However, the lay-down engine propelled a chassis that reclined its driver as far as possible. The BT55's lower fuselage left the rear wing in much cleaner air: early tests revealed a 30% gain in downforce. It was a major leap. The increased download together with a lower centre of gravity promised far more grip while an improved lift:drag ratio thanks to a more efficient rear wing and the reduced frontal area would assist fuel efficiency. Alas, it didn't quite work out like that...

Rio testing told the worst. Rosche got an oil temperature reading of 128 degrees – the end of his scale. Water temperature and charge temperature were also too high. The car was designed to be engine bay vented but the vacuum in its wake was insufficient to extract all the hot air. The entire cooling system had to be revised: engine

bay venting was supplemented by side venting, reducing downforce, and the oil and charge coolers had to be moved forward, compromising the weight distribution.

As a race car, the BT55 was a failure. Throughout the season it suffered a fundamental lack of acceleration. Properly sorted, it would corner quickly and would eventually reach a high top speed, but it wouldn't pull strongly from low to high speed. Rosche's abiding memory is of 'lots of wheelspin'. Murray says: 'it came out of corners and just stopped!' He adds that the BT54 had pulled from 2.0 to 5.0 bar in around 2.5 seconds, while early in the season the BT55 took almost three times as long. Traction was a problem thanks to the dynamics of the long, low car's weight distribution. Murray reflects: 'there were a lot of unsolved mysteries with the BT55'. He points to the engine's poor pick up, and to the fact that it wouldn't run as high qualifying boost as the upright engine.

The BT55 worked well at the Osterreichring, for example, Patrese fastest through the speed trap and fourth on the grid; his best position of the season. But the upright engined, similarly Pirelli shod BMW-Benetton was only a fraction slower through the trap, and sat on the front row. Murray reckons the BT55 was cornering faster but was only running 4.9 bar boost whereas the B186 was accelerating faster and was pumping 5.3 bar. Rosche admits that boost had been constricted by the charge pipe incorporated in the engine cradle prior to Hungary. However, thereafter the integral pipe was bypassed and with the same turbo the BT55 should have enjoyed the same boost...

While Arrows had a poor 1986, scoring but a single point, Benetton made excellent use of Mader's upright engines – '85 works specification (7.5:1 c.r./11,500r.p.m.) M12/13 units carrying Garrett turbos. The team's switch from Hart engines had given it an estimated 20% increase in race power, almost a 50% increase in qualifying power. It had also put up the cost of a season but Benetton took care of that, exercising its option to buy the Toleman operation outright.

By Francorchamps it was clear that the BMW-Benetton was an all round more effective package than the BMW-Brabham, in particular exploiting the acceleration that the troubled lay down car so badly lacked. For the later high speed European circuits Byrne had an improved aerodynamic package and Benetton livery went well to the fore at Hockenheim, the Osterreichring and Monza. In Germany, Berger set fastest race lap, then in Austria the team tried a larger qualifying turbo which didn't work, yet still buttoned up the front row. The cars majestically led one – two until Fabi bounced over a kerb and buzzed his engine, then Berger's battery failed...

If the Osterreichring speed was proof of the excellence of Byrne's aerodynamics, another illustration came in Italy where Berger used the big turbo and sky high boost to clock the fastest ever Formula One speed – 218.238m.p.h. Byrne says: 'Mader did a lot of development work on the qualifying set up. At Monza we saw a 5.5 bar flash reading – Mader estimated that was worth over 1300b.h.p. Qualifying boost was regularly 5.3 bar, with a charge temperature of 45 degrees. We pumped a lot of water onto the intercooler – we had 20 jets, spraying about three litres of water per lap!'

Byrne reports that race boost on 195 litres was generally around 3.7 bar, representing something in the region of 850b.h.p. After the splendid performance in Austria came Berger, Benetton and Mader's first Grand Prix win in Mexico, the result greatly aided by Pirelli longevity. Elsewhere, reliability was poor.

Zakspeed also failed to find good reliability. This year Zakspeed had a low pressure Motronic system as favoured by Porsche: BMW preferred high pressure electro-mechanical injection but a fully electronic four cylinder system had been developed by Bosch with the planned Alfa Romeo engine in mind. With inlet and exhaust pipes tuned to maximise its potential, Zakspeed's four was able to race at 3.5/3.6 bar (around 850b.h.p.)

while qualifying as high as 4.5 bar, on occasion.

Alas, throughout '86 the team lacked testing time and in '86 it failed to achieve its target of scoring World Championship points. As did Minardi, which likewise enjoyed improved engine control. This was the Marelli-Weber injection system introduced by Ferrari in 1984. Used with two injectors per cylinder, this was also loaned and overhauled by Ferrari, and was first tested on the 6VTC at Ferrari's Fiorano test track in February '86. Motori Moderni also benefited from an improved, now toluene-based AGIP supply, and an improved KKK turbocharger model. Chiti's relatively low compression engine was essentially unmodified internally and, with Motori Moderni unable to afford extensive engine mapping, needed to run a relatively rich mixture to preserve its pistons. Motori Moderni engines were used by both Minardi and in a couple of late season races by AGS, without success. Nor was there any success for the little Osella team which continued to employ Alfa Romeo V8 engines, having planned to switch to the 6VTC but failed to secure the necessary finance.

At the other end of the scale was the FORCE team, which started out with Hart engines once more as a stop gap measure then switched to the promised Cosworth Ford 120 degree V6. A 120 degree V6 was the smallest practical package, offering the least and lowest-located mass. The Cosworth engine was kept as compact as possible 'with no wasted space', designer Goddard points out. With the narrow (but undisclosed dimension) bore necessary to keep piston crown temperature under control, and little length added by a novel chain drive at the front, the tidy unit measured no more than 510mm. high and 450mm. long.

The heart of the new engine was an aluminium monobloc (with detachable heads) that extended well below crank axis. Plain bearings were supplied by Vandervell and the main bearing caps were formed within buttresses across the lower half of the crankcase, located both by bolts and interference fit (the walls of the block had to be jacked apart to allow installation or removal). In addition to the normal, vertical main bearing cap bolts, the buttresses held horizontal cross bolts spreading the bottom end loads and producing a structure well capable of handling immense loading.

The camshaft drive was taken off the nose of the crank. A gear either side of a helical cut take off at the front of the crank provided the half speed reduction and drove its respective bank via a short chain. Chains were compact – no wider than gears – light and introduced some damping. Compared to gears, chains were 'simpler and equally as effective'.

Driving H-section, steel con rods through steel gudgeon pins, the flat top, valve clearance notched three ring pistons were, of course, oil cooled, incorporating oil galleries. However, Cosworth employed a unique, secret, method of feeding the oil to the piston. It initially employed Mahle manufactured pistons, but planned to produce in-house. Cosworth had already produced its own pistons to run in the (similarly Nikasil linered) DFV engines. It made almost everything in-house, including the steel camshafts. The head was, says Goddard, 'a typical Cosworth design' and the valve angle at 40 degrees was (by coincidence) that of the FVA – wider than that of the DFV as keeping the valves well apart allowed more scope for valve cooling, a crucial consideration for an engine that would have to face extremes of exhaust valve temperature.

Detroit plumped for American turbos, turning to Garrett. Of course, Garrett had a special relationship with Renault. Cosworth became a development partner with Garrett, giving standard Garrett Formula One turbos its own 'embellishments'. While Detroit specified American turbos, its electronics boffins worked with Italian ignition and injection systems, Marelli-Weber supplying its capacitor discharge 'Raceplex' ignition and solenoid-operated injectors. Since Weber's injectors (like those from Bosch) were too small to meet the needs of a 1500cc turbocharged race engine, two were fitted for each cylinder.

Cosworth laid down the criteria that the Detroit developed engine management system had to meet. The system was based on Motorola's regular road car 'EEC IV' system, claimed to be the most advanced in the world, and controlled ignition timing and injection timing and duration, and was designed so that it could also regulate an electronically controlled wastegate, if required so to do. EEC IV was a very powerful, very sophisticated and very complex system. At the time the American auto industry led the world in the exploitation of engine management systems and Motorola produced both hardware and software, making its own chips. The company was expert in condensing electronics, allowing faster, more advanced processing. However, the EEC-IV's packaging was certainly a whole new ball game thanks to the unfriendly environment of a race car, and the boffins had to learn to work in a much hotter kitchen...

The prototype engine having been completed in mid '85, the original aim was to start track testing at the end of the season, soon after the Australian Grand Prix. In the event, the TEC Turbo was confined to the dyno until February 1986, problems sorting out its advanced electronics to blame. New to Formula One, Detroit appeared to have underestimated the task.

Nevertheless, if it took longer than anticipated, eventually an effective race engine control system emerged, one which Ford claimed was more sophisticated than Porsche/TAG's proven Bosch Motronic equipment. Soon up to 3.8 bar, Goddard reckons that Cosworth started out around Hart power, then strode ahead. The introduction of 'rocket fuel' in mid season was the key that unlocked the door. Soon the compression ratio was increased, matching fuel improvement. The first step was made at Brands Hatch, with a 7.5:1 compression ratio. Alas, there was a cooling problem, which FORCE blames upon local overheating within the engine and which called for larger coolers.

Monza saw a prototype engine having new pistons and a high compression ratio, which would appear to have been 8.0:1. Properly tuned into 'rocket fuel', Goddard says: 'the difference now was that 750b.h.p. was the minimum, rather than the maximum power!' On the regular engine Monza terminal speeds were poor, but Tambay tried the prototype high compression unit in the warm up and his speed trap readings soared.

Throughout, head and camshafts had remained the same – it was simply a question of the piston coming up the bore. Continual mapping had refined the map, concentrating on filling in the bottom end and transient conditions. The intention had always been to create a straight line power curve and that had been achieved: it could be drawn with a ruler. At Adelaide, Cosworth reckons it had an engine producing in excess of 1000b.h.p. on little over 4.0 bar, with a maximum of 12,000r.p.m.- and more revs and boost available beyond these 'sensible limits'. FORCE still wasn't producing results but it was clear that Cosworth had a very competitive engine ready for '87...

By 1986 Honda had taken a firm grip on turbocharged Formula One, though TAG/Porsche was by no means out of the reckoning. Ferrari had run out of development potential and Renault was struggling. Meanwhile Cosworth was starting to find its turbo-feet with this new FORCE car.

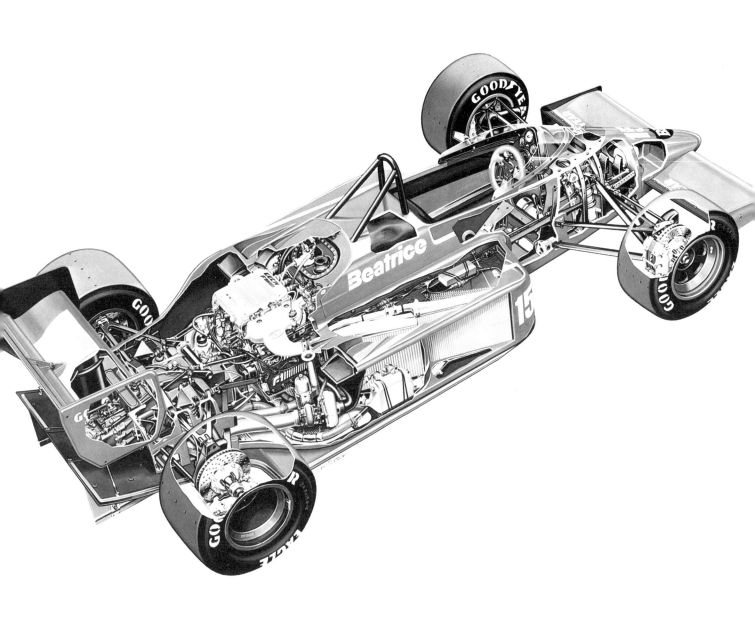

Grand Prix Cars 1987

In 1987 FISA introduced an Indy-style 'pop off' valve to restrict boost to 4.0 bar absolute. Nevertheless, by the end of the season Cosworth had managed to extract over 1000b.h.p. – arguably the most impressive power per litre per bar boost of the high boost era. At lower boost it is somewhat easier to match the theoretical boosted increase that multiplies the 175b.h.p. per litre of a typical Seventies four valve race engine at atmospheric pressure by 1.5 litres and manifold pressure. A theoretical 525b.h.p. at 2.0 bar boost is one thing, 1050b.h.p. at 4.0 bar is another.

How did Cosworth achieve such high efficiency? Essentially, it was able to run a very high compression ratio – at least 9.0:1. The four valve race engine was a highly efficient pump but to run a high compression ratio without incurring detonation at four times atmospheric pressure was no mean achievement. The engine clearly had to be mechanically sound, with good cooling. The fuel had to be as heat intolerant as feasible, and well atomised. Interestingly, with the development of toluene based 'rocket fuel' internal temperatures had actually fallen. Precise control of injection and ignition was another vital consideration and good charge cooling was essential.

Aftercooler water sprays had been outlawed for 1987 but Benetton's Rory Byrne had paid special attention to cooling requirements. The Benetton B187-Cosworth was a very effective package, but it took much of the season to extract its full potential. However, after working with an inexperienced team riddled by politics, Cosworth was happy to co-operate with the longer established, fast rising operation. For Benetton it was the third make of engine in as many years, and designer Rory Byrne offered yet another fresh and innovative design to maximise the potential of the compact engine. Boutsen and Fabi were signed to handle the B187 and fast Rio testing times suggested that Byrne had produced another fine chassis to follow his Grand Prix winning BMW-Benetton.

At the outset claimed 4.0 bar horsepower was 900b.h.p. at 11,500r.p.m. on a 7.5:1 compression ratio. Of course, in practice, everything was a little higher than that, other than boost. With two pop-offs, Cosworth would have found it hard to play 'beat the pop-off', in any case. As we have seen, essentially engine development had followed fuel availability and as the compression ratio had gone up a four figure output had been 'easily achieved' without going far over 4.0 bar. For '87, Mobil rather than BP supplied the necessary 'rocket fuel' and the compression ratio certainly rose above 8.0:1. Consequently, the engine was now more vulnerable, and could be lost through a missed shift...

Fabi was fastest of all in the Rio test immediately preceding the opening race, and both cars qualified in the top six, if not on the front row. There was further evidence of competitive speed at Imola with Fabi qualifying fourth again, and setting fastest race lap, but at Francorchamps and Monte Carlo the Benettons sank into mid field. And prior to Ford's important 'home' race the only points were two taken by Boutsen at Rio, the cars suffering an equal share of engine, turbo and transmission failures.

Detroit brought a new turbo package to provide a smoother power delivery. Goddard gives lie to the popular belief that Cosworth employed its own version of DPV. Unlike DPV (the Renault Sport licensed device) Cosworth's compressor performance-enhancer did not cause the pressure of the incoming air to drop. Needless to say, Cosworth kept its intriguing device secret. In conjunction with 'turbo development', it made throttle lag: 'virtually unmeasureable', none appearing on the ECU log! With the new system, Benetton was in the hunt again, and thereafter at least one B187 would qualify in the top six on all but two occasions, and only once was either car outside the top 10 qualifiers. However, Benetton was hot on the heels of the fast boys, not setting the qualifying pace. But chasing grid glory was still of secondary importance to Ford. Alas, race finishes were few and disappointing: only at the Osterreichring did a Benetton driver stand on the rostrum, and it took Senna's disqualification at Adelaide to give the team two third places. With the team fabricating c.v. parts in-house, the transmission weakness was cured around mid season, though not before Fabi had finished Ricard on one driven wheel. Engine reliability improved with new specification fuel introduced at the Osterreichring. Nevertheless, Benetton's disappointing total of points finishes was 11 from 32 starts. If after Detroit the reliability record was a little better, problems, often niggling little ones, continued to be rife and only at late season races did the Ford race challenge look really strong.

Towards the end of the '87 season Cosworth was running a 'very high' compression ratio and Goddard estimates that the V6 had 'just crept above' Honda race power. He reckons that Honda was running in the region of mid-900b.h.p., and confesses that Cosworth eventually got 'on the fringe of 1000b.h.p.' in race trim. Byrne says that qualifying power at Suzuka was a shade over 1000b.h.p., the team running on the edge of 4.0 bar. Bore and valve sizes remained as at the outset, and neither sodium filled nor Nimonic valves had been found necessary thanks to fuel development. At the same time, Motorola and Cosworth were improving the EEC IV management system, providing accurate fuelling over a wider range of conditions – the engine map was getting more refined as time went on. Goddard reckons: 'BMW had been running (computer control) five times as long, yet Ford went ahead in two years'.

He considers: 'it took a year to knit together, but towards the end of '87 Benetton was deserving of a place on the rostrum'. Indeed, Boutsen looked a good bet to win in Mexico until a gremlin in his ECU switched the engine off. Alas, in '87 the very capable combination of Cosworth and Benetton failed to reap the reward of its obvious potential.

Not so Honda which had moved from the Williams factory to a new base at Slough, where engines were prepared for both Williams and Lotus. Honda fitted a single pop-off at a point in the inlet manifolding that looked very much as if it was, in effect, a venturi throat. Through the venturi the airflow was faster, the pressure was lower...

The 1987 'G-spec' engine pushed revs, initially to 13,000r.p.m., though a later 'GE' version brought this down to 12,000, with superb economy and reliability. Osamu Goto had taken over as Formula One Project Leader and Chief Engineer and he confirmed that his team produced four different types of engine in '87 in the quest for better fuel consumption, though details of each had to remain confidential. The piston was still a flat top design, of conventional light alloy construction running in a four valve, single plug serviced Nikasil cylinder while the valves were still operated by finger cam followers. Honda further admitted that, while the compressor wheel was aluminium, the turbine wheel was Inconel. Inconel is an ultra high temperature tolerant alloy metal that is very hard to work.

According to Honda, 'since there were no boost pressure restrictions in 1985 and '86 our objectives had been to obtain higher power through increasing boost pressure and to improve engine reliability under high boost pressure operating conditions, particularly the reliability of the pistons and exhaust system. With maximum boost limited to 4.0 bar in 1987 two aspects became very important. One aspect was to increase the engine r.p.m. to a higher limit, which was required to obtain more power. The other was to develop an accurate boost control system, to keep the boost at its highest possible pressure under the pop-off valve limit'.

Wastegate control was a vital factor: running on the verge of 4.0 bar was safe but blowing the valve open caused an undesirable leak from the charge air system. In '87 Honda adopted a distributorless ignition system (as Ferrari) following the lead of Renault. This enhanced ignition control, helping to run closer to the detonation threshold. Crucially, throughout '86 and '87 Honda appeared to be able to race closer to that threshold than almost anyone.

For Williams, 1987 was another crushing success, this time with a World Championship for Honda favourite Piquet as well as the constructors title. And the overall tally for Honda was 11 pole positions and 11 wins, thanks to the efforts of Team Lotus which contributed one pole and two wins.

Ferrari also returned to the winner's circle in 1987 running a new 90 degree vee engine that exploited new materials. By the end of '86 it had been clear that Ferrari required a Formula One engine with a stronger block and smaller transverse dimension. Originally the designers considered a vee angle slightly narrower than 90 degrees, but the long experience gained by Chief Engineer His at Renault finally dictated 90 degrees. The 120 degree engine's bore and stroke (81 × 48.4mm.) were retained, and the engine construction was revised around these basic dimensions.

Structural requirements were catered for by a change to a linerless cast iron block: with the performance reached by turbo engines (in excess of 1000b.h.p.) causing very high internal pressures, and massive forces acting on the crank assembly, it was very difficult to maintain the required stiffness in an aluminium base, without resorting to weights and dimensions which would no longer have justified this type of material. Besides, notable progress had been made in metallurgy in the development of a special cast iron alloy with very interesting characteristics. This work involved the Teksid company within the Fiat Group, which had developed some very advanced casting techniques. That is why the excellent design engineer Renzetti was called in to participate in the project: Renzetti had been responsible for the development of the Fiat FIRE engine: a hi-tech engine with a resemblance to the sort of block envisaged in terms of materials.

For the Ferrari engineers, the main objective was to plan a strong engine block that would avoid distortion of the main bearings. Fears regarding excessive weight of the cast iron component were overcome through the fineness of design, with thin walls and perfect structural dimensions. The end result was so good that the total weight figure was slightly improved over the superseded alloy engine. A novelty was the move of the timing gear from the rear to a more conventional front position, with an included valve angle of 32 degrees. The crank retained a familiar vibration damper.

The entire technical formulation of the F1-87 was aimed at the highest thermodynamic efficiency. With due pride, Enzo Ferrari wanted to make clear at the launch the important achievement of his engine development team in for the first time achieving a specific consumption of under 200 gms. per h.p. per hour, reaching the value of 198 gms. This was considered essential, given the maximum tank capacity of 195 litres and the new 4.0 bar limit.

A contributory factor was an improvement in the digital electronics, with further modifications to the injectors and an operating pressure considerably higher than 10 bar. An important step was made with a new Marelli static ignition, providing a coil for each of the six plugs. Near the plugs was a three-point connector which carried current to the coil, placed in the well. The system was very reliable, minimised hi tension voltage leakage and, from the point of view of electronic control, enabled a valuable optimisation of the ignition for each cylinder, with instant correction.

With turbocharged engines, one looks at the compression ratio in order to understand the range of performance increase: with the F1-87 it rose from 7.5:1 to 8.0:1 for a stated power of 880b.h.p. at 11,500r.p.m.; equal to a specific power of 588b.h.p. per litre. In the new chassis, the engine was matched with a longitudinal gearbox, ending a long standing practice of setting a transverse gearbox ahead of the rear axle. Remarkable development brought the new engine to the top of the Formula One tree within only seven months of development, going from the initial placings (Berger fourth at Rio, Alboreto third at Imola) to victories in Japan and Australia. The most surprising aspect is that no striking engine modification was made from the first to the last race of the season, except for the routine variations in turbocharger. This means both that the 90 degree iron block engine was well produced and came out of an excellently formulated project, and that in this development phase of the turbo engine all the mechanical refinements had reached their peak and the highest performance levels were achieved only through electronic fuel control, ignition control and general turbo function.

The F1-87 chassis had been designed by Postlethwaite and newcomer Gustav Brunner, with finalisation of specification approved by newly arrived Technical Director John Barnard. Undoubtedly, the chassis matched the best ever encountered in the years immediately preceding, due to the arrival of Barnard and the commencement of operation of the Ferrari wind tunnel. These factors made for good overall success after two years of failures. But when an engine makes such significant advance as to reach the levels of the established best engines from Honda and Porsche, special credit is due.

The engine made its entrance with a split plenum chamber, but from the first race a single chamber was fitted to allow just one pop-off valve to be fitted. Thereafter, no external modification was made. Internally, there was a slight alteration to the combustion chambers and inlet tracts from Francorchamps. Although the quoted power was 880b.h.p. at 11,500r.p.m., the output looked less in early races. Subsequently came improvement at Francorchamps and Ricard, (while the slow circuits saw a resort to smaller turbos). Estimates relevant to the faster tracks showed 909-910b.h.p. at a maximum pressure of 4.0 bar, with 846-861b.h.p. at 3.71-3.78 bar race boost. The values increased at the German Grand Prix (to 932b.h.p. and 867b.h.p., respectively) and the Hungarian Grand Prix, where 950b.h.p. was reached during qualifying, 900b.h.p. during the race. Meanwhile, turbos utilising new materials had arrived and, above all, it was possible for the first time for the Ferrari engineers to surpass 4.0 bar by a few tenths, reaching levels of 4.1 and 4.2 bar, as Honda had been doing from the start of the season.

The die was cast and thereafter the Ferrari F1-87 was

highly competitive. Over the season as a whole Ferrari made all but one of its 32 starts from the grid top 10, while the second half of the season saw three poles: Berger at Estoril, Suzuka and Adelaide. During hurried turbo development, Ferrari had gone through the experience of Estoril: Berger, after taking pole position, missed victory by the skin of his teeth. New turbo equipment was supplied by Garrett as only left-hand units, as there had not been time to complete construction of left and right-hand versions. Ferrari compensated for the counter-rotation with the construction of different exhaust systems: a fast adaptation which produced good results. The new turbos had rotors with a silicon Nitride ceramic coating and notably emphasised the lightness of their rotating parts and their low friction bearings. The contribution was considerable, as regards performance and reliability, as a record on the test track and the two victories of Berger showed.

Prost took three victories for McLaren in this year of the Williams-Honda, a swansong year for the Porsche/TAG engine. Rosberg had now retired and was replaced by Johansson, sacked by Ferrari, and the MP4/2 package was further refined. In the last race of '86, Rosberg's engine had run an 8.0:1 compression ratio and this became standard for 1987. Again, the modification was allowed by a combination of the management system and fuel. For the engine's final year power in race trim went up to 900b.h.p. at 13,000r.p.m. running 3.5 bar (3.8 bar in qualifying).

To cope with the increased compression ratio, the pistons themselves became heavier, had heavier gudgeon pins and the con rods too were changed and became slightly heavier. These apparently minor modifications increased reciprocating weight which led to vibrations which caused other parts to break. Calculations had suggested that the modifications could be accommodated by the engine but apparently the calculations themselves were at fault since they had been based on adding all the additional weight together and not compounding the individual additions in weight. This was cured for Hockenheim by re-balancing the crankshaft.

At Hockenheim Prost led from half distance, with Johansson taking third a little later, but he was robbed of his 28th Grand Prix win, and the points which would have taken him to within a point of the top of the Championship table, by a broken alternator belt. This had previously happened early in the San Marino Grand Prix when he was lying second and to Paul Ricard when Johansson lost sixth, and a belt had broken during testing at Silverstone as well. After four years of reliable performance this spate of failures was a mystery but a cure was effected by a redesigned twin belt assembly rapidly supplied by the American firm Gates.

Although a deal with Honda for 1988 was announced in September, engine development continued and as late as Mexico there were visible modifications when, to service a revised version of the on-board computer, the cars sprouted small telemetry aerials. While the Honda-Williams was the cream of the field in 1987 Prost had emerged as the driver of his age. By his own standards, three wins in a season was below par but he was almost always among the top four qualifiers (typically Johansson would be half a dozen places lower down). With a little more luck Prost might just have taken a third world title, but it was not to be such a storybook ending for the TAG engine.

Alas, the fate of the BMW engine in 1987 was far worse. The Brabham programme – now without Murray – got underway late and the biggest panic was repackaging the transaxle to provide a shorter span between engine and differential for improved weight distribution. In the light of the BT55 experience the BT56 boasted large top vented coolers and it came out with a 40 – 60 static weight distribution which, in conjunction with a significantly shorter wheelbase transformed the traction problem. However, the team still suspected an engine scavenging problem.

Other than for electronic injection and a repackaged turbo system the '87 lay-down M12/13/1 was unchanged, still retaining a 7.5:1 compression ratio, according to Rosche. He says higher ratios had been tried on the dyno, without success. '86/'87 winter work had concentrated upon adapting to the pop-off valve. Clearly a four cylinder engine was harder hit by the 4.0 bar restriction than a six as it lacked revs: power is function of revs and boost. In '86 the Porsche/TAG engine had qualified at less than 4.0 bar whereas the BMW engine had raced at around 4.0 bar...

Rosche opinions that in '87, the four cylinder engine was at a significant disadvantage against a six for the first time. Lack of revs was the problem. To give it any sort of chance, the M12/13/1 had to be raced at 3.9 bar, which put it squarely in the area in which the pop-off started to come into play – the level at which any given valve operated was inexact. Patrese reckoned that for '87 there had been a small improvement in the engine, at high revs, but was critical of its response and low speed torque. After Rio his car was converted back to electro-mechanical injection in the interest of improved fuel economy, both cars running high pressure injection from Monaco. Rosche says the valves maintaining fuel pressure at 5.0 bar were inconsistent and that the significantly lower pressure (as against 40.0 bar) meant a longer injection period, with more fuel going through on valve overlap. Of course, a four cylinder engine requires more fuel per cylinder than a six cylinder engine, and BMW 'lacked time to develop 100% the low pressure system', which was beneficial at small throttle openings.

The season was one of mid field performance and the final tally was only three points finishes. Engine and transmission failures had been rife. Running Megatron badged Mader prepared upright BMW M12/13 engines, Arrows managed half a dozen points finishes but its drivers did not step on the rostrum. Ligier also ran Megatron engines, to no effect, after Fiat pulled the plug on new group member Alfa Romeo's deal to supply it with the long delayed four cylinder engine. With the 4.0 bar restriction a four cylinder engine looked a bad move and, just as bad, the Italian engine had an ominously large piston crowns thanks to a 92mm. bore.

Osella continued to employ the old Alfa Romeo V8. Alfa Romeo agreed to sell Osella the V8s and parts it held, on condition the marque's name was removed from the cam covers. Officially, the V8 became an 'Osella'. However, it was a back of the grid special, along with the Motor Moderni and Zakspeed cars...

After a shaky start in 1986, the Cosworth Ford 'TEC' Turbo emerged as one of the strongest runners under the 4.0 bar limit of 1987. By the end of the season turbo lag had been all but eliminated and the unit was offering a whisker over 1000b.h.p. in spite of the boost limit.

Grand Prix Cars 1988

Honda supplied McLaren and Lotus in 1988 and at McLaren's request it lowered its engine, the flywheel now matching a $5\frac{1}{2}$" clutch. This allowed Technical Director Gordon Murray to produce a chassis with a heavily reclined driving position, in the manner of his earlier Brabham BT55. Unlike the BT55, the MP4/4 had a competitive engine and a favourable weight distribution: it proved the worth of the low chassis concept as it left Lotus' classical design in its wake in dominating the 1988 World Championship.

For the 2.5 bar season Honda had three types of 'RA-168-E' engine, according to circuit conditions. It had responded to the boost cut with a higher compression ratio and higher revs: back to 13,000r.p.m., and beyond. With lower boost it could develop faster-responding turbochargers and perhaps most important of all, it found the way to atomise toluene fuel properly at the relatively low manifold pressure. Fuel chemistry and an unusually high injection fuel pressure played important roles in this. A high compression ratio and good atomisation were vital to 2.5 bar performance. With high revs, Honda was able to exploit something in the region of 650-680b.h.p.

Honda still ran its pop off in what appeared to be a venturi throat and early in the season had problems with the new European-produced, FIA supplied valve proving over-sensitive to throttle movement. Consequent pressure fluctuations in the inlet manifold upset the engine management system. It was necessary to relocate the throttles and from Imola the engine ran a throttle in each charge feed pipe just ahead of the single pop off on the carefully shaped plenum inlet.

Nevertheless, McLaren won every race on the calendar, bar one. A rare retirement for Prost and bad luck for Senna at Monza opened the door to a hugely popular Ferrari win. For the final season of turbocharging the Ferrari 90 degree V6 engine had needed a redesign of its cylinder heads. The 2.5 bar limit had made it particularly important to increase engine speed, the prime factor – all other things being equal – governing power output. Mechanically, a structure designed for 1000b.h.p. performance did not need the slightest modification. Indeed, the overall dimensions, which were fairly generous, were retained in the interests of reliability.

During the entire previous stage of development the turbocharged engine had never been required to breach the parameter of engine speed: the role of turbocharging pressure and its areas of application and the development of special fuels had always been dominant in the search for better performance. For the Ferrari V6, as for rival V6 engines, 11,000 – 11,500r.p.m. had been satisfactory, even at the 1987 season's level of 4.0 bar when the limiting valve's features (simplicity of design) permitted a certain amount of 'over boost'. The objectives for 1988 were set by a drastic reduction in pressure and by the arrival of a promised new and reliable pop off valve.

In the range of 25 b.h.p. per tenth of a bar super-charging pressure the 2.5 bar restriction could have meant a reduction from a figure of 900 – 930b.h.p. at the end of 1987 to a figure of 525 – 555 b.h.p. To achieve planned levels of 600 and more horsepower the technicians followed two routes. The first was via the variable operating characteristics of the turbo (dimensions, rotational velocity and electronic control) while the second was engine speed, which can be worth 40 –

50b.h.p. for every 1000 r.p.m.

Thus, in its version for the beginning of 1988, the Ferrari V6 was planned to have an engine speed of 12,000r.p.m. and a maximum declared power of 620 b.h.p. The engine specialists at Maranello achieved this result through marked improvements to the intakes, combustion chambers, valves and their control systems, both designwise and also in the use of more advanced materials.

Bore and stroke characteristics remained unchanged but the compression ratio was increased to an incredible 10.0:1. The increase in power obtained was determined by a leap from 18.5 to 19.4 meters per second in linear piston velocity. This is, nevertheless, still within broadly acceptable limits for a racing engine. Even at the first race of the year, in Brazil, 12,200 r.p.m. was reached, which brought this typical velocity up to 19.7 m./s.

All in all, a new season of championship success seemed to be opening up for the 1988 version of the Ferrari V6. However, the first confrontation with the most advanced contemporary turbo engine, the Honda V6, was pretty unsatisfactory. This triggered off a second and wider ranging process of development. It had less to do with power levels, which were already growing rapidly, than with the difficulties encountered with the new pop off valve. This valve was insufficiently tested and tended to open at the 2.5 bar threshold, with a sharp drop in power.

The on-board microprocessors and their sophisticated software allowed better control of the wastegate. At the instant of pressure drop (the pop off valve opening) the driver could press a button and quickly regain optimum performance. The next step (for the San Marino Grand Prix) was to produce a program which could control pressure jumps automatically and also rapidly re-adjust levels at the intermediate range.

After this, His had to fully exploit the latest resources in terms of materials and refinements: valves, camshafts, valve springs, pistons. On completion of the second stage of development the engine reached 12,400r.p.m. at the Mexican Grand Prix and 12,600r.p.m. (an average piston velocity of 20.3 m./s.) at the Canadian Grand Prix. From Canada onwards maximum power in the order of 650 b.h.p. was available during qualifying. The six butterfly valves (one per duct) were replaced by a single valve near the pop off. The pop off was fitted in a more rearward position over a venturi throat, Honda style.

· However, power yields during races, given the rigorous fuel consumption limit of 150 litres, were somewhat reduced to a band of 590 – 615 b.h.p. Other work was done on the electronic controls and on the fuel system pushing the injection pressure well over 10 bar. The aftercoolers, initially reduced by 25% compared to 1987, had to be enlarged. From the Hungarian Grand Prix on they were complemented by an automatic 'partialisation' system, with a Honda-style bye-pass valve for more efficient control of the charge temperature.

At the same time, work was done on the fuel after competitors appeared to have exceeded an 80% level of toluene (specific weight 0.867). A more easily atomised compound, but one retaining its other characteristics, was sought from the petro-chemical industry. One of the biggest ever technical commitments on the engine front was made in the search for a success in 1988.

Aside from Honda and Ferrari, the only turbo engines

running in 1988 were the Megatron-BMW, the Zakspeed and the Osella Alfa Romeo. The Megatron programme continued with the significant difference that Mader was now in charge of both engine and software development. He employed former BMW Formula One engineer Gerhard Schumann to carry out mapping on his Geneva dynos and throughout '88 that was a continual process.

Mechanically the upright BMW engine had to be modified to meet the 2.5 bar and 150 litre restrictions, of course, and Mader was understandably not prepared to disclose the compression ratio or valve sizes for '88. It is almost certain that the compression ratio was increased, even though previously, on 4.0 bar (or unrestricted) boost, Rosche had found no benefit from increasing the ratio above 7.5:1. Similarly, it is likely that the valve sizes were reduced. The 2.5 bar engine ran a smaller Garrett turbocharger and a standard size other than at Mexico.

After the cracking problem experienced in '87, some modifications to the block were made for '88 and 40 new blocks were cast by BMW on behalf of Megatron. Mader drew the strengthening modifications which centred around the area of the main bearing bulkheads (the caps remaining as before).

Mader admits he changed valve sizes as well as the compression ratio and says he also altered the con rod length and piston detailing. The replacement rod was to the regular H-section design and was still titanium. The new piston likewise retained the general characteristics of the '87 item but Mader altered the crown with the increased compression ratio which apparently became slightly domed. There were also different camshafts and different injectors for '88.

The high pressure electro-mechanical injection system was the biggest headache under '88 conditions. The lean burn engine had higher combustion chamber temperatures and this caused fuel atomisation to be a problem. Whereas the injector had been moved low to save fuel, in spite of the 150 litre ration it now had to be located high in the top of the plenum once more to assist atomisation. Atomisation was the poser of '88, according to Mader, who didn't have the possibility of developing a brand new injection system for one season. Nevertheless, Mader and the three engineers allocated to the Megatron programme (a stark contrast to the horde employed by Honda) were able to do a lot of mapping and with the engine run to a maximum of 11,400r.p.m. block cracking was a thing of the past. In contrast to '87, mid season Mader was able to report not a single breakage since the start of the season and he was running twice as many miles as in '87. Interestingly, the rev limiter was working better with less fuel since the servo didn't have to wind

the cam back so far.

The 1988 Megatron-Arrows was clearly much harder hit than the six cylinder turbo cars by the 2.5 bar restriction due to its lower revs and it was not surprising to find the cars, updated '87 models, typically mid field runners. The Arrows was more reliable this year but often was to be found fighting rivals running customer Cosworth DFZ engines – similarly prepared by Mader.

Zakspeed fared worse, finding it a struggle to even qualify. The major change to the other German in line four was an 8.0:1 compression ratio while the valve sizes were altered. However, the unit did not respond well to running at 2.5 bar. Zakspeed would have been better off with a DFZ engine, and the same goes for Osella. In the light of the 2.5 bar/ 150 litre restriction the old V8's compression ratio was increased considerably, to 10.5:1, and the valve diameters were reduced to help save fuel. The piston was altered to have a domed crown (needing deep cutouts) to achieve the desired compression ratio and the revised item was supplied by Mahle associate Mondial of Turin. New bronze based valve seats were introduced and the camshaft was reprofiled.

In addition to this work, the heads were substantially modified for a 2 degree narrower valve angle and for improved water circulation and the crankshaft design was revised to overcome the cracking problem. The crankshaft steel specification was also changed, the new cranks produced by Montepilli, another local supplier. Perhaps the most significant development, however, was the long overdue introduction of full electronic injection as a part of an engine management package supplied by Marelli Weber. This included control of the timing of a new Marelli CD ignition system and electronic wastegate operation. With the mandatory boost reduction smaller KKK turbochargers were fitted for a snappier response, one size serving race and qualifying needs.

The injection system offered one injector per cylinder, and this was located above the butterfly in the inlet tract. The mapped V8 was rated '600b.h.p.' on 2.47 bar with maximum r.p.m. 12,400 for qualifying and 12,200 on race day. Fuel consumption on 150 litres was claimed not to be a problem. Enzo Osella converted all his eight engines to electronic specification for 1988 and during the course of the season a two- rather than eight-butterfly throttle system was introduced, the butterflies then located ahead of the pop off valve. There was also a revised piston avoiding the deep cutouts for better flame propagation. And at Monaco the team had something to smile about. The inexperienced Larini brought its single, woefully underfunded and underpowered car home in the top ten!

Ferrari pressed Honda hard in 1988 but always seemed to be a step behind. For example, it was not until the late season races that its V6 ran on the same 84% toluene fuel exploited throughout their year of 2.5 bar/150 litre competition by the rival Japanese engine.

Back of the 1988 Ferrari (lower photograph) and front of the McLaren-Honda. Note the extremely low cockpit of the Gordon Murray designed McLaren. It adopted the same reclined driving position as the ill-fated Brabham BT55 in the interest of improved airflow to the rear wing.

Indy Cars 1988

Although 1988 was about V8 engines, it saw Buick achieve an all time high at Indianapolis. Since the Buick runners shook the establishment in qualifying for the 1985 500 there had been increasing doubt about the ability of the push rod engine to go a full race distance at a competitive speed. In the light of many piston failures in 1985, over 2000 miles of testing had been completed at the Brickyard prior to the 1986 '500' which saw three Buick cars, while a similar programme preceded a five car '87 onslaught – and still Buick didn't get a car home. The 1988 race was a turning point: Jim Crawford, a Buick driver since '86 who had broken both ankles after going 215m.p.h. in testing for the '87 race, managed to lead deservedly in Kenny Bernstein's Lola. And Crawford proved that a stock block engine could also finish, coming home sixth after a late race puncture.

The winner was Rick Mears, giving Penske and Chevrolet a historic victory after years and years of Cosworth domination. Indeed, with the Chevrolet Indy V8 raced at 11,800r.p.m. and more dependable, Ilmor victory followed Ilmor victory on the 1988 campaign. Ilmor was now supplying a fourth team, Galles Racing, though with Patrick down to one car it was still represented by only five regular runners.

New for '88 were better quality castings and a small valve spring heat treatment modification. Aside from such refinement the design was that established in '86 and even the same cam profiles were run. Inlet and exhaust pipes were still as established on the drawing board. However, development this season saw the introduction of an engine management system.

On the cards since CART had legalised engine management in '85, this was a joint project with GM and employed GM solenoid injectors and a GM digital ECU. The injectors were produced by Rochester Products and were not to the regular Bosch design. The fuel entered via the side rather than the top which made for a smaller, neater package. Two were fitted per cylinder with one or both activated according to engine load. The fuel pressure was a typical 5.0 bar.

The ECU monitored r.p.m., throttle angle and pressure and temperature in the plenum chamber and controlled the timing of the Lucas CD system and the timing and duration of injection. Originally the ECU, which packaged the microprocessor and the injector drives into a compact single box, had a plug in EPROM but by '88 it was programmable direct from a portable computer.

GM had designed the hardware specifically for Ilmor and there had never been any intention to race the system before '88 giving the engineers time to rid it of 'the usual noise problems'. An Ilmor-mapped fully electronic engine first won at Cleveland, Andretti the victor on this occasion. That was the sixth straight Chevrolet win since the season opener at Phoenix and the engine went on to take nine in a row.

The run was ended not by Cosworth but by Judd. The AV engine, now promoted by Truesports, was henceforth known as a Judd and new for '88 was direct operation of the valves through bucket tappets, following Judd Formula One practice. The 3.5 litre CV Grand Prix engine had a lower sump to match a 5½ inch clutch and this was also adopted by the AV. Now cast in the UK, the AV was essentially a short stroke version of the similar-bore CV with modifications to accept light turbocharging

and methanol fuel. Like the DFX it ran iron rather than Nikasil liners in view of the higher cylinder pressures, but there was no piston cooling spray. The AV ran to 11,700 r.p.m. rather than the 11,400r.p.m. of the CV and for Cleveland new pistons increased the compression ratio. With the involvement of Truesports, development had stepped up and the engine's maiden victory came at Pocono.

Cosworth, meanwhile, was clearly up against it. For some inexplicable reason, with the cut to 45ins. for '88 the short stroke DFX did appear to offer a real performance bonus – as much as 20b.h.p. The '88 engine had lighter, hollow camshafts following Formula One practice, and magnesium tappet blocks to take some weight off the top of the engine. It had slightly revised inlet porting but retained the same valve sizes, and for the first time the DFX was equipped with an oil spray to the underside of each piston. Following Ilmor practice, the sump was angled, with 19mm. shaved off its base at the rear. This allowed the engine to be run horizontal rather than – as previously – titled at 1.5 degrees to accommodate the diffuser upsweep. Tilting the engine had slightly increased its frontal area.

Frontal area was further reduced through a modified plenum. This smaller volume narrow plenum had been developed in the light of a rear wing rule threatened for '88 but in the event not implemented. It had taken a lot of work to get it to work without a power loss. The new design had a bottom feed right at the rear and the butterfly was positioned at this point with the pop off valve above it, in the rear of the plenum's arched roof.

The new plenum, far narrower than those run by Ilmor Engineering and Engine Developments in '88, had been developed in conjunction with inward curved inlet tracts and the lighter Cosworth turbocharger which now gained widespread acceptance. However, the development of what transpired to be an unnecessarily small plenum (given the late cancellation of the rear wing ruling) had cost valuable development time that might have been more profitably channelled into other areas.

The revised 1988 DFX was sold as a kit without fuel and intake systems allowing a choice of mechanical or electronic injection. Cosworth did the mapping for the electronic engine offering customers a chip that was suitable for all circuits with updates forwarded as found necessary. Mapping was done to increments of 800r.p.m., 5ins. boost and 10 throttle positions. In addition, there was a mixture control allowing adjustment from 12% rich to 10% lean in 2% steps to accommodate changing circuit or ambient conditions. A driver generally kept a given race setting unless drastic measures were called for by his fuel situation.

As we have seen, Truesports had won the Indy 500 and the 1987 Championship running a mechanically injected Weis-built DFX. Any power advantage from fuel system improvement or make of engine was marginal: far more important was the overall package and in '87 Truesports had that right. Alas, for 1988 Cosworth had lost Truesports to the Judd engine. Having already lost Penske and Newman Haas to Chevrolet, of the cream of Indy Car teams it was left with only Kraco. The DFX was still the most popular engine option but of the handful of competitors who could realistically hope to win races, only Andretti Junior had stayed faithful to it.

Worse, Cosworth admits that, 'we had penalised

ourselves to some extent over the winter of '87/'88 developing the compact plenum to suit published rules – that was three months development for nought. Much of the '88 season was spent clawing back ... with the DFS we were certainly even again, if not ahead'.

Introduced for Andretti Junior at Nazareth, the DFS was a radical rethink that took power on 45in. from the 670b.h.p./11,900r.p.m. of the original '88 spec DFX to 'over 700b.h.p.' Essentially, conversion of a DFX to DFS specification retained only the complete cylinder block assembly (block/sump/timing cover), the gear train and the flywheel. Just about everything else mechanical was new, as were the bore and stroke dimensions. Thus, the crankshaft was new, as were the liners, the rods, the pistons, the cylinder heads (still with a 32 degree included valve angle), the valves, the cam carriers, the cams, the cam covers and the manifolds. The DFS was ready to take the fight back against the Chevrolet Indy V8 to a new degree of intensity in 1989 ...

Also shaping up well for 1989 was Porsche, which had entered the fray in 1987 with its Typ 2780 Indy engine. Following the same logic as Ilmor Engineering, design chief Hans Mezger had plumped eight cylinders and a 90 degree vee angle for the new Indy project. With manifold pressure restricted to 1.62 bar absolute power had to be found from revs while a 90 degree vee angle was chosen in the light of considerations of engine balance and chassis installation. Mezger plumped for similar bore and stroke dimensions to those of the Chevrolet Indy V8 and produced a very tidy package as a fully stressed chassis member with a notably slim bottom end, reminiscent of the Porsche/TAG engine he had also designed for a wing car package.

Indeed, the front end gear drive was similar to that employed by the TAG PO1 V6, but now, of course, it faced the vicious torsionals transmitted by the flat plane crankshaft necessary for V8 exhaust tuning potential. Mezger says a number of anti-vibration measures were identified at the drawing board stage and were tested on the dyno. The solution eventually adopted was, he reports, a method of gear mounting simpler than the traditional Cosworth arrangement. Rather than employing miniature torsion bars to form a cushioning hub that allowed some angular movement in the gear train it used rubber rings to the same effect. 'In principle it was the same', Mezger admits.

Like the TAG PO1 the basis of the Typ 2780 was an aluminium block cast by regular Porsche supplier Honsel Werke AG that extended down to the depth of the crankshaft axis and to which was bolted a structural sump. The lower crankcase cum sump was again a magnesium casting and formed each of the five main bearing caps. Primary attachment bolts flanked each main bearing. The block carried Nikasil liners in the conventional manner with a flange at the top (and O-ring seals below) and the heads were sealed by metal sealing rings. The heads were aluminium with integral cam carriers and were closed by magnesium cam covers.

The crankshaft and camshafts each ran in five plain Glyco bearings. The crankshaft was a Nitrided steel forging produced by regular supplier Maschinenfabrik Alfing Kessler and had eight extended balancing webs. A steel flywheel was attached by eight bolts. As usual at the house of Porsche, the H-section con rods were titanium, with titanium big end bolts secured by steel nuts. The gudgeon pin was steel and was secured by conventional circlips.

Unique in Indy Car racing in 1987, the Porsche V8 ran oil gallery pistons. As yet, the DFX didn't even run a piston spray. As usual the piston supplier was Mahle while rings – initially three – came from Goetze. Mezger says the piston had a special crown design to provide the right compression ratio and the desired form to his combustion chamber. Intriguingly, he speaks not of a pent roof chamber but of a 'more advanced' four valve head with an undisclosed shape and valve angle.

The valves and valve seats were of unspecified material – not ceramic – while the valves were sodium cooled. The

valve guides were of a new, again undisclosed material. The engine ran dual Schmitthelm springs under a titanium retainer while the valves were directly operated through steel bucket tappets by steel camshafts. As we have noted, the camshafts were driven via spur gears at the front end in TAG PO1 fashion. The oil and water pump drives were also at the front, the pumps driven directly from the gear train. While there were two water pumps, Mezger was not at liberty to reveal the number of oil pumps he employed.

The Porsche Indy engine measured 88.2 × 54.2mm. for 2649.2cc. and ran an 11.0:1 compression ratio. For dyno testing only, the engine ran a distributor on the front of each exhaust camshaft. It was always the intention to run distributorless ignition as part of the Motronic MP 1.7 engine management system developed on the TAG PO1. The MP 1.7 system ran two injectors per cylinder, these feeding into the inlet manifold just below a short tract leading down from the common plenum. Upstream and downstream feeds were tested and there were two throttle packages available, offering either one or eight butterflies.

As usual Porsche looked to KKK for its turbocharger equipment but there was no contract for the Indy engine, and there was no electronic wastegate control in this application. The first test engine was fired up on December 11 1986 and bench testing continued through the first half of '87 while Porsche readied its own Indy Car chassis. Mezger says that there were no unexpected problems and, as we have noted, the best method of gear train relief was identified at this stage.

In February the marque had announced that it would make its CART debut late in the season prior to a full assault on the PPG World Series and the Indy 500 in 1988. Backing would came from Quaker State oil for a single car factory team to be run by Porsche Motorsport North America. In mid season Al Unser Snr. was signed as development driver.

The Porsche Typ 2708 Indy Car was readied later than scheduled, just in time for an official launch at the September 1987 Frankfurt Motor Show. At this stage power was impressively quoted as 750b.h.p./11,200r.p.m.,

with maximum revs of 11,800r.p.m. The show car then underwent Weissach trials while a second chassis was shipped to Holbert's Warrington, Pennsylvania base, this to act as the spare car. The race car did not arrive until October and Unser first drove it only three days before the penultimate CART race. His Portland test then Laguna Seca race test showed that Porsche had a steep learning curve ahead of it.

Unser was well off the pace at Laguna Seca and Holbert took over the controls for the Tamiami Park finale, only to fail to qualify. The problem was not the engine but was the chassis. Porsche had developed its aerodynamics using a fixed floor rather than rolling road tunnel, following Group C practice. For the more sophisticated Indy Car, that was a mistake. Porsche bought a March chassis for 1988.

Mezger describes an early oil scavenging problem on ovals as 'normal' and this was quickly overcome. Again, it had not been an unexpected problem. Engine development included the planned move to distributorless ignition, employing four rather than eight coils. Areas of experimentation included, as we have noted, injector position and throttle arrangement. There were also experiments with more injectors, with two ring pistons, with IHI and other turbos, and with alternative flywheel materials for use with a carbon-carbon clutch. Power on 45 inches manifold pressure was not officially quoted.

The combination of Teo Fabi and a Porsche-March proved much more promising in 1988 – and a top 10 runner at the outset. Long Beach was a disappointment with only a sixth row grid position and an engine failure after a mere four laps while at Indianapolis Porsche showed lack of speed and experience. Thereafter, Milwaukee brought a second top ten finish then the car picked up more speed and at Meadowlands in mid season Fabi was thoroughly competitive, qualifying third fastest. The '88 March chassis design had invariably proved inferior to the Lola and Penske alternatives so clearly, with revs up to 12,000r.p.m. and beyond and running a now undisclosed compression ratio, there was little wrong with the performance of Mezger's new generation Indy engine.

Bobby Rahal and the Truesports team won the 1987 Indy 500 and the CART Championship running a Cosworth DFX, then switched to the Judd engine for 1988. The number one car gave John Judd his maiden Indy Car victory at Pocono but 1988 was the year of the Ilmor-Chevrolet V8.

The 1988 Indy 500 front row: pole car entrant Roger Penske shakes hands with Mario Illien, designer of its Chevrolet V8 engine. Penske backed the Ilmor engine launch and secured the vital support of General Motors, this deal giving the British unit the Chevrolet tag.

Prototypes 1988

Outrun by Jaguar in 1987 other than at Le Mans and with Mercedes going ahead, Porsche clearly had some catching up to do on the Group C front in 1988. Its response was based around the more sophisticated Motronic MP 1.7 engine management system. As used already by Mercedes, this controlled the wastegate as well as injection and ignition, and offered more precise, more accurate control. It called not only for new (electronically governed) wastegates, but for a complete redesign of the exhaust and turbocharger and intake systems. The turbocharger and aftercooler plumbing was revised, there was just one throttle per bank at the inlet to the plenum, the injectors were repositioned and a new ignition system and new camshafts were introduced. The ignition was now distributorless having three coils, each firing two plugs twice per four stroke cycle and triggered by the ECU.

The more precise engine control upped the detonation threshold, allowing the 935/83 engine to run a 9.5:1 compression ratio. It unleashed more power from a given quantity of fuel and helped put Porsche more on terms with the 750b.h.p. Jaguar and turbo Mercedes engines that had taken over its pacemaking role in Group C. Indeed, the Porsche works team was only narrowly defeated at Le Mans where the MP 1.7 engine made its debut. Aside from Le Mans, in 1988 Porsche left Group C to its customers, as it had done over the latter half of 1987. Some of the key customers had received 935/83 units in 1987 following the withdrawal of the works team and after Le Mans 1988 a number of the high compression MP 1.7 versions were made available.

Nevertheless, aside from Le Mans, Jaguar's main challenger in 1988 was Sauber-Mercedes with engines supplied by the Daimler Benz R&D department. The R&D operation was headed by Doctor Panik while Doctor Hiereth was project leader for the development of the Group C engine. The engine designer was engineer Muller while engineer Withalm was in charge of development. The race engines were built from production castings which had been taken from the factory and sent to Mahle for a conventional Nikasil coating to be applied to the bores.

By 1988 Daimler-Benz had produced around 30 race engines. Each was reckoned to take two persons one week to strip and rebuild. There were no special qualifying engines but on 2.2 bar absolute qualifying power was rated as 'almost 800b.h.p.'. Maximum revs were 7,000 but the driver was asked to observe a limit of 6,500 on race day, aside from overtaking. At the 1.9 bar absolute race setting torque was a massive 800n.m. at 4250r.p.m. and the torque band was spread all the way from 3,000 to 6000r.p.m.

Sauber started the 1988 season in splendid form, winning at Jerez. It won again at Brno in mid season and thereafter looked to have the equal of, sometimes a slight edge over Jaguar. And that was the story of the 1988 World Championship: Jaguar versus Mercedes with Porsche the also ran, other than at Le Mans.

This year WM won a little glory at Le Mans. Its P88 was subtly modified in the aerodynamics department while engine work for '88 included a 93mm. bore, again in conjunction with the production stroke. At 2.8 bar and maximum revs of 8200r.p.m. Dorchy was now summoning approximately 910b.h.p. in his search for the elusive 400k.p.h. Qualifying saw him clock another 407k.p.h.

pass based on information recorded by the Motronic ECU log while on race day he was rewarded with official confirmation of mission accomplished – a 405k.p.h. clocking by the ACO.

Toyota and Nissan again only came out to play at Le Mans and Fuji. For Le Mans Toyota had two development ('88C') cars, both of which qualified just inside the top 10 and both of which finished, though again no higher than 12th. Meanwhile, back at base the Engine Research and Advanced Engineering Department was putting the finishing touches to a replacement 3.0 litre V8 twin turbo engine.

The Toyota V8 R32V commenced its national career at the Fuji 500 mile race in July 1988. The single 88C-V entry qualified seventh and retired with transmission trouble. First tested in mid April 1988, the engine displaced 3,169.0cc. (82.0 × 75.0mm.) and was pressurised by twin Toyota CT26 turbochargers. Running an 8.0:1 compression ratio it was officially rated '800b.h.p./8,000r.p.m.' on undisclosed boost.

Nissan also had a new V8 in 1988, the 'Hayashi engine'. In August 1987 Nissan had created a new department within its Central Engineering Laboratories to concentrate on the design and development of race engines, and immediately to produce a new Group C engine. The VEJ30 engine had been disappointing and a new man was put in charge of the replacement V8: Yoshimasa Hayashi. Work started in earnest in October and with Le Mans only eight months away Hayashi didn't have the completely clean sheet of paper he would have liked, and it was necessary to retain the vee angle and the stroke (66.0mm.) of the existing unit through retention of the crankshaft.

While the VEJ30's five bearing flat plane crankshaft was retained, the block pattern was extensively revised and 28 new blocks were cast. The revised alloy monobloc offered a half skirt rather than full skirt crankcase and modified water channels. The new detachable lower crankcase incorporated the five main bearing caps in a ladder frame attached by twenty vertical bolts. A pair of bolts was situated each side of each main bearing. A shallow magnesium sump pan closed the bottom of the engine. According to Hayashi, the design improved stiffness while lowering friction.

In view of the size of the bore the heads were attached by eight 10mm. studs around each cylinder. Sealing was by Cooper rings with an additional three-layer metal gasket fitted for Le Mans. Wet liners were located by a top flange, the liners being cast iron at Le Mans, elsewhere Nikasil. The four valve, single plug alloy heads were all new and had an integral cam carrier. Hayashi says he abandoned the production-based rocker system of the VEJ30 due to 'inertia problems'. He went for a conventional bucket tappet arrangement and narrowed the valve angle considerably from 45 to 28 degrees for a more compact pent roof chamber and smaller valve clearance notches in the flat top piston. The inlets were set at 16 degrees from vertical, the exhausts at 12 degrees.

The piston was of the oil gallery type, fed by a single spray. It was a light alloy forging from either Atsugi or Izumi, both Nissan subsidiaries, and carried three chrome plated Riken rings in conventional fashion. The con rod was driven through a regular, fully floating steel gudgeon pin located by circlips. The titanium rod was of I section, 144mm. long and drove the crankshaft through a plain bearing on a 50mm. journal. The main bearing journals were 60mm. in diameter, again wrapped by plain bearings. NDC supplied the conventional shell bearings for the engine.

The forged steel crankshaft was produced by Keio Juki and was lightened for the VRH30. A damper was fitted on the front end 'to be on the safe side', says Hayashi. The other end was a steel flywheel sized to match a 7 1/4 inch clutch and attached by 10 bolts.

The drive was taken off the front end and was via gears running in needle roller bearings. Above the crankshaft gear was a centrally located half speed with a smaller gear either side of it on the same shaft. Of those, the forward gear drove the left bank, the other the right bank. Both sides, the camshaft end gears were driven by a gear on the head, this in turn driven by a gear on the block.

The camshafts ran in five plain bearings and were cast iron at Le Mans, elsewhere steel. Steel bucket tappets were fitted over sodium cooled 'heat resistant alloy' valves closed by twin steel coil springs. With 33.0mm. diameter intake, 30.0mm. exhaust valves there was actually a little less valve area than in 1987. The intake valve was 2mm. smaller, saving weight. The valve gear was designed for 9,600r.p.m. with 9,000r.p.m. the normal maximum, reduced to 7,500r.p.m. for 24 hours at Le Mans.

The water system set a single pump on the front of the engine driven directly from the central half speed gear. Outside the block rather than inside as in '87, the oil pump was also at the front and was driven via an intermediate gear from the half speed gear. The oil pump was of the sandwich type incorporating one pressure and two scavenge pumps on the same shaft. While the lubrication system serviced the twin turbos, there were no additional pumps to scavenge them. Compared to '87, the turbocharger oilways had been enlarged for improved lubrication.

One size of RX6-type IHI turbocharger was available and this was of conventional, single entry design without exotic materials, water cooling or suchlike. The wastegate was also supplied by IHI and was electronically controlled throughout the rev range as part of a sophisticated engine management system based on an NEC ECU.

The electronically controlled injection was via two Bosch injectors per cylinder feeding into the inlet tract, one either side. The tracts were fed from an individual plenum chamber for each bank whereas the earlier V8 had carried a single plenum. There were only two throttle butterflies, one ahead of each plenum. In addition to the Bosch injectors, the NEC microprocessor controlled a distributorless ignition system that em-

ployed one coil per plug. The coil was built into the top of the 12mm. NGK plug. The system echoed that employed on certain Nissan production cars. The firing order was 1-8-5-4-7-2-3-6.

The ECU received readings of manifold pressure, r.p.m. (from a crank sensor), throttle position and intake temperature as its key inputs. In addition, a pressure-sensitive detonation sensor was fitted in the form of a special titanium and lead plug washer and this allowed individual cylinder timing retardation.

The mapping process was based on very fine readings for r.p.m. and boost pressure and a new map was produced for each circuit. The first engine ran on Christmas Day 1987 and early development included a cylinder head modification to overcome a cracking problem between the valve seat and the plug. The porosity of the casting was blamed and chill casting overcame the problem. With that cured, the engine managed to successfully complete a 50 hour reliability run.

Further development saw the position of the inner injectors raised to improve fuel economy and smaller plenum chambers for better response. The plenum capacity was reduced from 7.0 litres to 3.6 litres per bank. The '88 Le Mans arrangement of dual throttles, twin plenums and high and low injectors was said to help provide significant response, low speed torque and economy benefits over the unloved VEJ30 engine.

The VRH30 ran an 8.5:1 compression ratio and at 2.4 bar absolute was rated 'over 750 b.h.p.' Le Mans was raced at 2.2 bar while the maximum safe manifold pressure was 2.8 bar which was reckoned to offer over 950b.h.p. The unit weighed 185kg. without turbo system and dimensions were: length 675mm.; width 670mm.; height 730mm. It took five days to build a new one. The engine was run only semi-stressed, at Le Mans '88 in two R88C prototypes based on the '87 March chassis which had run the VEJ30 with extended wheelbase and improved aerodynamics developed by. Nissan. One finished, overcoming gearbox and brake problems to bag 14th place overall.

Not a great success, then, for Nissan in Group C. GTP was another matter, the Electramotive Nissan turbo overthrowing the 962. For 1988 IMSA forced turbo engines to run a 57mm. air inlet restrictor and Porsche responded with an 8.0:1 compression ratio and an engine tuned to offer far more torque if less top end power, under 700b.h.p. Response was faster, power building up very quickly – then the air restrictor cut in, flattening out the power curve.

Porsche did not have the advanced Motronic MP 1.7 engine management system introduced for Group C in 1988 available for IMSA. Consequently some Porsche

teams developed their own wastegate control systems. Nevertheless, Nissan-type performance remained out of reach. In 1988 Nissan had a new car designed by Trevor Harris and it took a string of victories. In the summer of 1988 it was the Electramotive Nissan rather than a Porsche or a Jaguar that was the car to beat in the Camel GT series and pilot Geoff Brabham easily shattered the GTP record of four consecutive victories for one driver.

The Electramotive Nissan's V6 heads were based on a stock casting supplied by Nissan. The head sealing incorporated a Cooper ring atop the liner flange, retained by an aluminium gasket, with Vitron O-rings for water passages. O-rings were used throughout the engine, there being no conventional gaskets. O-rings sealed the bottom of the liner, which was left free to expand. The head was closed by a magnesium cam cover cast in the UK by Kent Aerospace, while magnesium sumps were produced locally.

Electramotive ordered high strength iron liners from various US suppliers and these were run uncoated. The three iron piston rings were, however, molybdenum faced. While Sealed Power rings were generally used, others were supplied by Rieken, a Japanese company. The pistons, forged in California by the Ross Racing Piston company were run without oil gallery or even a spray. Designer John Knepp reckoned oil gallery pistons notoriously unreliable, and in any case considered a spray to be 'unnecessary'; indeed, a waste of power. A 3.2 litre Group C derivative seen at Le Mans was run with flat top pistons (having small valve clearance notches) while the GTP unit had shorter con rods and taller pistons for the same stroke, its pistons having a slightly domed crown to maintain the desired 8.5:1 compression ratio.

The four bearing, six pin crankshaft was machined from a solid billet of steel and featured wider journals and different webs compared to the stock item. By mid '88 it had been redesigned a number of times, saving a total of almost 2kg. The main bearing journals were of 2.5in. (63.5mm.) diameter while the big end journals measured 2.1in. (53.3mm.). A six-bolt steel flywheel (with integral starter ring) was supplied by Quartermaster. Sometimes a Quartermaster clutch was run but more often the 7 $\frac{1}{4}$ inch item was from AP. At the nose of the 9,000r.p.m. crankshaft, a hydraulic vibration damper was fitted in respect of 'shaft harmonics'. This was supplied by Hudi, an American company, and was designed for truck camshaft applications.

The crank ran in plain Sealed Power bearings and was turned by Crower Cams produced I-section rods. These were to Electramotive's design and specifications. The gudgeon pins were also devised by Electramotive and were 1" (25.4mm) steel pins retained not by circlips but by Teflon buttons. The buttons were a push fit and were free to rub the cylinder wall. Retained by 13 larger-than-standard studs, each head was of a regular (production) combustion chamber layout, accommodating two large valves. Electramotive ported and polished the stock heads, lightly machining the intake side and fitting new valves, seats and guides. Valves were solid, of titanium on the intake side, inconel for the exhaust, on which side Stellite seats were fitted. Dual steel springs were used, with a titanium retainer.

The valves were activated by aluminium rockers designed by Electramotive and reckoned to be five times stronger than the production item. The production car hydraulic lifter was replaced by a plain steel lifter running in the stock lifter guide – the only production part left above the camshaft. While the camshaft ran directly in the head, a needle bearing was fitted at the front of the right hand head, ahead of which was taken the alternator and fuel pump drive. As standard, there were four bearing bosses for the shaft which was machined to Electramotive specifications from a steel billet supplied by Nissan. The two camshafts were turned by a Uniroyal belt direct from a cog mounted at the front of the crank.

While the right hand shaft drove alternator and fuel pump the left hand shaft drove the distributor. Ahead of the timing pulley on the nose of the crank was a magnetic trigger, then the damper, then an oil pump drive pulley then the water pump pulley. Located alongside the block, the oil pump was of sandwich construction, incorporating three engine scavenge, one turbo scavenge and the pressure pump.

On the front of the block, the water pump was Electramotive's own design with a special impeller – 'to flow a tremendous amount of water. We use a high water pressure – 45p.s.i. – mainly to eliminate hot spots. This enables us to run more boost', Knepp explains.

The turbocharger installation variations between Group C and GTP engines saw the former having a conventional overhead plenum while the latter had it offset to one side to allow an overhead location for its single aftercooler. In each case the plenum was of magnesium with a single butterfly throttle at its entrance and an individual outlet pipe for each cylinder. The turbocharger was of conventional design, based on T31 parts with inconel turbine wheel and aluminium compressor wheel. Electramotive developed bespoke wheel profiles in conjunction with Garrett.

The wastegate was Electramotive's own product and with the use of titanium, aluminium, stainless steel and inconel it was reckoned to be 'the lightest in racing'. It featured an electro-pneumatic boost control capable of continual adjustment by the ECU. The Electramotive engine control system ran the wastegate, the fuel injectors and the ignition timing.

The fuel injection system incorporated a Lucas mechanical fuel pump and Bosch solenoid injectors, two per cylinder. Injector position varied according to the specific application, being regularly used as a 'tuning tool'. The ignition system supplied by MSD was modified by Electramotive. It was a conventional CD racing system triggered by the magnetic pick up on the crank and with advance/retard set by the ECU. It fired a single Bosch 14mm. platinum plug per cylinder. The distributor was a stock Nissan part with its internals ripped out. In addition to a new ignition rotor it was equipped with another magnetic trigger, this one for injector sequencing.

The ECU and its attendant parts was designed by Electramotive specifically for the V6. Knepp reckoned his system was 'eight times as powerful as Motronic', offering greater precision and flexibility. The ECU recalculated between each firing. Readings were taken of crank position (speed), manifold pressure and throttle position (load), boost control pressure, fuel pressure and air and water temperatures and either one or both injectors were driven, according to the given map. The production detonation sensor (screwed into the side of the block) was retained and apart from injection, ignition and wastegate control the ECU activated warning lights on the dashboard and provided a data logging facility.

Carefully honed, the Electramotive VG30 qualified as high as 9,000 r.p.m. and raced at 7,500 – in 1988 generally away from its Camel GT opposition. Aside from Porsche, that opposition primarily consisted of the new TWR Jaguar team. Indeed, after Nissan Jaguar was often the 'best of the rest'. The Hendick Chevrolet team switched to atmo engines early on and new private Buick and Ford operations found little success.

Le Mans in 1988 witnessed a historic victory for the 'atmo' Jaguar engine, ending a long run of Porsche turbo success. Meanwhile W. M. sought 400k.p.h. (250m.p.h.) (Photo overleaf.) from its V6 twin turbo machine and Toyota showed good speed from its single turbo four.

STATE OF

THE ART

STATE OF THE ART
GALLERY

Le Mans 1989 saw Mercedes proudly heading the grid, dispelling unhappy memories of the 1988 withdrawal. In 1989 everything worked for the Sauber team and the Silver Arrows pulled through to win the classic.

The 1988 McLaren-Honda was easily the most outstanding turbo car of the Eighties. It won 15 of 16 World Championship races: an unparalleled level of mid-engined era succes. This is Prost at Imola.

The 1989 Lola-Nissan was one of the last cars to be designed prior to the switch to 3.5 litre atmospheric engines for FIA Formula One and Sports-Prototype racing. Its strong heart was a 3.5 litre V8 turbo.

Senna in the low-line 1988 McLaren-Honda. The super-successful 2.5 bar turbo car did not only have a very effective engine, it also had the most advanced chassis of its year in Murray's BT55-influenced MP4/4.

Fuel stop for a Mercedes team en route to a historic 1989 Le Mans victory. The Mercedes turbocar was not swifter than the Jaguar V12 but stayed the distance in good health, unlike the defending trophy holder . . .

CITROËN
MICHELIN
AUTOMOBILE CLUB DE L'O
Castrol
SHOEI
MERCEDES-BENZ

McLaren-Honda

On the face of it Formula One technical regulations for 1988 limiting turbocharged engines to 2.5 bar and a 150 litre race fuel allocation gave rival 3.5 litre atmospheric engines with unlimited fuel a more than even chance. By the early Eighties atmospheric racing engines had shown a potential to produce 180 b.h.p. per litre so 630 b.h.p. was the target for the 3.5 litre runners. Turbocharged racing engines had never produced significantly more than 170 b.h.p. per litre per bar boost so a comparable output was conceivable for the pop off valve controlled 1.5 litre turbo pumping two and a half times atmospheric pressure.

Certainly, for the early Eighties when the pioneering turbo engines were exploiting that sort of level of boost 630 b.h.p. was a representative output at 2.5 bar. Power had subsequently climbed steeply with increasing boost. As we have seen though, the spiral of rising boost and power that started around 1982/'83 had been made possible only through the development of engine management systems and special fuels.

By the mid Eighties the Formula One turbo engine was a very special animal. Whereas the early Eighties turbo engine running 2.5 bar for 630 b.h.p. or thereabouts had a compression ratio in the region of 7.0:1, the highly developed 1987 4.0 bar engine sometimes ran a ratio as high as 9.0:1. The potential of a 2.5 bar engine with an advanced engine management system and special fuel and a high compression ratio was unknown.

Further, by 1987 Renault and Honda had built turbo V6 engines capable of running at speeds in excess of 13,000 r.p.m. Never before had Formula One engines spun that fast. Power is a function of boost and revs and each 1,000 r.p.m. would be worth an extra 40 to 50 b.h.p. to a 2.5 bar turbo. Equally, a 3.5 litre atmo could benefit from high r.p.m. and in 1989 new generation engines would soar towards 14,000 r.p.m. reaching for 700 b.h.p. However, the Cosworth and Judd V8s fielded in 1988 were traditional designs incapable of exceeding 12,000 r.p.m.

In the event, the lean burn, high compression 2.5 bar engines developed by Honda and Ferrari for 1988 ran to 13,000 r.p.m. and beyond. Cosworth admitted to no more than 565 b.h.p. for its 1988 DFZ engine at 11,500 r.p.m. with a shade under 600 b.h.p. at 11,000 r.p.m. for its modified DFR. Honda later admitted to 685 b.h.p. for its 2.5 bar turbo at 12,500 r.p.m., and to a 13,500 r.p.m. potential.

Of course, the 150 litre race ration must also be taken into account when considering the 1988 turbo versus atmo contest. The Honda engine was rated a very conservative 620 b.h.p./ 12,500 r.p.m. at its 'minimum fuel consumption' setting – which was required throughout an entire race only on rare occasion. The rival atmo engines drank over 200 litres per race, thus with refuelling banned the Honda runners – McLaren and Lotus – and the other turbo users had the enforced chassis advantage of a significantly smaller and lighter fuel tank.

That potential car packaging gain McLaren used to the full thanks to the arrival of Gordon Murray as Technical Director. As we have seen, Murray had been responsible for the disastrous 'lay down' Brabham BT55-BMW of 1986. Having moved to the McLaren team he spent 1987 evolving a similarly low-line car for McLaren, persuading Honda to lower the transverse dimensions, in particular the height of its V6 as far as was practical. The key development was a lower sump and crankshaft in conjunction with a smaller, 5½ inch diameter clutch.

Rival designers had only seen the BT55's dismal track record. Murray had seen its wind tunnel promise and knew that the concept of radically reclining the driver for an ultra-low fuselage was a major breakthrough. The McLaren MP4 chassis was straightforward but its fuselage was extremely low and the cramped cockpit was tailored very closely to its compulsorily laid back driver. The same thing had happened to Jim Clark in 1962 and Senna and Prost were similarly jockey-sized to the benefit of the operation. Damn comfort: improved airflow in Clark's day reduced drag, now the better feed to the rear wing provided a significant increase in downforce. In 1988 Lotus had the same engine and tyres as McLaren but its traditional chassis was beaten from the moment it rolled out of the workshop.

The success of a racing car is not the success of a chassis alone, or an engine alone, or a driver alone but is the success of an overall package in which all elements are essential. In 1988 McLaren had two superb drivers and an excellent team infrastructure to fully exploit the potential of its pioneering chassis and Honda's remarkable, highly developed if short lived 2.5 bar turbo engine.

The 1988 Honda engine, the RA168E, was notably light with aluminium for the block and heads and magnesium for most other parts. Its total weight was only 146kg. The bore was only 79mm. to keep the piston crown small leaving a relatively long stroke of 50.8mm. (a stroke:bore ratio of 0.643:1) while the included valve angle was a narrow 32 degrees to run with a lightly notched flat top piston in a pent roof chamber with a squish band surround. The compression ratio was 9.4:1.

The 13,500 r.p.m. potential was allowed by a gear driven valve actuation system featuring finger cam followers. The unusual finger followers allowed high load springs with a reduction in equivalent inertia weight. The RA168E also boasted a highly developed engine management system with distributorless ignition and two injectors per cylinder. The fuel was pre heated to assist atomisation, a crucial consideration under conditions of low boost.

The predecessor of the RA168E was the 4.0 bar RA167E run in 1987 which produced 1010 b.h.p. at 12,000 r.p.m. with torque of 67.7kgm. given a charge air temperature of 40 degrees centigrade, the optimum fuel:air ratio and a special fuel containing 84% toluene. The compression ratio of the RA167E was 7.4:1, significantly lower than that of the Ferrari or the Cosworth rival. The maximum 685 b.h.p. of the 2.5 bar engine was produced on a slightly richer mix (its higher compression ratio lowered the detonation threshold) at the same intake air temperature, with the same fuel. In both cases the ignition timing was adjusted in the light of detonation sensor readings. With the lower boost engine it was possible to improve the stability of combustion, this having been assisted by revised porting and fuel injection to suit the new conditions.

Honda discovered from engine data logging that full and closed throttle conditions dominated turbo engine race driving and thus concentrated upon full rather than part throttle fuel consumption. For a power output of 620 b.h.p./12,500 r.p.m. consumption was only 200gms./b.h.p./hr. given a very lean mixture, a charge air temperature of 70 degrees centigrade and a fuel temperature of 80 degrees centigrade. Where circuit conditions called for less strict consumption a richer mixture and a lower charge temperature were possible producing increased power.

The increased charge temperature promoting better atomisation was achieved through bye-passing a given proportion of the charge air from the aftercooler. Fuel consumption decreased – albeit at a cost in terms of power – as temperature increased from 40 to 70 degrees and at the same time the ignition timing was backed off since the higher temperature lowered the detonation threshold. By the time the charge temperature had reached 70 degrees the timing had been retarded as far as was practical – higher temperatures consequently had an adverse effect on consumption as well as power output.

Heating the fuel had a similar – though less pronounced – effect to that of higher charge air temperature, promoting good atomisation. The problem of atomisation was pronounced since a toluene-based fuel is difficult to atomise at ambient temperature, though has the effect of reducing combustion chamber temperatures. Leaning off the fuel mixture naturally decreased fuel consumption. The limit of mixture weakening was found to be a deterioration in transient engine response which

made the engine undriveable rather than detonation.

Honda revealed interesting studies regarding fuel composition, noting by way of introduction that 'it sometimes appears that differences in fuel ingredients effect knocking properties, even though the RON (octane rating) of the fuels is the same. The development of a fuel with good knocking properties under high speed and boost conditions is essential for adopting a high compression ratio'. Further, in the face of a race fuel ration it was clearly desirable to develop a dense – 'heavy' – fuel, thereby packing more energy into a tank limited by volume rather than fuel weight (in this case the ration was a volume of 150 litres, fuel weight unspecified).

Honda tested toluene contents of 30, 60 and 84%, mixing appropriate amounts of normal heptane and isoctane so as to register a RON of 102 as per Formula One regulations. Toluene is very dense and the 84% mix proved most effective in terms of power and consumption. The 84% mix was the best in terms of reduced susceptibility to detonation and this allowed advanced ignition timing which was in the interest of good consumption, as was the significantly increased density of the mix.

The 1988 Honda RA168E was a remarkable engine, producing almost 700 b.h.p. from only 2.5 litres in spite of a 2.5 bar boost limit. Engine management via computer and special fuel were the keys to high b.m.e.p., with unusually high r.p.m. producing unusually high power.

The low line McLaren MP4/4 with Honda 2.5 bar engine set a
new standard for turbocharged Grand Prix car success during the
1988 season. Here Senna leads team mate Prost en route to the
seventh one-two finish of the RA168E-dominated year in the
Hungarian Grand Prix.

The Lola-Nissan made its debut at Dijon in May 1989. It was an all-new package, specifically designed from a clean sheet of paper for Group C racing in 1989/'90. A lightly turbocharged V8 engine produced a highly impressive 800b.h.p. race power given Group C fuel limitations.

Lola-Nissan

Only two companies produced clean sheet of paper engines for Eighties Group C, Nissan and Toyota. Neither engine arrived before the late Eighties, by which time the fuel limitation formula was well established, its challenge well explored. Both Nissan and Toyota plumped for 90 degree V8s displacing 3.5 litres and pressurised by twin turbochargers. Nissan started its V8 programme over a year before Toyota and by 1989 with its mark three unit arguably had the more refined engine. This was married to an advanced chassis produced by Lola, a relatively large and long established British based company with more wide ranging expertise than the small Japanese operation which produced the Toyota V8 chassis.

The Nissan V8 programme emerged in 1987 with a 3.0 litre twin turbo engine that exploited production-based four valve head technology with finger cam followers. The VEJ30 engine was not a success and in August of '87 a new department was created within the Yokosuka, Japan based Nissan Central Laboratories to create a replacement V8 unit. The department was headed by Yoshimasa Hayashi, a new chief designer for the race engine programme who made a fresh start. Hayashi was able to produce new block and heads while for logistical reasons retaining the VEJ30 crankshaft and thus the bore and stroke dimensions and cylinder location.

The VRH30 was gear driven off the front end and this feature was retained for the new 3.5 litre VRH35 engine designed by Hayashi for 1989. A 90 degree V8 equipped with a flat plane crankshaft runs as two four cylinder engines sharing a common crankshaft and is subject to significant unbalanced secondary forces that manifest themselves as side to side shake of the crank. That torsional vibration is transmitted through a gear drive and can be a source of gear train failure, particularly in a lightweight drive system.

The VRH30 had a relatively heavy drive train but for the VRH35 Hayashi sought to lighten the gears and camshafts, this in turn reducing the capability of the system to absorb vibration. In response, the gears were mounted on needle or – as in the case of the majority – ball bearings and a mass damper was fitted at the head of each camshaft, acting like a flywheel. However, each damper weighed only 500gms so the desired effect was subtle.

The VRH35 was an all new engine designed with two major objectives in mind. Firstly, it was intended to meet the requirements of Lola as part of a fully integrated engine and chassis package. The VRH30 had been designed without such co-operation and ran in a suitably adapted March chassis as a semi-stressed member. Lola requested a fully stressed engine with accessories carefully located to fit its desired ground effect aerodynamic package. Secondly, it was intended that the VRH35 should be lighter and more powerful than the VRH30 and this called for the freedom to alter the bore and stroke dimensions and the bore pitch.

Granted such freedom, Hayashi opted to retain the 85mm. bore of the VRH30 while introducing an 11mm. longer, 77mm. stroke for a total displacement of 3496cc. His aim was to design the engine to operate at a low maximum speed – 8,000r.p.m. – and with only light turbocharging for good fuel efficiency. The chosen displacement and stroke provided good torque, Hayashi looking to strong yet fuel efficient b.m.e.p. rather than

engine speed for power.

An 8.0:1 compression ratio was found optimum with 99 RON pump petrol and the long stroke configuration and an improved combustion chamber design helped give the 3.5 litre unit a massive 80kgm. torque from 4,500 right through to 7,200r.p.m. pumping 2.2 bar. Indeed, from 3,600 to the 7,600 maximum Le Mans race rev limit torque was never less than 75kgm. Race power was a solid 800b.h.p. at 7,600r.p.m. on 2.2 bar.

The combustion chamber design was the product of a lot of research and the new chamber featured a narrower valve angle – the exact angle undisclosed – and a squish band. The VRH30 porting was retained while the compression ratio was lower. The only gap between the piston crown and the head squish band at top dead centre was the thickness of the steel head gasket which replaced the Cooper ring plus optional metal gasket of the VRH30.

The bore pitch – the distance between the axis of adjacent cylinders – was reduced from 120mm. to less than 110mm. which called for thinner cylinder walls but produced a shorter, lighter, more compact engine of increased rigidity. As well as saving weight this improved chassis packaging potential and assisted the move to a stressed structure.

In terms of basic construction, the VRH35 followed the VRH30, with Nikasil liners in a half-skirt block, oil gallery pistons driving titanium rods and so forth. This year an aluminium liner was retained for Le Mans while the sump pan and cam covers were strengthened in line with the change from semi to fully stressed engine. Further, head retention was improved via a switch from six to eight bolts per cylinder while there were extra bolts, and larger diameter bolt specifications for the ladder frame.

The EMS was changed from NEC to JECS, with wastegate control, the detonation sensors and distributorless ignition retained. The prototype VRH35 first ran on the dyno in November 1988 and very few problems were experienced, with the target 800b.h.p. seen from the outset. Already Lola was working on the '89 chassis, discussions having commenced at Le Mans in 1988. The unveiling of the carbon fibre chassis Toyota V8 Group C car in October 1988 spurred the Nissan board into finalising the deal with Lola for a state of the art machine embodying Formula One knowledge.

Lola was supplying Grand Prix cars for the Larrousse team and had produced the base car from which Electramotive had developed its highly successful Nissan V6 turbo GTP challenger. As we have seen, Lola had requested a stressed engine with improved packaging potential, and this requirement Hayashi had been pleased to accommodate. Lola had developed a deep understanding of the application of advanced composite materials to racing car construction – running its own composite production department – and was thus well placed to produce an enormously rigid yet light chassis structure.

Aerodynamic considerations dominated the chassis design. Lola had a long standing relationship with the Cranfield research centre, home of one of the finest rolling road wind tunnels in the world and here a lot of scale model work was undertaken. Early on Lola boss Eric Broadley was supplied with a very accurate mock up of the V8 and he was able to optimise the body and underwing shape to a very fine degree of tolerance

149

without seeing a finished engine.

Wind tunnel work commenced in October 1988 with the major parameters the dictates of the 1989 Group C regulations and the V8 engine configuration. The aim was to produce a Le Mans aerodynamic package first, which would them be adapted for regular circuits. In essence, the Lola followed the TWR Jaguar approach to Group C aerodynamics with the entire underbody region ahead of the rear diffuser tunnels forming a flat area headed by the nose splitter. The Le Mans package had a shorter splitter and shorter tunnels than the sprint alternative for less drag on the three and a half mile long Mulsanne straight.

Le Mans also saw a lower mounted single rather than twin element rear wing. The body shape was standard for both applications and featured a front mounted water radiator and front fed but side mounted aftercoolers. The sides of the car were fitted at the base with horizontal lips to confuse air rushing down the flanks of the body towards the low pressure underbody region. Further, the rear wheels were sealed in via detachable covers. The regulation height restricted tunnels rose either side of the engine block and transaxle with the sides of the transaxle smooth and forming part of the tunnel wall in the interests of both maximum tunnel width and transmission cooling. The dampers were mounted over the transaxle to help keep the tunnels free of suspension components.

The monocoque tub was formed of carbon fibre skins over Kevlar honeycomb with Nomex honeycomb in areas of complex shaping. A steel roll cage was added as per the regulations while the engine was bolted to the back of the tub with sump, cam cover and block mounting points. The bellhousing was a bespoke magnesium casting with integral oil tank and linked the engine to a standard Hewland heavy duty five speed VGC gearbox.

Brakes were supplied by Brembo, cross-drilled ventilated discs stopped by four pot calipers. Special attention was paid to disc and wheel bearing cooling with the uprights designed to carefully feed air adjacent to the bearings thence out through the disc. The suspension – pushrod front and rear – employed steel fabricated uprights and wishbones and steel springs over Koni dampers, the spring/damper units scuttle mounted at the front. Lola's experience with Formula One and Formula 3000 chassis saw the car initially very stiffly sprung in the interest of avoiding pitch and roll to the benefit of the operation of the underwing. However, it was found that a significantly heavier sports-prototype with a higher centre of gravity intended for longer races involving a change of driver required more suspension movement.

More suspension movement gave a more supple ride and was more 'driver friendly' if slightly compromising of aerodynamic performance. The higher degree of suspension movement combined with the very stiff chassis saw excellent tyre wear rates while the car was set up to promote sufficient rearward weight transfer under acceleration for good traction. The Nissan V8 supplied impressive torque but it was necessary to get that onto the track.

The combination of high torque and a stiff chassis saw Nissan request a new sports-prototype tyre from Dunlop: a high profile 19" rear radial. The large diameter ensured a longer and thus larger footprint area to the benefit of traction but the bespoke tyre did not appear before mid season, which was a major development headache for the new car. Another problem was poor braking preformance, for which there was no obvious cause. It was not until the car was tuned into carbon brakes that it stopped well and one cast iron disc equipped car was shunted out of contention at Le Mans when the driver lost control under braking. The Lola-Nissan was too new to shine at Le Mans in 1989 but its performance in the early part of the race confirmed its excellent engine and chassis potential.

Sauber-Mercedes

The Sauber-Mercedes was not the most advanced of the 1989 sports-prototype contenders but it was the most successful and it won the Le Mans 24 hour race. That was the last great stock block triumph of the Eighties. It was also somewhat unexpected given Sauber's pre-'89 Le Mans record with Mercedes: three years of participation but only one year at the start, let alone the finish!

As we have seen, the Sauber-Mercedes adventure began in 1985 with Mader engine preparation and a single – C8 – Le Mans entry that dramatically somersaulted out of contention at the Mulsanne brow during qualifying. Highlight of a short, five race 1986 programme was an unexpected victory in the wet at the 'Ring. In 1987 the programme was again only five races but there was a new C9 chassis and two examples, still with Mader engines, were pushed onto the Le Mans grid. Although neither made it through the night Sauber came away from Le Mans with the lap record and there was another record at Spa Francorchamps, where the C9 model secured pole position.

For 1988 Daimler Benz came out and gave the improving Sauber team full and open works backing and the increased commitment was immediately rewarded with a win at Jerez. Following a second disappointing withdrawal from Le Mans – this time due to tyre failures – Sauber bounced back to win at the Norisring and Brno. Indeed, over the second half of the 1988 season the Sauber-Mercedes was the fastest Group C sports-prototype and a total of five World Sports-Prototype Championship wins matched defending Champion Jaguar's '88 total. Nevertheless, TWR Jaguar lifted the '88 World titles.

Sauber went into 1989 still with the 1987-launched C9 chassis but with a new four valve version of the Mercedes engine. The chassis, in fact, was based on a Sauber aluminium monocoque designed in the early Eighties for a BMW in line four propelled car. It was produced in-house at Sauber's Hinwal, Switzerland base and was fitted with carbon fibre based side and nose boxes. A frames ran from the back of the tub to carry the Mercedes V8 semi-stressed, while further projecting tubular structures linked a transaxle-straddling rear crossmember to the back of the tub.

The rear spring/damper units were positioned horizontally and longitudinally, running along one of the upper engine bay tubes and worked through a compact rocker and crank arrangement from the forward leg of the upper wishbone. This kept the units out of the high tunnels that ran either side of the engine on the '87 car. In '88 the tunnels had to be reduced in height following regulation changes but the damper position remained. The C9 ran heavy duty dampers and hard rear springs and only rarely a rear anti roll bar. Leaving the bar off was good for traction and enhanced rear tyre life.

With bags of torque from its big capacity V8 turbo the Sauber-Mercedes was notoriously harsh upon its rear tyres, and was hard work to keep running in the transmission department. Sauber ran a specially fabricated c.w.p. and differential in its strengthened Hewland VGC five speed gearbox, fed from a conventional triple plate clutch. A magnesium bellhousing was a bespoke Sauber production while the case and its internals was essentially standard Hewland. Gears, c.w.p. and half-shafts were new for each race.

Aside from the rear damper location, the suspension was conventional front and rear. Wishbones and uprights were steel while the hubs were aluminium without drivepegs. The pegs were formed with the wheel rim and were thus fresh with each change of rim. The rear rims were of 19″ diameter and were shod with Michelin radial tyres.

The water radiator was located in the nose, the aftercoolers in the sides where they were fed through NACA flank ducts. The body was of conventional shape with the rear wing outrigged on a single central post. The underwing was a conventional late Eighties design, flat apart from the tunnels and headed by a variable-length splitter. The car was stopped by Brembo four pot brakes, carbon generally for 1989 when the so called C9/88 chassis carried the four valve V8.

Tests showed that the four valve version of the M117 engine offered slightly enhanced fuel consumption, giving Sauber a little more race power. The four valve engine retained an 8.5:1 compression ratio and had a pent roof chamber with a 37.5 degree included valve angle surrounded by a squish band. The piston crown was slightly dished within the squish area and had shallow valve clearance notches. Ignition was via a single central plug. Seven different head and piston designs were tested prior to finalisation of the combustion chamber detailing, though the overall chamber architecture was dictated via the engine's production base.

The four valve engine was derived from the 500SL four valve production car engine, this retaining a linerless alloy block derived from the two valve M117 engine. However, the block was a little lower and the con rod was shorter, lowering the centre of gravity which was an important consideration given the weight added to the top end.

The same 'super tuning' process was employed to produce the M119 four valve race engine as for the same displacement two valve unit and thus the internals included Mahle oil gallery pistons and so forth. The four valve head had an integral tappet block and was driven via chain, as per the two valve head. The race camshafts were of the same built up type running in five plain bearings and driving steel bucket tappets with the usual shim adjustment. Twin steel springs closed the valves which were sodium cooled with a nimonic foot. Valve dimensions and porting was as per the production engine, each head a production line casting.

The four valve engine was fitted with a Motronic MP2.7 rather than 1.7 EMS, with two injectors per cylinder, one pointing into each inlet valve's channel. Otherwise the injection and ignition systems were as per the two valve engine, as was the throttle system. However, the twin injector arrangement posed a problem of inferior atomisation since each injector passed only half as much fuel. On the other hand volumetric efficiency was improved at high speed, though with forced induction this was not a major gain. The key advantage was slightly improved combustion thanks to a more compact chamber with a central plug and for a given power level the four valve unit was more fuel efficient than the two valve engine.

The normal race boost was 1.6 bar absolute, providing 700 – 720b.h.p. race power at 7,000r.p.m. with up to 2.0 bar and 820b.h.p. for qualifying when the same 7,000r.p.m. limit was imposed. The engine posed few development problems but its 220kg. weight was a challenge for Sauber, as was its 5mm. higher centre of gravity. However, for 1989 minimum weight was up from 850kg. (a target that the two valve car had never reached) to 900kg.

Le Mans 1989

TURBO versus ATMOS

It was the last great confrontation of the Eighties between atmospheric and turbocharged engines. A confrontation with no clear-cut favourite. From the inception of Group C in 1982 until 1987 a Porsche turbo engine had won Le Mans without fail. In 1988 a Jaguar atmo engine had finally broken the stranglehold. In 1989 Jaguar was back with its proven equipment while Nissan and Toyota made greater efforts than ever before with new turbocharged cars. With well tested turbocharged machines Porsche, giving factory support to tough private teams, could not be counted out, nor could Daimler Benz. Le Mans 1989 was a battle between five manufacturers, with the weight of numbers on the side of the turbo.

Although Jaguar was the defending World Sports-Prototype Champion marque, since June 1988 the Mercedes turbo challenge had been growing ever stronger. Indeed, by June 1989 the Sauber C9 was the car to beat in regular World Championship races. Statistics, however, were against a Daimler Benz Le Mans victory. History had demanded time and again that a major manufacturer should wait until at least its third attempt to win the great 24 hour race. With Mader Mercedes engines the Sauber team had started once, in 1987. With works Mercedes engines, not at all.

Experience is vital not only to seek out and eradicate every weakness of the car but also to find the secret of a competitive Le Mans race pace. The three and a half mile long Mulsanne straight puts a unique premium on drag reduction. Set up for a normal circuit, a ground effect sports-prototype produces enough downforce to run upside down on the ceiling at 130m.p.h. while enjoying a lift to drag ratio in the region of 3.5:1. In this high downforce 'sprint' configuration it runs to around 180m.p.h. with downforce increasing as the square of speed, exceeding twice the car's weight at top speed.

On the endless Mulsanne designers seek a maximum speed well in excess of 180m.p.h. Since downforce increases with the square of velocity, clearly it can increase alarmingly on the Mulsanne where it is unwanted and brings the danger of excessive component stress. Less downforce, the lower drag that implies and consequently improved Mulsanne speed can pay dividends. Often there is a choice between a high speed/low drag configuration and a higher downforce/higher cornering speed configuration for a given Le Mans lap time. The first option offers less component stress and – significantly – will be lighter on fuel consumption, allowing a faster Group C race pace.

Final preparations for the Sauber-Mercedes trio prior to the 1989 Le Mans 24 hour race. This was the first year of Sauber participation with works Daimler Benz V8 turbo engines yet all three cars would pull through to the finish. With two of the three in the top two places . . .

The specialised low drag Le Mans aerodynamic package is particularly difficult to optimise since a good lift to drag ratio is harder to achieve at lower levels of downforce. For example, a ratio of 3.0:1 is easily surpassed by a well designed high downforce package but is an exceptional figure for an effective low drag Le Mans car. The arrival of TWR Jaguar to challenge Porsche saw a higher level of research into this area than ever before.

TWR started its Le Mans aerodynamic studies over the winter of '85-'86 and by the 1988 race had conducted something in the region of 400 scale model Le Mans runs in the Imperial College London rolling road wind tunnel. The XJR-9LM had arguably the most highly developed of all low drag Le Mans aerodynamic packages (with L:D undisclosed). In contrast, Porsche and Sauber had employed fixed floor wind tunnel model testing. Porsche had the underbody handicap of a wide flat six engine while Sauber had a lot less wind tunnel experience than either of the '87 front runners. Arguably, the tyre failures that kept the C9 out of the '88 race were provoked by excessive downforce on the Mulsanne, though this theory has never been confirmed.

The highly developed TWR aerodynamic package was the key to Jaguar's 1988 atmo success and, further refined, promised to keep the 7.0 litre two valve V12 engine in front in 1989. For 1989 TWR had a round 750b.h.p. from its proven Le Mans engine specification. That was unimpressive by the qualifying standard of '89 but allied to effective aerodynamics was sufficient to produce a second row grid position for two of the four cars and a potential race winning pace. Indeed, as the race shaped up it was clear that Jaguar had the speed to beat its German rivals fairly and squarely, so long as weather conditions remained fair and there was no extended pace car period to save fuel that could subsequently be used more effectively by a turbo engine.

The weather did indeed stay fair and there was no lengthy pace car period yet from early on the multi-car Jaguar challenge crumbled. Overnight the team tried unsuccessfully to claw back. Eventually two cars fell out with valve train failures. The two valve TWR V12 engine employs production based head castings and retains the production valve train design, albeit with bespoke components. In its production roots lies the Le Mans danger: head castings and valve train components – particularly the large and consequently heavy valves themselves, and the springs needed to close them – are a potential source of failure over 24 hours. TWR had come to expect to lose one car to head casting or valve train failure each year at Le Mans. In 1989 it lost two cars, and its two other cars were afflicted by a transmission problem. Lammers/Tambay/Gilbert-Scott could manage no better than fourth, Ferte/Ferte/Salazar eighth.

Like the earlier TWR Group C cars, the XJR-9 employed a well proven heavy duty March gearbox evolved from the classic Hewland dog-selection design with additional bearing support for the gear shafts. It appears that on this occasion a sub-contracted component had been incorrectly manufactured, leaving a weak link in the transmission that the stress of the 24 hour race unforgivingly brought to light. There was an air of disbelief in the TWR camp after the race, in stark contrast to the quiet confidence of Saturday afternoon.

By Saturday evening it had become evident that only Nissan had the race pace to beat Jaguar in a straight fight, though two of the Joest Porsches looked very strong. While Joest could hope to sustain its challenge, Nissan – beset with teething bothers – was by no means ready to turn its speed into a win. In fact, within just four laps one of three Nissan R89Cs had fallen by the wayside, victim of an accident caused partly by an under-developed braking system. Poor braking was a mysterious ailment of the otherwise generally impressive if rather stiffly sprung new Lola produced chassis. In the light of the problem the Nissan Motorsports Europe team had enthusiastically adopted the high Mu-value carbon-metallic pads used so effectively by the Electramotive

Nissan IMSA team. However, not until the car was equipped with carbon-carbon discs and pads later in the season would it stop well. Cast iron discs are essential at Le Mans and it was the volatile combination of difficult braking and a keen, impatient young driver finding himself in an extremely competitive car that had cut the Nissan challenge.

The superb race pace of the Lola-Nissan was confirmed by the Brabham car during Saturday night, though brake disc changes kept it well back from the front. The surprising speed of the Japanese car is explained by a combination of a good aerodynamic package and an 800b.h.p. race engine. The aerodynamic form had been developed by Lola specifically for Le Mans using sophisticated rolling road wind tunnel model testing. Lola had a long sports-prototype involvement on which to draw and although 1989 was the first year of life for the RC89 it must have been only marginally less aerodynamically efficient than the XJR-9. That supposed deficit was more than bridged by a superior race engine.

As we have noted, Nissan and Toyota were the only two companies ever to have produced clean sheet of paper Group C Le Mans engines. The 3.5 litre Nissan V8 was effectively the marque's third attempt and its claimed 800b.h.p. in race trim was realistic given the compromises under which the stock block Jaguar V12 produced Allan Scott's 'no bullshit' "750b.h.p." As we have seen, the '89 Nissan V8 had been optimised for Group C in every respect – right from basic configuration to compression ratio – following two learning years and was fully tailored to its state of the art chassis.

The Nissan V8 was specifically a race rather than a qualifying engine and maximum r.p.m. for the Le Mans grind was 7,600. Right from 3,600r.p.m. up to that level torque was in excess of 75kg.m. and from 4,500 to 7,200r.p.m. it was a steady 80kg.m given the regular 2.2 bar absolute in the plenum. At 2.2 bar absolute the third generation Nissan V8 was 24 hour dependable on the bench but success first time out in a 'raw' chassis would have been asking too much.

The two other RC89s both suffered engine failure. One failure was due to a broken water pipe on the chassis, the other was a consequence of excessive charge cooling. The team hadn't had much time in which to get the cooling right on the Brabham car and an overcooled charge led to poor atomisation which in turn led to droplets of fuel squeezing past the piston. The fuel mingled with the oil, diluting it and after 19 hours a main bearing seized.

In qualifying trim the Nissan V8 hadn't shone as brightly as the rival Toyota V8, but that only reflected contrasting approaches to the exercise. For Nissan the engine adaptation had been an alternative chip to run with a richer mix plus an extra 200r.p.m. for 820b.h.p. (as quoted for the Mercedes engine). Meanwhile, Toyota had run a special higher power qualifying-only version of its new engine reputed to develop four figure horse-power.

The Toyota V8 was a clean sheet of paper replacement for the marque's 2.1 litre in line four cylinder production-based turbo engine. A displacement of 3.2 litres had been identified as ideal for a Group C turbo engine and given that figure eight cylinders was seen as the optimum, with a 90 degree configuration the best in the light of chassis considerations. Bore and stroke were set at 82mm × 75mm. and the unit was designed to run to 9,000r.p.m. in qualifying (with a 10,000r.p.m. potential). It was an all aluminium four valve d.o.h.c. engine run as two four cylinder engines thanks to a flat plane crankshaft.

A conventional late Eighties racing engine in terms of basic technology, the electronically managed Toyota 89CV ran an 8.5:1 compression ratio and was designed to be blown to a maximum of 2.9 bar absolute plenum pressure. Race boost was set at 2.4 bar absolute at which the engine was rated 800b.h.p. at 8,000r.p.m. with 80kg.m. torque at 5,000r.p.m. In qualifying 9,000r.p.m. and 2.9 bar in the plenum released 950b.h.p. The truth is that only on the bench had the magic 1000b.h.p. been witnessed, an ambitious 3.1 bar pumping out 1060b.h.p. – arguably a record for a pump-petrol-fuelled race engine.

Of course, 950b.h.p. was comfortably in excess of the qualifying power run by Jaguar, Nissan, Porsche and Mercedes. It propelled a brand new chassis designed and produced in Japan by the Toms team in conjunction with Toyota. This was a clean sheet of paper design with ground effect aerodynamics tested in the full sized Toyota fixed floor wind tunnel, with the downforce checked via a load cell on the advanced Toyota test track.

Nevertheless, the Toyota 89CV was not as aerodynamically sophisticated as the European chassis it ran against. Toyota announced the unimpressive lift to drag ratio of 3.3:1 in sprint trim falling to the superficially excellent figure of 3.2:1 at Le Mans. In fact, the Japanese car had exceedingly high downforce by Le Mans standards with few changes from the regular sprint package. Given 950b.h.p. Toyota could afford to pull a lot of drag in qualifying and still reach high speed on the Mulsanne. Its 250m.p.h. clocking was matched only by the fastest Mercedes which ran 820b.h.p. and far less drag in a successful quest to pip Toyota to pole.

The 950b.h.p., 250m.p.h. Toyota Q-car was the team's T-car and consequently its second fastest qualifying time

was disallowed: Toyota started its two regular 89CV cars from mid grid. Without a slippery fuel efficient chassis its race pace was unimpressive, particularly in view of the claimed 800b.h.p. (from higher revs and higher boost than the similar Nissan figure, it should be noted). One car suffered driveshaft failure, stranding it out on the circuit. Rival marques ran a spool – a solid link between the driveshafts which replaces the differential – to be able to limp back to the pits in such an event. The second Toyota had earlier suffered engine failure, after only three hours...

So it was that with the collapse of the Jaguar challenge the 1989 Le Mans race was left a battle of German turbocars: Porsche flat 6 versus Mercedes V8. Although Porsche had withdrawn its works Group C team it had spread its factory race engineers among its key privateer teams and had supplied a number of factory engines. With a total of 17 962 models plus a pair of Cougar-Porsches fielded by nine teams – the list including the super-professional Joest, Kremer, Brun, Lloyd and Schuppan outfits – Porsche had half the Group C1, category 1 field, a highly enviable depth of representation.

Joest Racing was the top-rated Porsche Le Mans team given its past back to back victories ('84/'85) and from Weissach Norbert Singer, father of the 956/962C joined

 Nissan V8 in the Lola that showed excellent race speed at Le Mans in 1989. The car was too new to hope to run without teething troubles but it was very quick, thanks to an excellent engine output married to very effective aerodynamics. The V8 performed at very low revs.

The key to Group C Le Mans car performance is the ground effect underbody, as revealed here on the scrutineering lift. The Nissan has a flat underbody ahead of its tunnels aside from a slight indent between the front wheels fed from a short nose splitter.

it for the weekend. Significantly, Joest had engine expertise and thus shunned the factory engines, its own units prepared as usual by the unassuming Mike Demont. Superficially, the Demont engine was similar to the 3.0 litre Motronic MP1.7 equipped, 9.0:1 compression ratio factory engine of 1988 and Demont used the Weissach dyno for his mapping. However, he would not confirm the '89 compression ratio and spoke of only 700b.h.p. at 2.1 bar absolute as race power running to 8,400r.p.m. (as in qualifying when 2.4 bar was employed). He did admit that his engine was firmly based on the experience of the factory in '88 – the first year the MP1.7 system had been employed – and in practice Joest's race power was clearly a very healthy figure, a match for Jaguar . . .

The three Joest cars were all based on conventional 962C chassis adapted to suit Goodyear radial tyres and ran the Singer-devised Le Mans aerodynamic package first seen on the '88 factory cars. Singer will not disclose aerodynamic performance figures for this design. His '88/'89 package was a clever redesign to suit the low tunnel regulations introduced for 1988 and it retained the classic Porsche long tail. To some extent Porsche had benefited from the regulation revision relative to rival cars since its wide flat 6 engine had then become less of a handicap.

Singer's retention of a full length tail with a sideplate mounted wing sitting over the rear deck was unusual. Rivals generally opted for a shorter tail plus a remote wing on a central gearbox-supported post (a pattern followed by some private Porsche efforts including an '89 Joest sprint car). The rear wing acts as a powerful underbody extractor device, pulling air from the diffuser tunnels, and the wing/rear deck/underbody spatial relationship is crucial to ground effect aerodynamic performance. For Le Mans TWR Jaguar had introduced the concept of a short tail plus a long chord wing at deck height. The wing then acted, in effect, as an extension of the tail: the air saw the XJRLM as a long tail car.

Extensive rolling road wind tunnel modelling by Mazda suggests that the Jaguar aerodynamic solution was particularly effective, but that a higher mounted shorter chord (similarly single element) remote (gearbox post supported) wing could be made to work well for Le Mans. Sauber ran the latter option but Mazda – significantly – followed Jaguar's lead for its 1989 Le Mans package. The little rotary engined GTP class car ran very swiftly, too, gaining useful Mulsanne speed.

Meanwhile, Porsche clearly had another sound answer to the Le Mans challenge, and a very strong engine given the Daimler-Benz pioneered MP1.7 engine management system. Indeed, in '88 the Stuck/Bell/Ludwig MP1.7 factory car had given Jaguar a good run, finishing on the same lap as the winner, in spite of losing a couple of laps early on. The '89 combination of Stuck and Wollek saw the star Joest car move into the lead as the Jaguar effort crumbled and well in command at midnight. Alas, just over an hour later Demont found air in the water. A nut had vibrated loose, a problem that had never previously occurred he shrugged. Thereafter, the water system had to be regularly topped up and further delays included a pits fire and a clutch malady. The upshot was third place, just seven laps adrift of the winning Mercedes after 24 often trying hours.

The second 'fast' Joest car crewed by Jelinski and Raphanel was equally unfortunate, a cracked head casting leading to retirement before midnight after a strong challenge for second had underlined similar winning potential. Again the unprecedented failure mystified Demont. It was clear that either key Joest car could have won given the sort of untroubled run that brought the team victory in the mid Eighties. No other Porsche propelled team featured strongly but Reinhold Joest had (as in '84) provided a good substitute for the factory effort and his third car (Pescarolo/Ballot-Lena/Ricci) finished a comfortable sixth – less than 20 laps adrift – after a steady run.

With Joest finishing third and sixth and the best surviving Jaguar fourth, the remaining top six placings were filled by Sauber-Mercedes. By any standards first, second and fifth is an outstanding result, and the fifth placed Silver Arrow was only 11 laps behind the winner . . .

As we have seen, equipping the Sauber C9 in '89 was the new four valve version of the Mercedes V8 turbo engine on which work had commenced in September '88. Over the winter this version successfully completed a number of 40/50 hour continuous running tests on the bench. After each test the engine – one of three prototype units – had been disassembled and carefully checked. The only significant weakness that had to be overcome was a lack of strength in the camshaft. With its MP2.7 Motronic engine management system the unit had an 8.5:1 compression ratio and ran 1.6 bar absolute and to 7,000r.p.m. for a quoted '720b.h.p.' race power and 2.0 bar and to 7,000r.p.m. for its official '820b.h.p.' in qualifying.

For Sauber the '89 Le Mans programme had commenced in November '88 with 20% model tests in a fixed floor Daimler Benz tunnel. Technical Director Leo Ress explored modifications to the existing 'sprint' package – he did not have the scope to produce an entirely new aerodynamic form in the manner of the XJR-9LM. The C9 had TWR/XJR-influenced aerodynamics with the undertray flat aside from the carefully sculptured diffuser tunnels. A splitter led air into the underwing while a remote, central post mounted wing helped extract it.

The '89 Le Mans package – checked in the full sized Daimler-Benz tunnel in March '89 – essentially set an alternative wing as high and as far back as possible while reshaping the tunnels and removing the splitter, closing off the front wheel arch air bleeds and removing the rear deck spoiler. The Le Mans wing was single element and ran almost flat and the most important settings as regards downforce were front and rear ride height, the influence of the pitch crucial. Ress talks of the excellent lift to drag ratio of 3.0:1 for his low drag Le Mans package, reducing from 4.0:1 or more in sprint trim. However, emerging from fixed floor tunnel work, these figures are not directly comparable to those quoted for English rolling road modelling.

Clearly, after the tyre failures of '88 tyre loading was of major concern and Michelin arranged for high speed testing on a 3.6km. Canadian military runway located near Karlsruhe and the base of Michelin Germany. Over 400 troublefree kilometers were recorded at sustained high speed. However, downforce was reduced a little from the tunnel settings during these tests. Michelin specified the maximum acceptable load and the car was trimmed to this via pitch and the rear wing setting.

Satisfied with its Le Mans aerodynamics and tyres, Sauber ran a 24 hour Le Mans test with two cars at Paul Ricard immediately after Karlsruhe. Indeed, within this busy two week period in March the team ran Michelin's Clermont Ferrand, France base (where 380k.p.h. was seen), Karlsruhe and Paul Ricard in that order. The Ricard test was over the long circuit with a chicane added to simulate hard braking. A day was spent setting up the cars for the track, then at midday the following day the 24 hour trial kicked off. One car soon ran into problems with a broken wastegate that allowed over-boost, thus breaking its engine before quarter distance. The other car ran well apart from an engine oil leak that filled the cockpit with smoke, making the driver feel sick. Drivers from the sidelined car had to be brought in for relief duties and 24.5 hours continuous running clocked around 3800km. with no other problem of note.

At Le Mans the only modification compared to the Ricard settings was a one degree reduction in the rear wing angle – the wing virtually flat – as tyre loadings were carefully monitored. The straightforward set up process made for a stress-free week and Ress says that was a major factor contributing to the team's success.

'Our work was calm and cool and the mechanics could relax. That is very important if a team is to win Le Mans.'

The only drama of practice was a broken fifth gear on one car that saw the Sauber encampment closed after pre-race preparation at 10.00pm. on Friday evening rather that Ress' target 8.00pm. The cause of the problem was a dog failure. The team was running a long fifth gear that was actually smaller in diameter than its dog and in response the switch was made to a shorter fifth. During qualifying Schlesser had set the pole time in chassis 05 and for the race the nominated T car – 02 – was used instead, as planned. However, this car's engine was found to be a little down on revs and early on Cudini was hit in the eye by dirt entering through the ventilation system, suffering a bodywork-crunching spin as a result. Later a spate of tyre bothers wasted time, though after midnight the run was clear. Fifth place was the upshot for Schlesser/Cudini/Jabouille.

The second placed car of Baldi/Acheson/Brancatelli was well in the hunt for victory until breakfast time on Sunday when a spin by a brake-bothered Baldi let the winning sister car ahead. Just over an hour from the finish Acheson found himself stuck in fifth gear, a selector finger having broken. The engine was so flexible that this wasn't a major problem, other than for restarting from the pits. Thankfully one further fuel stop was all that was required. Meanwhile, the winners had strode purposefully home having overcome early delays. During Saturday evening a stray exhaust pipe had punctured the underbody and later a tyre had turned on its rim, setting up a disquieting vibration. Nevertheless, Mass/Dickens/Reuter lay fifth at midnight. Soft tyres as the track cooled under the veil of darkness and fast night driving were key factors in the successful recovery. 'They drove better than us', one of the drivers of the second placed car sportingly admitted.